**READERS' GUIDES TO ESSENTIAL CRITICISM SERIES**

CONSULTANT EDITOR: NICOLAS TREDELL

Published

| | |
|---|---|
| Thomas P. Adler | Tennessee Williams: *A Streetcar Named Desire/ Cat on a Hot Tin Roof* |
| Pascale Aebischer | Jacobean Drama |
| Lucie Armitt | George Eliot: *Adam Bede/The Mill on the Floss/ Middlemarch* |
| Simon Avery | Thomas Hardy: *The Mayor of Casterbridge/Jude the Obscure* |
| Paul Baines | Daniel Defoe: *Robinson Crusoe/Moll Flanders* |
| Brian Baker | Science Fiction |
| Annika Bautz | Jane Austen: *Sense and Sensibility/Pride and Prejudice/Emma* |
| Matthew Beedham | The Novels of Kazuo Ishiguro |
| Richard Beynon | D. H. Lawrence: *The Rainbow/Women in Love* |
| Peter Boxall | Samuel Beckett: *Waiting for Godot/Endgame* |
| Claire Brennan | The Poetry of Sylvia Plath |
| Susan Bruce | Shakespeare: *King Lear* |
| Sandie Byrne | Jane Austen: *Mansfield Park* |
| Sandie Byrne | The Poetry of Ted Hughes |
| Alison Chapman | Elizabeth Gaskell: *Mary Barton/North and South* |
| Peter Childs | The Fiction of Ian McEwan |
| Christine Clegg | Vladimir Nabokov: *Lolita* |
| Jay Corwin | Gabriel García Márquez |
| John Coyle | James Joyce: *Ulysses/A Portrait of the Artist as a Young Man* |
| Martin Coyle | Shakespeare: *Richard II* |
| Sarah Davison | Modernist Literatures |
| Sarah Dewar-Watson | Tragedy |
| Justin D. Edwards | Postcolonial Literature |
| Michael Faherty | The Poetry of W. B. Yeats |
| Sarah Gamble | The Fiction of Angela Carter |
| Jodi-Anne George | *Beowulf* |
| Jodi-Anne George | Chaucer: The General Prologue to *The Canterbury Tales* |
| Jane Goldman | Virginia Woolf: *To the Lighthouse/The Waves* |
| Huw Griffiths | Shakespeare: *Hamlet* |
| Vanessa Guignery | The Fiction of Julian Barnes |
| Louisa Hadley | The Fiction of A. S. Byatt |
| Sarah Haggarty and Jon Mee | William Blake: *Songs of Innocence and Experience* |
| Geoffrey Harvey | Thomas Hardy: *Tess of the d'Urbervilles* |
| Paul Hendon | The Poetry of W. H. Auden |
| Terry Hodgson | The Plays of Tom Stoppard for Stage, Radio, TV and Film |
| William Hughes | Bram Stoker: *Dracula* |
| Stuart Hutchinson | Mark Twain: *Tom Sawyer/Huckleberry Finn* |
| Stuart Hutchinson | Edith Wharton: *The House of Mirth/The Custom of the Country* |
| Betty Jay | E. M. Forster: *A Passage to India* |
| Aaron Kelly | Twentieth-Century Irish Literature |
| Elmer Kennedy-Andrews | Nathaniel Hawthorne: *The Scarlet Letter* |
| Elmer Kennedy-Andrews | The Poetry of Seamus Heaney |
| Daniel Lea | George Orwell: *Animal Farm/Nineteen Eighty-Four* |
| Rachel Lister | Alice Walker: *The Color Purple* |

| | |
|---|---|
| Sara Lodge | Charlotte Brontë: *Jane Eyre* |
| Philippa Lyon | Twentieth-Century War Poetry |
| Merja Makinen | The Novels of Jeanette Winterson |
| Stephen Marino | Arthur Miller: *Death of a Salesman/The Crucible* |
| Matt McGuire | Contemporary Scottish Literature |
| Timothy Milnes | Wordsworth: *The Prelude* |
| Jago Morrison | The Fiction of Chinua Achebe |
| Merritt Moseley | The Fiction of Pat Barker |
| Pat Pinsent and Clare Walsh | Children's Literature |
| Carl Plasa | Toni Morrison: *Beloved* |
| Carl Plasa | Jean Rhys: *Wide Sargasso Sea* |
| Nicholas Potter | Shakespeare: *Antony and Cleopatra* |
| Nicholas Potter | Shakespeare: *Othello* |
| Nicholas Potter | Shakespeare's Late Plays: *Pericles/Cymbeline/ The Winter's Tale/ The Tempest* |
| Steven Price | The Plays, Screenplays and Films of David Mamet |
| Berthold Schoene-Harwood | Mary Shelley: *Frankenstein* |
| Nicholas Seager | The Rise of the Novel |
| Nick Selby | T. S. Eliot: *The Waste Land* |
| Nick Selby | Herman Melville: *Moby Dick* |
| Nick Selby | The Poetry of Walt Whitman |
| David Smale | Salman Rushdie: *Midnight's Children/The Satanic Verses* |
| Enit Steiner | Jane Austen: *Northanger Abbey/Persuasion* |
| Patsy Stoneman | Emily Brontë: *Wuthering Heights* |
| Susie Thomas | Hanif Kureishi |
| Nicolas Tredell | Joseph Conrad: *Heart of Darkness* |
| Nicolas Tredell | Charles Dickens: *Great Expectations* |
| Nicolas Tredell | William Faulkner: *The Sound and the Fury/As I Lay Dying* |
| Nicolas Tredell | F. Scott Fitzgerald: *The Great Gatsby* |
| Nicolas Tredell | Shakespeare: *A Midsummer Night's Dream* |
| Nicolas Tredell | Shakespeare: *Macbeth* |
| Nicolas Tredell | Shakespeare: The Tragedies |
| Nicolas Tredell | The Fiction of Martin Amis |
| David Wheatley | Contemporary British Poetry |
| Martin Willis | Literature and Science |
| Matthew Woodcock | Shakespeare: *Henry V* |
| Gillian Woods | Shakespeare: *Romeo and Juliet* |
| Angela Wright | Gothic Fiction |
| Michael Whitworth | Virginia Woolf: *Mrs Dalloway* |
| Britta Martens | The Poetry of Robert Browning |

*Forthcoming*

| | |
|---|---|
| Nick Bentley | Contemporary British Fiction |
| Kate Watson | Crime and Detective Fiction |
| Andrew Wylie and Catherine Rees | The Plays of Harold Pinter |

*From the same author*
Browning, Victorian Poetics and the Romantic Legacy: Challenging the Personal Voice. Farnham: Ashgate, 2011.

# The Poetry of Robert Browning

BRITTA MARTENS

Consultant Editor: NICOLAS TREDELL

BLOOMSBURY ACADEMIC
LONDON • NEW YORK • OXFORD • NEW DELHI • SYDNEY

BLOOMSBURY ACADEMIC
Bloomsbury Publishing Plc
50 Bedford Square, London, WC1B 3DP, UK
1385 Broadway, New York, NY 10018, USA
29 Earlsfort Terrace, Dublin 2, Ireland

BLOOMSBURY, BLOOMSBURY ACADEMIC and the Diana logo are trademarks of
Bloomsbury Publishing Plc

First published in Great Britain 2016 by Palgrave
Reprinted by Bloomsbury Academic 2022

Copyright © Britta Martens 2016

Britta Martens has asserted her right under the Copyright, Designs and Patents Act, 1988, to be identified as Author of this work.

All rights reserved. No part of this publication may be reproduced or transmitted in any form or by any means, electronic or mechanical, including photocopying, recording, or any information storage or retrieval system, without prior permission in writing from the publishers.

Bloomsbury Publishing Plc does not have any control over, or responsibility for, any third-party websites referred to or in this book. All internet addresses given in this book were correct at the time of going to press. The author and publisher regret any inconvenience caused if addresses have changed or sites have ceased to exist, but can accept no responsibility for any such changes.

A catalogue record for this book is available from the British Library.

A catalog record for this book is available from the Library of Congress.

ISBN: HB: 978-0-230-27331-3
       PB: 978-0-230-27332-0

To find out more about our authors and books visit www.bloomsbury.com and sign up for our newsletters.

For 'wee boy', who allowed me to write this book, 'wee gello', who made finishing it so difficult, and their wonderful dad

# CONTENTS

INTRODUCTION                                                           1

Changing Perspectives in Browning Criticism

The introduction gives a brief overview of Browning's life and major works and his changing critical fortunes, followed by an outline of the chapters that follow.

CHAPTER ONE                                                            8

Romanticism: Browning and Shelley

This chapter surveys criticism on Browning's response to Romantic poetics, covering his own critical prose and its interpretation by Philip Drew and Thomas Collins. It presents readings of Browning's ambiguous attitude towards Shelley's poetics by John Maynard, John Stuart Mill, William Clyde DeVane, Herbert Tucker, Michael Yetman and Harold Bloom, who vary in their conclusions about how and when Browning overcomes the influence of this literary predecessor.

CHAPTER TWO                                                           25

Romanticism: Debt and Defiance

This chapter contrasts analyses of Browning's response to Wordsworth by John Haydn Baker and Lawrence Kramer. It also discusses Clyde Ryals' and Patricia Diane Rigg's readings of Browning in terms of Romantic irony. Catherine Maxwell's interpretation of Browning's ideal of the imperfect in relation to the Romantic sublime is contrasted with Herbert Tucker's deconstructive approach to the same concept. While David Latané examines Browning's Romantic elitist aesthetics through the lens of reader-response criticism, Britta Martens focuses on his engagement with Romantic self-expressive poetics.

## CHAPTER THREE 41

### The Dramatic Monologue: Form and the Reader

This chapter concentrates on formal definitions of the dramatic monologue by Ina Beth Sessions, Michael Mason, Alan Sinfield and Philip Drew. Robert Langbaum's influential reader-centred definition of the genre is juxtaposed with E. Warwick Slinn's reading of it as creating a fictional identity, Ralph Rader's emphasis on the genre's poetic form and Cynthia Scheinberg's feminist approach. The chapter also covers criticism on the role of the genre's audience both within and outside the text by John Maynard, Jennifer Wagner-Lawlor, Dorothy Mermin and Lee Erickson, and analyses of the genre in terms of speech act theory by Cornelia Pearsall and Slinn.

## CHAPTER FOUR 67

### The Dramatic Monologue: Causes and Context

This chapter focuses on approaches which situate Browning's development of the dramatic monologue within various literary and cultural contexts, including Isobel Armstrong's concept of the 'Victorian double poem', J. Hillis Miller's foregrounding of the Victorian Crisis of Faith, Loy Martin's Marxist reading and Britta Martens' analysis of the genre in the context of social change and other prose genres. Special attention is paid to the genre's relationship with Victorian psychology, as explored by Ekbert Faas, Michael Mason, Ellen O'Brien and Barry Popowich with reference to psychiatry and by Gregory Tate with reference to Victorian theories of mental processes.

## CHAPTER FIVE 82

### Aesthetics: Realism and the Grotesque

This chapter presents critical appreciations of Browning's realism by Walter Bagehot, John Woolford and E. Warwick Slinn and the related issue of Browning's use of the grotesque, as discussed by Bagehot, Woolford, George Santayana and Isobel Armstrong. Readings of Browning's famous painter poems are also covered, including David DeLaura's and Laurence Lerner's focus on the political and religious dimensions of their aesthetics, a psychoanalytical approach by Harold Bloom and a Marxist reading by Loy Martin.

CHAPTER SIX                                              104

Love and Gender Relations

This chapter examines Browning's attitude towards gender issues, opening with criticism about biographical and intertextual influences of Elizabeth Barrett Browning on his work by Betty Miller, William Clyde DeVane, Daniel Karlin, Corinne Davies and Nina Auerbach. Karlin and Isobel Armstrong discuss Browning's interest in unhappy love relationships. Divergent assessments of Browning's attitude towards women are offered by Joseph Bristow, U. C. Knoepflmacher, Ann Brady, Susan Brown, Penelope Gay, Shifra Hochberg, Catherine Maxwell and Ernest Fontana. Browning's concept of masculinity is scrutinised by Michael Ackerman, Herbert Sussman and Evgenia Sifaki. His celebration of divine love through the dogma of the Incarnation is explored by William Whitla and Jochen Haug.

CHAPTER SEVEN                                            131

Historical and Geographical Distancing

This chapter reviews analyses by William Raymond and Elinor Shaffer that relate Browning's religious poetry to contemporary developments in biblical scholarship, the so-called Higher Criticism. It then presents criticism by Mary Ellis Gibson, Morse Peckham and Hilary Fraser that classifies Browning's concept of history in relation to rivalling nineteenth-century schools of historiography. Assessments of the political motives for Browning's fascination with the Italian Renaissance by Stefan Hawlin and of his denigration of contemporary Italians by Robert Viscusi are complemented by Alison Chapman and Britta Martens who focus on Browning's critique of English patriotism and his parodic use of national stereotyping for the Italians.

CONCLUSION                                               147

Browning at 200 and Beyond

The final chapter highlights the main preoccupations of Browning criticism as covered in this Guide and, with the help of some major

Browning scholars celebrating the poet's Bicentenary, suggests where scholarship about the poet may be heading at a time when the emphasis of Victorian studies is shifting from traditional literary analysis to cultural studies.

NOTES 150

BIBLIOGRAPHY 163

INDEX 170

NOTE

References to Browning's poems are by line number in the version as it appears in his last lifetime edition, *The Poetical Works of Robert Browning* (London: Smith, Elder, 1888–89), which almost all modern editions of Browning's poetry use as their copy text.

Wherever possible, dates have been given for authors and other significant figures and for titles when they are first mentioned in the Guide. In some cases, however, dates were unavailable.

# INTRODUCTION

# Changing Perspectives in Browning Criticism

Alongside Alfred (Lord) Tennyson (1809–92), Robert Browning (1812–89) is the most famous and most frequently studied Victorian poet, valued for his acute psychological insights, engagement with key Victorian concerns and poetic innovation. However, unlike Tennyson, the son of an Anglican clergyman who took the conventional route of studying at Cambridge and later became Poet Laureate (1850–92), writing poetry which reflected the concerns and sensibilities of the nation, Browning is a strangely marginal figure. His poetry seems less immediately accessible than Tennyson's – hence the arguable usefulness of a critical guide such as this. He spent much of his life abroad – a fact which is reflected in the themes of his poetry – and his background and interests were not exactly mainstream. This introductory chapter will provide a brief outline of his life and major works, followed by an overview of his changing critical fortunes and a summary of the chapters that follow.

## Life and Work

Browning was born in 1812 in the South London suburb of Camberwell, the son of an imaginative and book-loving father who had been obliged to pursue a career as a clerk at the Bank of England but who made sure his son could have the kind of gentleman's life he could not indulge in himself. The young Browning was educated privately, and the sometimes esoteric references and allusions in his poetry result in part from the independent reading he undertook in his father's eclectic library. As a religious Dissenter, he could not attend Oxford or Cambridge. He chose instead to study Latin, Greek and German at the new University of London, but he broke off his studies after only a year.

1

In the meantime, he had begun to write poetry, initially in imitation of the Romantics, especially under the influence of Percy Bysshe Shelley (1792–1822). Browning's first (anonymous) publication, the long poem *Pauline* (1833), is alternatively seen as an unsuccessful attempt to imitate Romantic self-expressive poetry or as a first step towards his innovative impersonal poetics. Over the next few years, he wrote several longer works that are indebted to Romanticism such as the closet dramas (i.e. dramas that are intended to be read rather than performed) *Paracelsus* (1835) and *Pippa Passes* (1841) and the obscure, historical long poem *Sordello* (1840). Like so many other nineteenth-century poets, he also dreamt of a career as a dramatist – and like others he failed.

Between 1836 and 1846, he wrote eight plays but managed to get only two of them performed, with less than modest success. His plays were characterised by complex speeches and character analysis and lacked the external action that is essential in staged drama. At the same time he was writing short poems that distinguished themselves by a dramatic quality that his plays lacked. Many of these poems belong to the genre of the dramatic monologue, of which Browning is the most famous exponent. Briefly defined, this genre represents the speech of a character other than the author in a dramatic situation of utterance, directed at a silent listener. Most of Browning's publications of the 1840s to early 1860s are collections of dramatic monologues, the best known being *Men and Women* (1855) and *Dramatis Personae* (1864).

Although Browning is famous for these collections now, he was relatively unknown and unappreciated at this stage of his career. A far more popular poet at the time was his wife Elizabeth Barrett Browning (1806–61). Browning wooed her in a romantic twenty-month courtship, conducted initially only by letter and later on through secret visits to the invalid poetess' family home, as her father did not approve of his children getting married. The couple eventually married in 1846 and eloped to Italy, where they spent most of their life until Barrett Browning's death in 1861. Browning immediately returned to London with the couple's only son and spent the rest of his life in the capital with frequent visits to France and Italy, where he died in 1889.

The period after Barrett Browning's death was his most productive, resulting in a number of collections and several long poems. Most of these are not widely studied these days, with the notable exception of the monologue sequence *The Ring and the Book* (1868–69), which represents the events of a historical seventeenth-century Italian murder story from the divergent points of view of nine different characters and the poet himself. From the mid-1860s onwards, Browning's reputation began to improve, although he would never be as popular as Tennyson. He was, however, the first living author in whose honour a literary society was founded, the (London) Browning Society (1881).

## Critical Reception

The various Browning societies and clubs which sprouted in the UK and especially the US from the 1880s onwards offer a good starting point for a brief survey of the poet's changing literary reputation.[1] Browning Society members were not put off by Browning's linguistic and intellectual complexities, which they undertook to unravel at their meetings. Some, though not all, of them were also more appreciative of his impersonal poetry than his Victorian reviewers, whose taste was still largely dominated by the Romantic tradition of self-expressive lyrics in the poet's own voice. Reviewers were frequently made uncomfortable by the fact that the ideas and views of Browning's dramatic speakers – including such marginal figures as madmen, murderers and adulterers – were not counterbalanced by an authorial voice passing a clear moral judgment on these characters. Some therefore even attributed the immorality of Browning's speakers to the poet.

By contrast, the Browning societies saw the poet as a great moral thinker and optimist, often concentrating on the religious and philosophical issues that were raised by poems which engaged with debates about truth and human knowledge or Victorian religious scholarship.[2] It is telling that some members of the London Browning Society referred to him reverently as 'the Master'.[3] The title of Sir Henry Jones' 1891 book *Browning as a Philosophical and Religious Teacher* is an indicator of this attitude towards the poet's work. This book and the essay 'The Poetry of Barbarism' (1900) by the Harvard professor of philosophy George Santayana (1863–1952), though both highly critical of Browning's philosophy, are among a number of papers which demonstrate that the poet's work was judged worthy of serious consideration by academic philosophers (see Chapter 5).[4]

Browning's reputation declined with the advent of modernism in the 1910s. While Ezra Pound (1885–1972) was a great admirer of Browning and acknowledged the influence of his most difficult work, *Sordello*, in his poetry and criticism, T. S. Eliot (1888–1965) distanced himself from Browning and other Victorian poets.[5] In his essay 'The Metaphysical Poets' (1921), he claimed that unlike the seventeenth-century Metaphysical poets surrounding John Donne (1573–1631), whose works combined feeling and intellect, the Victorian poets suffered from a 'dissociation of sensibility'.[6] According to Eliot, 'Tennyson and Browning are poets, and they think; but they do not feel their thought as immediately as the odour of a rose'.[7] This denigration of Victorian poetry must be understood within the historical context of emerging literary movements. To assert its independent identity, any new literary movement needs to present itself as distinct from its immediate predecessors – in the case of the modernists, the Victorians.

While this rejection of the predecessor works for the response to the realist novel by modernist novelists like Virginia Woolf (1882–1941), who introduced new techniques like the stream of consciousness, it does not really apply to poetry. In 'Tradition and the Individual Talent' (1919), Eliot's statement that '[t]he progress of an artist is a continual self-sacrifice, a continual extinction of personality' seems to be closely indebted to Browning's impersonal poetics, and many of Eliot's poems such as 'The Love Song of J. Alfred Prufrock' (1915) and *The Waste Land* (1922), with their use of dramatic voices, are a development of the dramatic monologue as used by Browning.[8] Eliot's criticism strongly influenced the main representative of the new Cambridge criticism of the 1930s, F. R. Leavis (1895–1978), who in turn influenced academic criticism and what was being taught at universities for several decades. In his *New Bearings in English Poetry* (1932), Leavis more or less reiterated Eliot's judgment of the Victorians, thus pushing them to the margins of English syllabuses.[9] While readers and critics over the first two decades after Browning's death had valued the poet as a Victorian sage, his work was now predominantly seen as irrelevant to modern concerns.

The critical tide changed again in the 1950s, when a general rehabilitation of Victorian poetry began. As a result, the 1960s saw the foundation of a number of Victorianist literary journals, most importantly for our purposes *Victorian Poetry* (1962), and specialist Browning journals attesting to the popularity of Browning and his wife in particular. These are the *Browning Newsletter* (1968), renamed in 1973 *Studies in Browning and His Circle*, and the *Browning Society News* (1969), renamed in 2010 the *Journal of Browning Studies*. Sadly, due to changing constraints within academia and the publishing world, these journals have not published issues since 2006 and 2012 respectively. *Browning Institute Studies*, founded in 1973, only ran until 1990 and was later relaunched as *Victorian Literature and Culture* (1997) – an indicator of the more recent turn in Victorianist research from literary to cultural studies that will be discussed below.

A seminal text for the positive revaluation of Victorian poetry and especially of Browning is *The Poetry of Experience: The Dramatic Monologue in Modern Literary Tradition* (1957) by Robert Langbaum (born 1924), which is still the most influential study of the dramatic monologue.[10] Langbaum traced the Romantic roots of the genre but also presented Browning's work, especially *The Ring and the Book*, as a precursor of modernism in its formal characteristics and relativism. Critical interest now began to shift from discussions of the poet's philosophy and sensibilities to considerations of the ironies and ambiguities of individual poems and to the literary portrayal of character. Under this new lens Browning's poetry, with its intricate representation of complex and often dubious speakers, fared much better.

Browning's poems also proved to work well as test cases for many theoretical approaches during the high tide of literary theory from the 1970s to the 1990s. With his wide variety of subjects and rich palette of speakers, Browning has received ample attention from feminist and gender critics as well as postcolonial critics (see Chapters 6 and 7). The most notorious critical paradigm applied to his work is the 'anxiety of influence' formulated by Harold Bloom (born 1930), which draws on Sigmund Freud's (1856–1939) concept of repression to argue that a 'strong' poet is distinguished by his creative misreading of an overpowering predecessor. Bloom expounded his theory in several publications, making Browning's fraught relationship with Shelley one of his favourite examples (see Chapter 1).[11] His approach also overlaps with the methods of deconstruction which presented Browning's work as characterised by unresolved tensions and contradictions. Thus Herbert F. Tucker in *Browning's Beginnings* (1980) focused on the rejection of closure in Browning's texts (see Chapter 2), and E. Warwick Slinn, in *Browning and the Fictions of Identity* (1982), examined the implicit irony of characters whose self-knowledge is illusory (see Chapter 3).[12] Referring to the nineteenth-century paradigm of Romantic irony, Clyde de L. Ryals (1928–98) developed a related argument about Browning's pervasive use of irony (see Chapter 2).[13]

The dramatic monologue with its silent auditor and the high demands that the absence of an authorial voice makes on the reader also attracted the interest of reader-response critics. These either focused, like Dorothy Mermin, on *The Audience in the Poem* (1983) or on the poem's reader, as in Lee Erickson's *Robert Browning: His Poetry and his Audiences* (1984, see Chapter 3).[14] Erickson's interest, and even more so John Woolford's in *Browning the Revisionary* (1988) and David E. Latané's in *Browning's 'Sordello' and the Aesthetics of Difficulty* (1987, see Chapter 2), lay in Browning's historic nineteenth-century audience and the poet's response to audience expectations and reactions.[15] This attention to context is even more pronounced in analyses which are inspired by New Historicism, such as Mary Ellis Gibson's examination of Browning's engagement with contemporary concepts of historicity in *History and the Prism of Art* (1987, see Chapter 7) or Loy D. Martin's Marxist reading in *Browning's Dramatic Monologues and the Post-Romantic Subject* (1985, see Chapters 4 and 5).[16]

These two studies also announced the latest big shift in Victorian and Browning criticism, that to cultural studies, which considers literature as just one of many forms of cultural expression. Once more the variety of Browning's themes and his rootedness in Victorian culture, problematic for the modernist, makes his work an interesting site of enquiry for a variety of approaches, though mostly in the form of articles and book chapters rather than monographs. Also, the interest in theory over recent decades does not mean that no attention has been paid to textual scholarship and biographical criticism. Students of Browning are spoilt by a choice of three critical editions of his work as well as the ongoing edition of *The Brownings' Correspondence* with 40 projected volumes.[17] While publishers these days are more reluctant to publish books about single authors, and especially poets, Browning scholarship is therefore in a robustly healthy state.

## The Structure of This Guide

This guide is divided into thematic chapters. It groups together critical perspectives on poems from different periods which share key characteristics, although where appropriate chapters or sub-sections present criticism in chronological order to reflect critical developments over time. The chapter themes reflect the perspectives from which Browning's poetry is most commonly studied these days.

Most students first encounter Browning on survey courses about nineteenth-century literature, which explain his distinctiveness as a Victorian poet through a comparison with his Romantic predecessors. This is why Chapters 1 and 2 focus on the critical debate surrounding his complex responses to the Romantic tradition. Chapter 1 examines Browning's own critical essays in which he implicitly situates himself in relation to Romanticism as well as criticism on his changing attitude towards his early hero Shelley. Chapter 2 considers his response to other Romantic poets and abstract concepts, such as Romantic irony and the use of the poet's personal voice.

Browning is the prime exponent of the most important poetic genre of the Victorian period, the dramatic monologue. Chapters 3 and 4 cover criticism on Browning's use of this genre. Chapter 3 opens with an overview of formal definitions of the genre. It then focuses on the most influential analysis of the dramatic monologue in terms of the reader's experience and on a variety of approaches which consider the genre primarily as a communicative act. Chapter 4 is devoted to the genre's context, its literary origins and its relationship with the cultural environment of the 1830s when Browning developed it, especially the rise of the discipline of psychiatry.

As some of Browning's most famous poems share concerns with aesthetics and the correspondences between different art forms, Chapter 5 considers Browning's two key aesthetics, his poetic equivalent of the nineteenth-century novel's realism and his related use of the grotesque. Special attention is accorded to the aesthetics articulated in Browning's famous painter poems, with interpretations ranging from the religious to the political.

Browning's work also offers rich material for the analysis of gender relations. Chapter 6 is devoted to the representation of (mostly unhappy) love and gender relations and presents the critical debate over whether Browning is a feminist or a defender of patriarchy. The chapter explores the possible influences on his work of his wife's strong interest in gender issues, assessments of his concept of masculinity and his celebration of divine love.

Another striking and sometimes confusing feature of many Browning poems is their setting in earlier historical periods and/or foreign locations, especially Italy. Chapter 7 presents criticism on the implications of this historical and geographical distancing. It examines definitions of Browning's concept of history and his engagement with contemporary debates about the writing of history and biblical scholarship. It also covers criticism about Browning's contradictory attitude towards Italy, exploring his national stereotyping of the Italians despite his support for Italian independence. His sense of Britishness and his critique of British national prejudices are also critically examined.

CHAPTER ONE

# Romanticism: Browning and Shelley

This chapter and the one that follows discuss criticism on Browning's poetry in relation to the Romantic poetry which dominated the literary scene during his youth and fashioned literary taste well into his maturity. The chapter opens with a consideration of Browning's own critical writings in which he seems to define his poetics in opposition to Romanticism and proposes a narrative about the historical development from one literary period to the next. Opposing critical views by Philip Drew and Thomas J. Collins are presented on whether Browning is, in his own terminology, an impersonal 'objective' poet or whether he strives for an ideal that incorporates elements of Romantic poetics. The chapter then examines Browning's statements about the need to move beyond an imitation of literary predecessors and explores how critics have applied these to Browning's early work, especially in relation to the hero of his youth, Percy Bysshe Shelley. Interpretations by John Maynard and William Clyde DeVane (1898–1965) of Browning's first publication, *Pauline* (1833), as an autobiographical record of his early emulation of Shelley, are juxtaposed with a reading by Herbert F. Tucker, who sees the poem as already signalling Browning's overcoming of Romanticism. This is followed by Michael G. Yetman's analysis of *Sordello* (1840) as the text in which Browning frees himself of Shelley's influence. The next section considers Harold Bloom's scrutiny of Browning's attitude towards Shelley to illustrate his famous 'psycho-poetic' theory of the 'anxiety of influence'.

Logical starting points for the study of any author are their early reading, their first literary endeavours and the literary influences which they either adopt or reject. The Victorian poets (writing in the period ca. 1830–1900) are usually studied in relation to their immediate predecessors, the Romantics (ca. 1780–1830). Romanticism is the most pivotal period for English poetry, as it saw the most radical changes in poetics, and it still largely influences our concept of poetry today. Romanticism established the short, self-expressive lyric in the poet's own voice as the archetypal poem. This genre allowed poets to explore the workings of their creativity within the very poems which were the products of this creativity. On the downside, the Romantics' intense self-consciousness about their imaginative process could also lead to writer's block or to the accusation of egotism or solipsism, i.e. an inflated sense of one's own importance and a detachment from other people. Like any new generation of authors, the early Victorian poets had to overcome the temptation to merely imitate the style and concerns of their predecessors in order to lay claim to a distinctive, original artistic identity. This valuing of original genius was itself, it should be said, a key Romantic tenet.

Browning is the Victorian who can be considered the most radical in his rejection of Romantic poetics, as so much of his poetry replaces the Romantic personal voice of the poet with that of fictional, dramatic speakers. He thus avoids the dangers of the poet's solipsism inherent in the Romantic self-expressive lyric. He can be seen as a test case not only for how Victorian poets created their distinctive poetics but also, more generally, for how literary movements situate themselves in relation to their predecessors. Browning's case is also interesting because he reflected on this issue in his only two pieces of critical prose, now known as the *Essay on Chatterton* (1842) and the *Essay on Shelley* (1852), which in turn have influenced how his critics have analysed his poetics and artistic development. The next two sections will present the key ideas in these essays and examine how critics have applied these to Browning's own poetry.

## Browning as Critic: Subjective and Objective Poetry in the *Essay on Shelley*

At a moment in his career when he had developed his mature impersonal poetics, Browning was asked by his publisher to write an 'Introductory Essay' to a collection of newly discovered letters by Shelley, which appeared in 1852.[1] Embarrassingly, it was revealed shortly after publication that the letters were forgeries, and the volume was swiftly withdrawn from sale. Browning's essay was not reprinted until 1881 but has since then been used as a way of explicating his poetics and his sense of his position within the poetic tradition with reference to his own terminology. Considering that they turned out to be forgeries, it is fortunate that Browning does not comment on the specific letters to which the essay served as preface. Instead, he uses the second half of the essay to defend Shelley against his detractors, arguing that his premature death prevented him from expressing all his greatness in his poetry. The first half of the essay makes a more general case for the importance of considering the biography of some poets, such as Shelley, in order to better understand their poetry. Drawing on the terminology of German Romantic criticism, probably via the mediation of critical writings by Samuel Taylor Coleridge (1772–1834), Browning defines two opposed types of poets, 'objective' and 'subjective' poets.[2]

The subject matter of objective poetry is the external world or characters other than the poet himself. The poetry is distinct from his personality, giving as little indication of the author's self as a play reveals about the dramatist's identity. Moreover, the objective poet with his superior perception and acute sense of his audience's abilities writes for the benefit of readers who are less perceptive than he, and so his poetry should be easily accessible.[3]

By contrast, the subjective poet is the Romantic self-expressive visionary. Unlike the objective poet, he is not interested in relating to his audience and strives instead for the ideal in the hope of reaching the absolute perspective of God. Paradoxically, the subjective poet reaches for the ideal and absolute truth by looking inside his own soul as a reflection of the divine. Man and work cannot be separated. Although there is no guarantee that he will attain his lofty aim, Browning's enthusiastic choice of words can be read as suggesting that this type is superior to the objective poet: he is a visionary 'seer [...] rather than a fashioner'.[4] However, this apparent bias is balanced by Browning's explicit rejection of any kind of hierarchy between the two types and his emphasis on the importance of dealing with the real world, the subject matter of the objective poet.[5]

The standard critical interpretation of these contrasting definitions is that, despite the overt reference to the dramatist William Shakespeare (1564–1616) as an archetypal objective poet, the covert reference here is to Browning himself. His impersonal poetry, especially the dramatic monologue with its psychological insight into a speaker who is distinct from the poet, seems a perfect fit for his characterisation of objective poetry as 'reproducing things external' to the poet, 'the manifested action of the human heart and brain'.[6] Browning adds that the objective poet 'chooses to deal with the doings of men, (the result of which dealing, in its pure form, when even description, as suggesting a describer, is dispensed with, is what we call dramatic poetry)'.[7] The absence, as in drama, of an authorial voice to evaluate the speaker was a key difficulty for Browning's contemporary audience. Browning himself did not use the term 'dramatic monologue' for his poems, but he did call them 'dramatic lyrics', as in the titles of his collections *Dramatic Lyrics* (1842) and *Dramatic Romances and Lyrics* (1845), or 'Dramatic Pieces', as in the 'Advertisement' to the former where he declares that his poems are 'always Dramatic in principle, and so many utterances of so many imaginary persons, not mine'.[8]

To support this reading of Browning as an objective poet, Philip Drew, in his article 'Browning's *Essay on Shelley*' (1963), asserts that

Browning 'filled his poems with the doings of mankind, whereas almost all the other poets of the nineteenth century found their inspiration in solitude or in the countryside'[9] – a somewhat contentious generalisation about the subject matter of most Victorian poetry. In Drew's view, the relevance of the essay lies in Browning's marking of his 'sense of difference between his own poetry and that of the Romantic poets of the first half of the nineteenth century'.[10] Drew reminds his readers that

■ Browning resisted throughout his career any attempt to interpret his poems in the light of his life or, conversely, to establish his personal opinions from those of the characters in his poems. [...] Browning's inveterate dislike of those who drew parallels between his poems and his life is given a theoretical justification in the Essay.[11] □

Drew's identification of Browning as an unambiguously objective poet is called into question by Thomas J. Collins, whose article 'Browning's Essay on Shelley: In Context' (1964) is a direct response to Drew's. He argues instead that Browning strives to combine the objective and subjective modes in his work. Collins examines a selection of poems about artists, arguing that

■ Browning not only tries to unite the subject matter of both poets, but that he also frequently judges the success or failure of the artists who are his own poetic creations by their ability to accomplish that fusion.[12] □

However, this fusion of objective and subjective *in the same work* is not quite the ideal that Browning promotes in his essay. He actually states that there is no

■ reason why these two modes of poetic faculty may not issue hereafter from the same poet in successive perfect works. A mere running-in of the one faculty upon the other, is, of course, the ordinary circumstance. Far more rarely it happens that either is found so decidedly prominent and superior, as to be pronounced comparatively pure: while of the perfect shield, with the gold and the silver side set up for all comers to challenge, there has yet been no instance.[13] □

Browning's highest praise is thus reserved for poets who can produce both purely subjective and purely objective poetry *in separate works*. The 'perfect shield' with two opposing sides of gold and silver represents the two pure types of poetry. His ideal is not the combination of both within a single poem.

Browning's essay makes another important point that invites an application to the poet's own work. It sketches out a schematic development of literary history as progressing through an alternation of objective and subjective phases. According to this model, one type of poetry, say objective poetry, will dominate for a certain period until the possibilities of that mode are exhausted, at which point a poet of the opposite type will appear and initiate a new phase in the subjective mode, until this, too, is succeeded by a new phase of objective poetry, and so on. The sign that a phase comes to its end is the work of inferior imitators of an original genius who can only create a faint imitation of the work of the initiator of that phase.[14] Being at the end of a phase is thus the worst historical moment for a poet to be in. This could be the very young Browning or any other first-generation Victorian poet whose earliest poetic endeavours imitated the Romantics. But having made the transition to the impersonal dramatic monologue in his mature work, Browning can lay claim to being the initiator of a new objective period in literary history.

According to Drew, the application of Browning's theory to his own age is as follows. When describing the end of a subjective phase in the poetic tradition,

> ■ it seems likely that Browning has particularly in mind the Romantic poets of the early nineteenth century. If this is so his contemporaries are either the heirs of the great traditions of Wordsworth and Coleridge, or, equally possible, they are even later in the great period of poetic change and merely chew the straw of last year's harvest. [...] whether his contemporaries were working in a fruitful or in an exhausted tradition, Browning does not reckon himself of their number, for, unlike them, he is a predominantly objective poet [...].[15] □

A similar reading of an essay by Browning, ostensibly about a different poet, as a hidden discussion of his own poetics has been suggested in relation to his other critical essay, the *Essay on Chatterton*.

## Overcoming Romantic Imitation: The *Essay on Chatterton* and Browning's Early Work

The text which is now called the *Essay on Chatterton* was published in 1842 in the *Foreign Quarterly Review* as an anonymous review of a book about the Italian poet Torquato Tasso (1544–95), but it soon digresses into a discussion of Thomas Chatterton (1752–70), whom the Romantic poets celebrated as their predecessor and a tragically unacknowledged and precocious poetic genius. Chatterton, a Bristol attorney clerk, surprised the literary world with his 'discovery' of poems by the medieval monk Thomas Rowley, which were actually Chatterton's own forgeries. After unsuccessful attempts to establish himself as a literary writer in London, Chatterton committed suicide at the age of eighteen. Browning uses Chatterton's case to present an argument about the importance of imitation as a necessary first stage in an author's development. The problem of the accomplished forger Chatterton is that he does not manage to take the next step in the poet's development from imitation to original creation:

■ Genius almost invariably begins to develop itself by imitation. It has, in the short-sightedness of infancy, faith in the world: and its object is to compete with, or prove superior to, the world's already recognised idols, at their own performances and by their own methods. This done, there grows up a faith in itself: and, no longer taking the performance or method of another for granted, it supersedes these by processes of its own. It creates, and imitates no longer.[16] □

This passage explains imitation as a desire to emulate one's artistic heroes but also stresses the necessity to then overcome imitation. It and the essay's sympathetic portrayal of the misled genius Chatterton can be read as a veiled defence of Browning's own imitations of the Romantics in his unpublished *juvenilia*, and perhaps also as a justification for the anonymity of his first publication *Pauline* and his use of pseudonyms in some very early publications. Unlike Chatterton, however, Browning will make a successful transition to original work.

The dominant critical narrative about Browning's artistic development centres on this overcoming of Romantic imitation, especially in relation to Shelley, whose work Browning first read at the age of fourteen and who impressed him so much that he even temporarily copied Shelley's vegetarianism and atheism.[17] Shelley's idealistic poetics and his radical politics had a significant influence on the young Browning. Detailed biographical research on Browning's reading of Shelley has been conducted by Frederick A. Pottle in *Shelley and Browning: A Myth and Some Facts* (1923) and by John Maynard in *Browning's Youth* (1977).[18] The influence of Shelley is directly acknowledged in *Pauline*, where the speaker apostrophises Shelley as the 'Sun-Treader' (l. 151). The poem's speaker is a young poet who initially writes idealistic and self-expressive poetry inspired by Shelley, but he eventually becomes disillusioned with his hero and enters a phase of unproductive, misanthropic solipsism, from which he hopes that his selfless lover Pauline, the addressee of the poem, will save him. The speaker's development is usually read as thinly veiled autobiography. Maynard, for instance, takes quotations about the speaker's attitude towards Shelley and reads them as Browning's own, concluding:

> ■ By the time [Browning] wrote *Pauline*, he had not only become disillusioned with Shelley's political ideas but was even able to put this entire part of his intellectual development in a cogent and coherent autobiographical perspective.[19] □

Maynard's reading of *Pauline* as autobiographical is a more elaborate version, backed up by contextual research, of one of the earliest commentaries on the poem which is based only on a close reading of the text. This is a note in a review copy of *Pauline* by John Stuart Mill (1806–73), who would later become a major social and political thinker of the Victorian age. Mill had intended to write a review of *Pauline*, but when he found he could not place the review in two periodicals, he abandoned the project and returned his annotated copy to the poet. Raised in the tradition of Romantic, self-expressive poetry, Mill assumes that the poem's protagonist is a representation of his author. No distinction is drawn between the speaker and the writer, whose state of mind Mill diagnoses as a quasi-medical condition:

> ■ With considerable poetic powers, this writer seems to me possessed with a more intense and morbid self-consciousness than I ever knew in any sane human being [...] the psychological history of himself is powerful and truthful, *truth-like* certainly all but the last stage. *That* he evidently has not yet got into. [...]
> Meanwhile he should not attempt to shew how a person may be *recovered* from this morbid state – for *he* is hardly convalescent, and 'what should we speak of but that which we know?'[20] □

According to Mill, poetry should only depict experiences that the poet has undergone himself, and Browning in his poem transgresses this rule because he has not yet reached the speaker's final phase of recovery from solipsism in which he despises his former state. William Clyde DeVane, in his influential *Browning Handbook* (1933, revised 1955), integrates Mill's note into his narrative of Browning's career. According to DeVane, as Browning read Mill's criticism,

> ■ he realized that he had exposed his callow soul to the gaze of a stranger, a thing hateful to him the rest of his days. The thought of *Pauline* became repugnant to him; he hid it from sight. Henceforward, his poetry would be objective and dramatic, the utterances of created characters, not of himself. The perfect bard hereafter was one who 'chronicled' the souls of others, preferably historical persons. At the end of his own note in Mill's copy

of *Pauline*, Browning wrote, 'Only this crab remains of the shapely Tree of Life in this Fool's paradise of mine.' The whole episode of *Pauline* rankled in the heart of the young poet. The poem itself is, perhaps, an admission of defeat, for Shelley had meant to the young Browning rebellion against his parents, the church, and society. *Pauline* is a record of his capitulation, and in some ways his loss of freedom.[21] □

DeVane's assertions here about the poet's emotional reaction to Mill's scathing criticism, which are based on Browning's note in the Mill copy of *Pauline* and on the fact that Browning recovered the unsold copies of the poem (probably all of them) from the printers, may strike the modern reader as problematically speculative. However, they are plausible in that Browning's subsequent publications seem to turn towards a more impersonal style with protagonists who are less likely to be equated with the poet himself. DeVane's analysis also depends on his interpretation of the poem's elaborate paratextual framework, which consists of two epigraphs in French and Latin, a date and place at the end of the poem and a note in French by Pauline. Like Mill, he reads these as devices that are meant to hide the autobiographical nature of the poem.[22]

These paratextual devices are interpreted very differently by Herbert F. Tucker. In 'Browning as Escape Artist: Avoidance and Intimacy' (1998), he calls into question the common critical view that Browning tried to 'run away' from the embarrassment of *Pauline*.[23] Tucker focuses on the poem's paratext discussed by DeVane and also on the two prefatory notes about *Pauline* in Browning's *Poetical Works* of 1868 and 1888–89. Here Browning acknowledges the poem 'with extreme repugnance' and, quoting his own 'Advertisement' to *Dramatic Lyrics*, claims that *Pauline* 'was my earliest attempt at "poetry always dramatic in principle, and so many utterances of so many persons, not mine", which I have since written according to a scheme less extravagant and scale less impracticable than were ventured upon in this crude preliminary sketch'.[24] Tucker comments:

■ The poet seems genuinely ashamed of his first published work – and yet he could hardly have done more to rivet our attention on that work if he had meant to. But then, to anticipate matters a bit, maybe he did mean to. The one idea (among all others) that inescapably belongs in [Browning's] (among all poets') self-presentation to posterity is the idea of dramatic composition. While this idea does make its way into the prefaces of [1868] and 1888, it does so only by attaching itself to the problematically impersonative *Pauline*, which [Browning] is at pains to defend as a piece 'dramatic in principle', a 'performance' like all the rest. If the profuse apologetics of these prefaces tell us, in effect, not to skip *Pauline* whatever we do, that may be because the poet regarded this poem not as an exception but as a paradigm for the collection it headed [i.e. his *Poetical Works*, which are mostly dramatic poems]. Far from an indulged piece, granted pseudo-dramatic status on the strength of all the poetry that followed it, *Pauline* may come first in the *Poetical Works* because it is [Browning]'s primer [...].[25] ☐

*Pauline* is, in Tucker's view, not a disguised Romantic self-expression but already a truly dramatic performance that demonstrates Browning's overcoming of Romanticism. The paratextual apparatus displays the characteristics of the mature Browning, an impersonal poet who is absent from his text and distances himself from it through various textual layers. Tucker sees

■ in the proliferating apologetics of *Pauline* the signature of the Victorian escape artist par excellence. *Pauline* stands at the head of [Browning's] collected poems as a virtual contract with the reader. The poet undertakes to be dependably, consistently elusive, and the reader undertakes to seek him out not as an essence – an integral self – but as an act or method: a way of making tracks towards a vanishing point. It is only fitting that such a contract be ghost-written and solemnized in disappearing ink, for these ways of escape are the very behaviors that [Browning] from the first challenges us to know him by. He makes his mark on us as the one who disclaims, the one who isn't there, the one for whom to abdicate is to be in character.[26] ☐

For Tucker, Browning is an impersonal poet from the very start and never tempted by Romantic self-expression. The reader has to recognise that Browning is an 'escape artist' whose self cannot be pinned down but who is characterised by his avoidance of the reader's direct scrutiny.

Other critics locate the overcoming of Shelley's influence and the turn to impersonal poetics in later works, above all the historical long poem *Sordello*. In 'Exorcising Shelley Out of Browning: *Sordello* and the Problem of Poetic Identity' (1975), Michael G. Yetman reads the poem's hero, the thirteenth-century troubadour Sordello, as Browning's representation of himself during his formative years when he is torn between the opposed poles of subjective poetry in the vein of Shelley and objective poetry. Sordello begins his career as an egotistical Romantic poet, but then decides to devote himself to the cause of humanity. However, he dies without having acted on his newly found altruism, under the strain of having to choose between his attraction to one political faction, which he thinks is committed to the cause of the common people, and the offer to become the leader of the opposed political faction. For Yetman, the poem acts as a justification for Browning's abandonment of subjective poetry after *Sordello*, which reflects his waning belief in the Shelleyan supreme authority of the poet and his recognition, associated with objective poetry, that the poet needs to relate to society. *Sordello*

> ■ might be called negative autobiography, by which I mean to designate details that link the developing sensibility of the hero to a rejected or bypassed stage in the author's own poetic evolution, a stage dominated by Romantic ideas of art and the artist's relation to society. [...] As I see it, what *Sordello* actually records is a symbolic exorcism of the adopted Shelleyan sensibility. At the same time, in the curious manner of such relationships it constitutes a special pleading with the rejected or former self to understand the necessity for its dispossession.[27] □

Sordello acts as a negative alter ego of Browning; he dies unable to overcome the Romantic aesthetics which Browning himself exorcises through the writing of *Sordello*, albeit still with a sense of having to apologise to his former self for this change of heart.

Yetman pays particular attention to the 'surprisingly strong antagonism' between the protagonist and the poem's intrusive narrator, who seems to be Browning himself and who 'has little that is kind to say about Sordello until the day the poet dies'. Sordello and the narrator, Yetman suggests, should be seen as 'two conflicting sides of the same personality (Browning's), which will be reconciled considerably, though never completely, as the poem moves tortuously to a conclusion. [...] Sordello begins to think more and more like the maturing Browning.'[28] As his aesthetics develop from Romantic solipsism towards Browning's new aesthetics, Sordello becomes more and more like Browning as represented by the narrator. Focusing on Sordello's eventual inability to act on his devotion to the cause of the people, Yetman concludes that Browning's hero fails because he lacks his author's altruism:

> ■ Sordello's tragedy stems from our realization that – even given more time – he would never have become a poet of humanity. Browning has neglected to provide Sordello with what was in his view the single most important possession of the artist: a dedication of one's art to the illumination of other men. [...]
>
> For Browning, perhaps more than for any other of his contemporaries, the idea of poetry that went nowhere beyond a sterile communion with the self was morally irresponsible. [...] the development of Sordello's soul is really Browning's nightmare vision of himself as he thought he might have become had the quandary stemming from his possession of two distinct and contradictory poetic personalities never been resolved. By transferring

to his creation his own anxieties concerning the nature of the true poet in himself and dwelling dispassionately on the phenomenon of the divided self *in extremis*, Browning was better able to see a way out of his personal dilemma. More specifically, he was able to show himself what might have occurred had the originally dominant and unqualified Shelleyan identity held sway.[29] □

Projecting his own conflict between egotism and altruism onto his fictional hero, who fails to solve it, allows Browning to resolve the conflict in favour of altruism and to move on artistically, leaving Shelley behind and developing his impersonal poetics. Yetman's thesis that Browning needs to exorcise the influence of Shelley from his work is indebted to Harold Bloom's theory of the 'anxiety of influence'. The following section will summarise the foundations of this theory and discuss Bloom's applications of it to Browning's work.

## Harold Bloom's Anxiety of Influence

Unlike the critical sources covered so far in this chapter, which focus on Browning's early work, Bloom's interest lies in how Browning revisits his turn away from Shelley's model in his mature poetry. Bloom's famous theory, which he expounded in a number of books, is not based on what we might normally understand by intertextuality and what he dismisses as mere 'source-study', i.e. the analysis of verbal echoes or close resemblances in the styles and themes of two texts. Instead, the texts that he connects can be significantly different, as in the case of Browning and Shelley. Bloom's theory develops out of his conviction that all poetry is generated through the poet's reading of work by earlier poets and out of Bloom's particular interest in Romantic poetry. He observes that the Romantics, who place great value on the ideal of original genius, suffer from a sense of 'belatedness', i.e. the uneasy feeling that they have come too late and may only be able to repeat what an overpowering precursor has accomplished before them. Bloom analyses the successor poet's strategies for coping with this pressure through a 'psycho-poetics' based on the psychoanalytical theory of Sigmund Freud, in particular the Oedipus complex, according to which sons desire to possess their mother and wish to kill the rival for their mother's affection, the father.

Bloom is not the first critic to apply Freudian theory to Browning. In her biography *Robert Browning: A Portrait* (1952), Betty Miller (1910–65) presents Browning as having an Oedipal attachment to his mother, which is later replaced by what Miller considers his submissive attachment to his wife. She reads Browning's turn away from the radical atheist Shelley as a consequence of his stronger allegiance to his mother, a deeply religious Evangelical:

> ■ The ideals of Shelley and those of Sarah Anna Browning could not continue to exist under the same roof: the moment had come in which he must either deny his 'wild dreams of beauty and good', or irreparably wound and alienate his mother, 'the one being', we are told, 'whom he entirely loved'. Faced with this deadlock between head and heart, Browning found his own solution. Reason divided him from the one he could love: reason, therefore, must be sacrificed. With a truly Herculean effort, which seems to have absorbed all of his youth's strength, Browning performed upon himself an act of re-grafting: reversing, deliberately, the laws of his own growth.[30] □

For Miller, Browning goes against his reason and artistic instincts, which would align his work with Shelley's, in order not to disappoint his mother. Miller therefore sees the whole of Browning's career as reflecting his guilt at having betrayed Shelley's free spirit to submit to his mother's Evangelicalism.

Freud's controversial mother–son relationship is not relevant to Bloom's theory, which focuses on relations between texts rather than individuals and only concentrates on the rivalry with the 'poetic father'. Unsurprisingly, given his Freudian inspiration, Bloom's examples are all males. He argues that in order to rid himself of the crushing influence of his precursor and become a 'strong' poet with his own distinctive identity, the successor poet, like Freud's male child, must reject his poetic father. He overcomes his sense of inferiority by creatively 'misreading' the precursor's work, i.e. by proving to himself that the precursor is in some sense wrong or inferior, which then allows him to improve on the precursor's work. This misreading makes the creation of poetry possible and lies at the heart of the poetic tradition since the Renaissance:

> ■ Poetic Influence – when it involves two strong, authentic poets, – always proceeds by a misreading of the prior poet, an act of creative correction that is actually and necessarily a misinterpretation. The history of fruitful poetic influence, which is to say the main tradition of Western poetry since the Renaissance, is a history of anxiety and self-serving caricature, of distortion, of perverse, wilful revisionism without which modern poetry as such could not exist.[31] □

Bloom sets out his theory in *The Anxiety of Influence: A Theory of Poetry* (1973), where he presents six 'revisionary ratios', textual strategies which strong poets can employ to misread their predecessors. These are derived from three sources: first, the unconscious psychological defence mechanisms an individual employs to maintain a certain self-image as theorised by Freud's daughter Anna (1895–1982); second, the

Kabbalah, the ancient and esoteric Jewish tradition of mystical interpretation of the Bible; and third, classical rhetorical figures. Bloom's terminology comprises the ratios of: *clinamen* (a reading which assumes that the precursor poem swerved away from the right path, so that the successor poem can claim to correct the wrong turning, associated with the rhetorical trope of irony and the defence mechanism of reaction-formation); *tessera* (completing the precursor because he seems not to have gone far enough, associated with synecdoche and a turning against the self); *kenosis* (a breaking away from the precursor or emptying through self-humbling which in the end humbles the precursor more than the successor, associated with metonymy and isolation or regression); *daemonisation* (a displacing which calls into question the uniqueness of the precursor's work, associated with hyperbole and repression); *askesis* (a diminishing or self-purgation through curtailing the successor's, and hence implicitly the precursor's, work, associated with metaphor and sublimation); and *apophrades* (the return of the dead which suggests that the successor himself could have written the precursor's work, associated with metalepsis and introjection or projection).[32]

This idiosyncratic terminology can be disorientating, and Bloom's application of the theory to Browning's '"Childe Roland to the Dark Tower Came"' (1855) in his next book, *A Map of Misreading* (1975), is far from an easy read. Bloom opens by stating that the poem's real subject is interpretation, which can only be misreading.

> ■ Roland's monologue is his sublime and grotesque exercise of the will-to-power over the interpretation of his own text. Roland rides with us as interpreter; his every interpretation is a powerful misreading; and yet the union of those misreadings enables him to accept destruction in the triumphant realization that his ordeal, his trial by landscape, has provided us with one of the most powerful texts that any hero-villain since Milton's Satan has given us.[33] □

Browning's speaker thus stands for the successor poet whose misreading of his precursor, represented by the landscape, creates a great poem by a strong poet.

The poem uses the medieval quest motif, which was favoured by the Romantics. Its speaker is engaged in a belated Romantic quest which parallels Browning's own sense of belatedness in relation to Shelley – a link which is made through Bloom's assertion that Browning's Dark Tower is an allusion to the tower in Shelley's *Julian and Maddalo* (1824) and his association of Roland's blowing of his slug-horn with Shelley's 'Ode to the West Wind' (1820).[34] Roland deals with his belatedness through various mechanisms of creative misreading that can be analysed through Bloom's terminology as summarised above. Bloom divides the poem into three parts. The first part (stanzas I–VIII), which retells Roland's encounter with a 'hoary cripple' (l. 2) who points him the way to the Dark Tower, illustrates *clinamen*:

■ The poem's opening swerve is marked rhetorically by the trope of irony, imagistically by an interplay of presence and absence, and psychologically by Roland's reaction-formation against his own destructive impulses. [...] Roland says one thing and means another, and both the saying and the meaning seek to void a now intolerable presence.[35] □

Roland says that he 'first thought' (l. 1) the cripple lied and pointed him in the wrong direction but he is being ironic because he believes that 'the cripple inevitably speaks the truth' and takes the path the cripple has indicated.[36] His reaction-formation, i.e. his managing of his anxiety to succeed in the quest by exaggerating a directly opposing tendency, is to manifest a will to fail in the quest. He then moves on to *tessera*, characterised by synecdoche, or a standing in of a part for the whole, and a turning against the self. Bloom states that 'Any quest is a synecdoche for the whole of desire; a quest for failure is a synecdoche for suicide.'[37]

The second part (stanzas IX–XXIX), which is dominated by the description of the grotesque landscape through which Roland travels, illustrates *kenosis* as it 'alternates between the psychic defense of isolation and the more Sublime defense of repression, but collapsed here into the Grotesque [...] Roland's landscape is a kind of continuous metonymy [i.e. a concept replacing a closely related concept], in which a single, negative aspect of every thing substitutes for the thing itself'.[38] This part ends with Roland's recognition that he is trapped, 'yet paradoxically this entrapment alone makes possible a fulfilment of his quest'.[39]

The poem's third part (stanzas XXX–XXXIV), in which Roland faces the Dark Tower, watched by his predecessors who also failed in the quest, 'alternates between an *askesis* of defeated metaphor and a magnificent, perhaps triumphant metaleptic return to earlier powers'.[40] The ending thus also illustrates metalepsis, i.e. the replacement of a concept by a more remotely related one such as cause for effect, and Bloom's ratio of *apophrades*. Bloom reads the Dark Tower as a metaphor for art or a metaphor of

■ misprision, for the over-determined and inescapable meanings that belated creators impose upon poetic tradition. The [blind] Tower stands for the blindness of the influence-process, which is the same as the reading-process. Fresh creation is a catastrophe, or a substitution, a making-breaking that is performed in blindness. [...] Roland is giving us a parable of his relation to his brother-knights, which becomes a parable of Browning's relation to the poets who quested for the Dark Tower before him.[41] □

Roland's creativity, like Browning's, is not a fully conscious act, which is determined by the relationship with his precursors.

Eventually, Roland manages to turn his sense of belatedness into one of earliness when he blows his slug-horn uttering the message and closing line of the poem, *'Childe Roland to the Dark Tower came'* (l. 204), which is a kind of prophecy. In the final analysis, Roland has both triumphed and failed:

> ■ Roland has triumphed by failing precisely as his precursors failed, and by recognizing and so *knowing* that their 'failure' was a triumph also. Each one in turn found himself alone at the Dark Tower, facing himself as opponent at the Scene of Instruction, measuring himself always against the composite form of the forerunners. [...]
>
> The Childe's last act of dauntless courage is to will repetition, to accept his place in the company of the ruined. [...] Childe Roland dies, if he dies, in the magnificence of belatedness that can accept itself as such. He ends in strength, because his vision has ceased to break and deform the world, and has begun to turn its dangerous strength upon its own defenses. Roland is the modern poet-as-hero, and his sustained courage to weather his own phantasmagoria and emerge into fire is a presage of the continued survival of strong poetry.[42] □

Failure and belatedness are paradoxically reinterpreted as a triumph because the successor poet accepts them and can thus claim to be a strong poet and of the same status as his predecessors.

There are several essays in which Bloom returns to what he acknowledges to be a personal obsession with 'Childe Roland'.[43] One of these, which also has the merit of covering a range of other Browning poems, is a chapter in *Poetry and Repression: Revisionism from Blake to Stevens* (1976), 'Browning: Good Moments and Ruined Quests', which attempts 'to show our tendency to read his epiphanies or "good moments" as ruinations or vastations [i.e. devastations] of quest, and our parallel tendency to read his darkest visions-of-failure as if they were celebrations'.[44] We see here at the reader's level the same paradoxical connection between failure and success that Bloom identifies at the end of 'Childe Roland'. Bloom describes Browning's general attitude towards Shelley as quite untypical of successor poets. While others usually feel 'ambivalence towards the prime precursor [...], Browning loved Shelley unbrokenly and almost unreservedly' throughout his life. His anxiety of influence arises from

> ■ the guilt or shame of identifying the precursor with the ego-ideal [i.e. one's ideal self-image], and the living on in the sense of having betrayed that identification by one's own failure to have become oneself, by a realization that the ephebe [i.e. the successor] has betrayed his own integrity,

and betrayed also the covenant that first bound him to the precursor. That guilt unmistakably was Browning's as Betty Miller and others have shown, and so the burden of belatedness was replaced in Browning by a burden of dissimulation, a lying-against-the-self, rather than a lying-against-time.[45] □

Browning does not reject his precursor like other successor poets but suffers from the realisation that he does not live up to Shelley's model.

Bloom contrasts 'Childe Roland' with the late lyric 'Thamuris marching' from *Aristophanes' Apology* (1875) about the Thracian bard Thamuris, who according to the *Iliad* (ca. 800 BC) challenged the Muses to a singing contest which he lost. The poem depicts him marching purposefully towards his meeting with the Muses but breaks off before the contest, thus omitting the defeat. Thamuris' joyful quest seems to reverse the belated Roland's defeat. But he also revels in the anticipation of his destruction. He

> ■ *knows* he is marching to an unequal contest, a poetic struggle of one heroic ephebe against the greatest of precursors, the Muses themselves. [...]
> Browning's Thamuris marches to a Shelleyan *terza rima*, and marches through a visionary universe distinctly like Shelley's, and overtly proclaimed as being *early*: 'From triumph on to triumph, mid a ray / Of early morn—' [ll. 5197-8] Laughing as he goes, yet knowing full well his own doom, Thamuris marches through a landscape of joy that is the deliberate point-by-point reversal of Childe Roland's self-made phantasmagoria of ordeal-by-landscape [...]
> Roland's band of failures has become the glorious band of precursors among whom Thamuris predominates. [...] There is the true triumph of Browning's art, for the ever-early Thamuris is Browning as he wishes to have been, locked in a solitary struggle against the precursor-principle, but struggling *in* the visionary world of the precursor.[46] □

In 'Thamuris marching' Browning can write like Shelley and contend with the precursor as Thamuris does with the Muses. However, both the reader and Thamuris know that the successor will fail in the end even though this outcome is not included in Browning's poem.

Bloom's theory has itself generated a certain anxiety of influence among Browning critics who cannot avoid the precursor Bloom when discussing Browning's attitude towards Romanticism. Given that Bloom focuses only on a few poems in addition to his favourite 'Childe Roland', there have been opportunities to apply his theory to other poems, either early or late. Three conspicuous limitations of Bloom's approach are worth noting. Firstly, the theory is anti-historicist, paying no attention to the broader contemporary cultural context of the successor poet. Secondly, this is a purely antagonistic approach, which leaves no space for a grateful acknowledgement of the predecessor. Bloom's antagonism between Browning and the Romantics is in line with Browning's own theory of poetic history as progressing through opposed stages, but Bloom's black-and-white approach does not make visible ways in which Browning may have developed elements of Romanticism. A section in the next chapter on the reading of Browning's use of Romantic irony will show the potential of such an approach. Thirdly, Bloom only focuses on a single precursor. Although his analysis concentrates on texts rather than personal psychology, this does reduce the complexity of Browning's engagement with Romantic poetry as a whole or as an abstract. The next chapter broadens this perspective by considering criticism about Browning's attitude towards another major Romantic poet, William Wordsworth (1770–1850), and by presenting other critical paradigms that have been applied to Browning's attitude towards Romanticism.

CHAPTER TWO

# Romanticism: Debt and Defiance

This chapter extends the survey of criticism about Browning's complex relationship with Romanticism that is so crucial to understanding his work. Much of the criticism covered here situates itself, either explicitly or implicitly, in relation to Harold Bloom's theory of the anxiety of influence as discussed in Chapter 1, either by adopting aspects of it or by suggesting alternatives. The first section on Browning and Wordsworth contrasts a Bloomian reading by John Haydn Baker with one by Lawrence Kramer which locates the intertextual dialogue between two poems in the wider context of Victorian revisions of Romantic textual strategies. This is followed by an analysis of Browning's poetry in terms of the paradigm of Romantic irony by Clyde de L. Ryals and Patricia Diane Rigg. Competing interpretations of Browning's aesthetics as explained either through the literary-historical context of Romanticism or through the perspective of modern theory also characterise criticism on his ideal of the imperfect, as demonstrated by Catherine Maxwell's reference to the Romantic sublime and Herbert Tucker's deconstructive reading of the same concept. Closely combining historical and modern approaches, David E. Latané situates Browning in relation to Romantic elitist poetics but also draws on twentieth-century reader-response theory. The chapter closes with Britta Martens' discussion of Browning's dramatised confrontation with Romantic self-expression in the poems in his own voice.

## Browning and Wordsworth: More Anxiety?

Shelley might have been a huge influence on Browning and other Victorian poets, but William Wordsworth, who became Poet Laureate in 1843, was certainly the most popular Romantic poet among the general public. The influence of Wordsworth's aesthetics on Browning's has been explored in John Haydn Baker's *Browning and Wordsworth* (2004), which applies Bloom's theory to this other poetic precursor. Baker summarises Browning's changing attitude towards Wordsworth throughout his career, focusing first on the young Browning:

> ■ Browning's early poetry, especially *Paracelsus* [1835], demonstrates that as a young man Browning was so influenced by Wordsworth – mainly by Wordsworth's attempt to fuse romantic idealism with practical realism [...] – that he was in danger of producing pastiches of Wordsworthian doctrines.[1] □

Baker defines the 'idealist' as the opposite of the 'realist' in that he strives to transform the 'real' world into a perfect world:

> ■ Idealism is humanistic, but it may not be *actively* so; the idealist may strive to create his utopia, or he may rest content with merely imagining it, and thus contribute nothing to the humanistic mission of alleviating human suffering. As will be shown, these flaws in romantic idealism troubled Browning. As for 'humanism', the term is used to signify the humanitarian concern with the alleviation of human suffering that was such a strong motivating factor in the careers of many of the romantic poets; neither idealism nor realism are incompatible with this sort of humanism, but both have potentially antihumanistic flaws. For the romantics, this humanitarian belief was inextricably linked with political radicalism, in that many of the sufferings of humanity could be ascribed to oppressive governments; through fighting these rulers, the romantic humanist was helping mankind. [...] Browning's poetry, particularly that produced before 1840, is deeply imbued with this sort of 'romantic humanism'; much of this influence came from Wordsworth.[2] □

The young Browning subscribes to Wordsworth's Romantic attempt to create an ideal world for suffering humanity; but a close emulation of Wordsworth in Browning's early work does not allow him to become a strong poet, so that he has to change his approach and 'misread' and seemingly reject Wordsworth. He does this in *Sordello* (1840) where Wordsworth is 'brutally dismissed', but '[a]n examination of Browning's career after the apparent defeat or erasure of Wordsworth in *Sordello* shows how Browning's consciousness of the unfairness of his "misreading" troubled him for years'.[3]

Baker's focus is thus primarily on the relationship between aesthetics and ethics. He reads the closet drama *Paracelsus* as Browning's most Wordsworthian work in terms of the lesson it teaches the initially self-centred protagonist about humanism and its fusion of idealism and realism, whereas in *Sordello*, Browning distances himself from Wordsworth, because 'it is precisely as a "rival" of Wordsworth that Browning needs to redefine himself if he is to escape his influence and speak with his own voice'.⁴ Baker argues that in *Sordello*, where the narrator is converted to humanitarianism through an encounter with the allegorical figure of 'suffering humanity', Browning 'misreads' Wordsworth as ignoring the human suffering which surrounds him and depicts him as an egocentric, antihumanistic visionary. Between 1840 and 1869 Browning 'erases' Wordsworth's influence from his work, but in later works Browning's bad conscience forces him to make belated amends and acknowledge the precursor's humanitarianism.

Baker traces Browning's conflict with Wordsworth all the way to the 'Prologue' to Browning's final collection *Asolando*, which was published on the day of his death in 1889. In the 'Prologue', Baker detects a late resurgence of rivalry with the poetic father that is, in Bloom's view, typical of strong poets who 'return to origins at the end, or whenever they sense the imminence of the end'.⁵ An alternative approach which broadens the perspective to Browning's engagement with a pervasive Romantic pattern rather than just one predecessor is taken by Lawrence Kramer in 'The "Intimations" Ode and Victorian Romanticism' (1980). The article compares Browning's reply to Wordsworth's 'Ode: Intimations of Immortality from Recollections of Early Childhood' (1807) in the 'Prologue' to *Asolando* to similar poems by Tennyson and Matthew Arnold (1822–88). In Wordsworth's poem, the mature poet mourns the loss of visionary joy and spontaneous perception of meaning in nature which he enjoyed as a child, but he ultimately finds some consolation in memories of his earlier abilities and in his 'primal sympathy' (l. 186) with other humans. A similar line of argument can be found in a number of major Romantic lyrics, so that Kramer's article can be said to analyse the response to a key aspect of Romantic aesthetics despite the apparent focus on a single predecessor text. Kramer examines what he calls 'the Victorian dialectic of compensation', defined in opposition to the Romantic poem which finds a replacement for the youth's loss of vision:

■ As it appears in major Romantic poems [...], this compensatory movement achieves a saving moment in which the present is relieved of the burden of loss and projected into the future under the sign of the replacement. Thus Wordsworth in the Ode exchanges grief for 'primal sympathy'; [...] the compensatory rhythm depends upon the growth of what is in effect a new self, an altered subjectivity to which the diminished external world is not the radically deprived place it has been to the troubled and restless self that preceded it. However tentatively, a balance is regained: the depleted world is weighed against a replenished self.

Victorian versions of this pattern are very different. The major Victorian poets all seem to feel a deep skepticism about the power of the self to generate compensation by regenerating itself, and the compensatory rhythm in their poems tends to look for things outside the self in order to make up its losses.⁶ □

Romantic poems make up for the feeling of having lost the joyous experience of the outer world by finding compensation within a new, replenished self. By contrast, the Victorians no longer believe in the resources of the self and search for compensation outside the self.

Kramer dismisses Bloom's approach here, arguing that a struggle with the precursor is not the purpose of Browning's 'Prologue': ☐

> ■ Though it does offer some 'misreadings' of the Ode as part of its rhetorical strategy, Browning's poem is not concerned with revising its precursor's dialectic but with the self's inability to escape that dialectic – the hard balance of visionary loss and compensation, regardless of how those terms are defined. A profoundly self-subverting poem, the 'Prologue' takes a tortuously ironic course in order to rebuke and revoke its own concern with the loss of a visionary gleam in nature, while at the same time finding an unshakable external compensation for the loss it deprecates.[7] ☐

The 'Prologue' tries to make up for the loss of youthful vision outside the self, and it goes further than the Romantics by criticising and ironising the Romantic sense of loss. The poem opens with two stanzas spoken by a 'Friend' which are a Wordsworthian pastiche summarising the mature self's sense of loss of visionary power. To this Browning responds in his own voice that the youth's vision was coloured by 'falsehood's fancy haze' (l. 20) and that the mature self's sober perception of reality and fact is preferable. Kramer focuses on two 'startling formal discontinuities'[8] towards the end of the poem. Firstly, having just critiqued the Wordsworthian nostalgia for the youth's vision, Browning now echoes it by reminiscing about his first visit to the Italian town of Asolo, when he had a visionary experience of nature which he conveys by likening it to Moses' encounter with God in a burning bush (Exodus 3): 'Even more than the young Wordsworth, the young Browning sees nature as literally sacred; and he emphasizes more than Wordsworth the terror in the beauty, the uncanniness that identifies perception of the sacred with transgression.'[9] Compared to this ecstatic past experience, the present self's untainted perception of reality seems strangely demystified and inferior. But in a second, final twist, the poem ends with the voice of God which

> ■ speaks out to rebuke the poet for seeking transcendence in the creation rather than in the creator: 'At Nature dost thou shrink amazed? / God is it who transcends' (ll. 44–45). At this, of course, the dialectic of visionary loss is wholly collapsed. Regret for the lambent flame stands revealed as a kind of sacrilege, or a sacrilegious nostalgia. Yet at the same time, the self

that has been deprived of theophany [i.e. an encounter with God] in nature has been compensated by an unmediated colloquy with the divine – a compensation by transcendence. Browning underscores this new reversal by insisting on a distinction between the 'purged ear' [of the mature self] that 'apprehends / Earth's import' and the 'eye late dazed' [of the younger self, ll. 41–2] which cannot. The shift from seeing to hearing as the medium of revelation is an attempt to degrade the specifically visionary character of a 'Palpably fire-clothed' [l. 25] world beyond innocent self-projection to an absurd optical illusion, and at the same time an attempt to revalue language as a vehicle for truth.[10] ☐

The visionary perception of God through his creation that is valued so highly by the Romantics is dismissed by Browning as inferior to the direct aural communication that his speaker claims to experience. But Kramer sees this move as a sign of desperation rather than a genuine compensation for the loss of Romantic vision. The better-than-visionary experience relies on the awkward device of recruiting the supreme authority of God, and it replaces a joyous communion with a divine rebuke.

Kramer's approach differs from Baker's in that, instead of applying twentieth-century theories to the nineteenth-century text, it analyses Browning's use of Romantic textual strategies. The next two sections of this chapter present one approach which works on the same principle as Kramer's, analysing Browning's work in terms of the Romantic paradigm of Romantic irony, and a related approach which combines attention to the nineteenth-century context with twentieth-century theory.

## Romantic Irony

In his three books *Browning's Later Poetry, 1871–1889* (1975), *Becoming Browning: The Poems and Plays of Robert Browning, 1833–1846* (1983) and *A World of Possibilities: Romantic Irony in Victorian Literature* (1990), Clyde de L. Ryals (1928–98) reads Browning as an exponent of Romantic irony.[11] He sees the poet as inheriting and developing a Romantic belief in dynamic change:

■ [W]here his immediate poetic predecessors envisioned change as part of a revolutionary process leading to a new heaven and a new earth, Browning views change as a process without *telos* [aim]. The idea of an open, evolving universe is, to a certain degree, antithetical to the Romantics' notion of union of self and nature and of the work of art as a revelation of the meeting of the self and the Absolute. [...] Browning, on the other hand, maintains that it is the function of the imagination not to reconcile opposites but to transcend them by accepting them as antinomies, thereby substituting for the Romantics' circle of enclosure an upward-tending spiral.[12] ◻

Ryals sees Browning's belief in, and celebration of, perpetual change and unresolvable oppositions as something which always distinguishes him from Shelley and other English Romantics, who believe in the possibility of closure and union. Browning's conviction that the Absolute always remains out of reach is clear from his definition of the subjective poet quoted in Chapter 1. This idea is central to the paradigm of Romantic or philosophical irony as theorised by Friedrich Schlegel (1772–1829). Patricia Diane Rigg (born 1951), who conducts a reading of *The Ring and the Book* (1868–69) in *Robert Browning's Romantic Irony in 'The Ring and the Book'* (1999), summarises the stance of Schlegel's Romantic ironist thus:

■ To the Romantic ironist – both writer and reader – the self is a creative entity always in the process of creating 'self'; this creative impulse arises out of self-conscious criticism the goal of which is self-knowledge gained through a work which is, as Kathleen Wheeler says, 'self-consuming' because it resists closure or fixed meaning.[13] The writer as Romantic ironist defines himself or herself as 'becoming' rather than as 'being', as one in the constant process of striving rather than in stasis. The reader as Romantic ironist must define himself or herself in precisely the same terms. In other words, 'the true reader must be an expanded author'.[14] ◻

In Romantic irony, the state of becoming applies to the universe, the poet and the reader. A text which uses Romantic irony eludes closure and neat solutions. It obliges the reader to accept this open-endedness and become as critically self-conscious as the author. Turning to how this applies to Browning's poetry, Ryals explains:

■ When translated into psychological terms, this conception of the universe entails a tension in the individual, who simultaneously desires order and coherence – being – and chaos and freedom – becoming. The drive toward stability is usually experienced as love, the drive toward change as power. [...] the conflict between love and power is dramatized in all of Browning's early poetry. [...]

Schlegel's dialectic allows for no synthesis; his contradictions remain always unresolved. It is the function of philosophical irony as he expounds it to permit an individual to hold the two contrary states of being and becoming in mind at the same time and to recognize that they cannot

be harmonized. Browning too espouses this view, but he introduces the element of progress, which is not clearly a part of Schlegel's philosophy. [...] Browning does not envision a synthesis; for him the dialectic remains unharmonized. He sees, however, a growth of consciousness resulting from the dialectic interplay that allows the individual and the race to evolve into ever higher spiritual, moral and artistic states or conditions; for him becoming involves the notion of creative evolution. [...]
Browning's conception of philosophical irony has profound implications for his art, ultimately determining not only the content of his verse but its form as well.[15] ☐

Browning not only adopts Schlegel's eternal becoming without synthesis, he goes beyond it by conceiving of this open-ended process as spiritually and artistically elevating.

Ryals proceeds to analyse the tensions between love and power in Browning's work and also the self-consciousness of his characters who have an ironic awareness of how they construct and deconstruct their own existence. Wit, as displayed, for instance, by the *in propria persona* (in his/her own person) speakers of *Sordello* and the framing monologues of *The Ring and the Book*, is an important component, as Rigg points out:

■ Wit allows the Romantic ironist to be self-deprecating and self-critical without being humble; he or she hovers above the work, endorsing its integrity [...] all the while drawing attention to its inadequacies as a finite and limited version of the unlimited possible forms of truth.[16] ☐

Romantic irony is formally manifest in generic experimentation and innovation, and this, too, in Ryals' view, is illustrated by Browning's early work up to 1846 and again in the late work from 1868 onwards, both periods in which he experimented with a variety of different forms. By contrast, it might surprise the reader that Ryals describes Browning's middle period during his marriage, in which he worked primarily in the innovative genre of the dramatic monologue, as less ironic in the sense that the monologues 'have more moral design upon the reader than do the earlier poems'.[17] There are ironies in these poems 'but they are ironies that by and large point to some fixed meaning'.[18] We will see in the chapters about the dramatic monologue that not all critics would agree with this analysis of the genre as less ambiguous than Browning's early and late work. Indeed, as the next section will show, the unresolved tensions which Ryals explains as manifestations of Romantic irony can also be analysed in terms of deconstructive theory which constantly defers closure or as manifestations of the Romantic sublime.

## The Imperfect

Most critics would probably agree that Browning's highest abstract aesthetic ideal is the imperfect or incomplete. He advocates an eternal striving for an unattainable ideal but acknowledges that it always remains just out of reach. In the *Essay on Shelley* (1852), he defines the subjective poet as aspiring to – but unable to attain – a divine apprehension of 'all things in their absolute truth' (see Chapter 1).[19] Here, as in Andrea del Sarto's exclamation, 'Ah, but a man's reach should exceed his grasp, / Or what's a heaven for?' ('Andrea del Sarto' (1855), 97–8), the imperfect is conceived as an attribute of the Christian who aspires towards divine perfection. Indeed, perfection in the human sphere is dismissed in 'Old Pictures in Florence' (1855) as leading to deathly sterility: 'What's come to perfection perishes' (l. 130). Here the pre-1500 primitive painters, whose painting is less technically advanced than that of the artists of classical Greek antiquity, are presented as superior to their predecessors because their imperfection makes them more human. The speaker imagines them saying:

> ■ What if we so small
> Are greater, ay, greater the while than they [the classical Greek artists]!
> Are they perfect of lineament, perfect of stature?
> In both, of such lower types are we
> Precisely because of our wider nature;
> For time, theirs – ours, for eternity. [ll. 114–20] □

Catherine Maxwell sees Browning's promotion of the incomplete as a modified version of the Romantic sublime. She argues that the incomplete and the sublime are linked in a key text on the sublime, *A Philosophical Enquiry into the Origin of Our Ideas of the Sublime and Beautiful* (1757) by Edmund Burke (1729–97). The *Enquiry*

> ■ links the sublime to obscurity and infinity. Burke contends that both in nature and in painting 'dark, confused images have a greater power on the fancy to form the grander passions than those have which are more clear and determinate'. [...] Certainly the notion that incompletion lends itself to sublime effects becomes a familiar conceit in nineteenth-century literature.[20] □

For Maxwell, Browning's interest in this version of the sublime explains his famously difficult and elliptical style:

> ■ The language of Browning's texts, which is often apparently dramatic, is shot through with small hesitations, lacunae, divergences, disturbances

which run counter to the overt dramatic intention and allow something else to happen. These moments have the capacity to function as lyric epiphanies allowing access to what he called the infinite.[21] □

Such a moment of sublime insight occurs in '"Transcendentalism": A Poem in Twelve Books' (1855):

> ■ In this poem the speaker addresses an aspiring poet who, believing that lyricism is a juvenile concern and that 'grown men want thought', has taken to writing a rational unadorned verse. Unimpressed by the poet's 'dry words', the speaker points out that he might just as [well] 'speak prose', exchange the harp, the symbol of lyrical song, for the stentorian blast of the swiss horn. Repudiating the notion that lyricism is only for boys, he compares Jacob Boehme's intellectualising of vegetable nature with the inspired wizardry of the 'Mage', John of Halberstadt. For while we wrestle with the meanings of Boehme's 'tough book', 'life's summer' slips past:[22] □

As the poem puts it, 'John [...] made things Boehme wrote thoughts about' (l. 38):

> ■ He with a 'look you!' vents a brace of rhymes,
> And in there breaks the sudden rose herself,
> Over us, under, round us every side,
> Nay, in and out the tables and the chairs
> And musty volumes, Boehme's book and all, –
> Buries us with a glory, young once more,
> Pouring heaven into this shut house of life. [ll. 39–45] □

Maxwell comments:

> ■ The 'sudden rose' is the lyric moment or interlude which lets the sublime as imaginative energy break through into the quotidian, into the more regular perfunctory serviceable language which is then irradiated and altered by its presence.[23] □

Contrasting with Maxwell's tracing of Browning's advocacy of the incomplete back to Romantic lyricism, Herbert F. Tucker, in *Browning's Beginnings: The Art of Disclosure* (1980) proposes a twentieth-century perspective on Browning's aesthetics of the imperfect. Tucker's book is called *Browning's Beginnings* not only because it focuses on the poet's early works but also because it argues that Browning's poetics favour openings rather than neat endings. In Tucker's view, Browning is a poet of the future and of anticipation, and his ethical belief in the value of the incomplete is mirrored by the form of his poetry, ranging from the micro level of language to the plotlines of his long poems and plays:

> ■ Often at the end of these works the expected deed remains uncommitted, the complex issue unresolved, so as to suggest a residue of action exceeding the formal and temporal limits of the plot. In Browning's lyric poems, likewise, the traditional weight of closure feels less like exhaustive aplomb than like a force temporarily compressing a spring that remains tensed for further speech. Such tension may be located in Browning's reader as well as in his speaker, and it is essential to an understanding of Browning's dramatic irony to see irony as a way of composing a question for the reader's benefit without resolving it. Those occasions where a poem does snap shut, where action or speech does appear to have played itself out satisfactorily, are usually also those occasions where Browning's irony emerges at its strongest. Browning forges poetic forms that dramatize the relationship of accomplishment to desire, of heritage to initiative, and of present to future. Far from eschewing the closural resources of traditional poetic form, he uses those resources for the purpose of calling attention to closure in order to question its validity and worth.[24] □

The tension created by the lack of closure in Browning's poetry is meant to have an effect on the reader's critical mind. Even if there is closure in a poem, Tucker suggests, this apparent neatness is only an ironic device designed to make the reader question the value of closure.

As its theoretical basis, Tucker's study combines Harold Bloom's concept of poetic belatedness (see Chapter 1) with Barbara Herrnstein Smith's analysis of poetic closure and the deconstructive theory of philosopher Jacques Derrida (1930–2004). Herrnstein Smith's formalist book *Poetic Closure: A Study of How Poems End* (1968) is mostly focused on poems with a 'strong' or 'successful' closure.[25] This is in line with the main tradition of literary criticism before the 1980s (especially New Criticism) which valued works that offer a neat resolution. By contrast, Tucker is interested in Browning as an exponent of 'the anticlosural tendencies of poetry since the romantic period'.[26] Browning's avoidance of closure goes against the expectations of Victorian readers who largely still believed in religious and moral certainties, Tucker argues, while for Browning avoiding the certainty of closure was a way of coping with the sense of belatedness identified by Bloom:

> ■ The principal beneficiary of Browning's moral and aesthetic philosophy of incompleteness may have been Robert Browning – not as a man of his era, but as a poet, especially a poet writing in what was to him inevitably a late romantic era. His intricate preservation of the future helped preserve his own future as a practicing poet; not least among its many uses, Browning's defense of anticipation offered a means of self-defense against that

familiar hobgoblin of the poetic latecomer, the threat that there may be nothing left to say.[27] □

Tucker also draws on Derrida's deconstructive semiotics, according to which all experience is rooted in texts and meaning is intangible because every signifier refers to another signifier which refers to yet another signifier, so that meaning is constantly delayed. As a result, deconstruction values the open-endedness that more traditional critics would label as weak closure. Poetic language is particularly suited to convey the deconstructive deferral of meaning. Its so obviously artistic structure and use of figurative language draw attention to the fact that it is a representation, that is, it points to the absence of the thing it represents. Browning's psychology illustrates Derrida's concept of *différance*, 'a coinage that puns on the French verb meaning both "differ" and "defer," to describe the process of representation whereby language displaces and postpones indefinitely the verities it ostensibly signifies'.[28] He plays on yet another meaning of 'defer' in that his

> ■ characters tend to place themselves in secondary or deferential postures; by deferring to their ideals or to each other, they defer to the future and thus heighten the climate of anticipation in which Browning's poetry thrives. Juxtaposing the senses of temporal deferral and emotional deference not only can show how the oddities of Browning's characters have a place in his poetry of the future, it can give to the formidably dispassionate tone of much deconstructionist theory a welcome human resonance. Deconstructionist criticism has generally slighted character analysis, probably because the notion of 'character,' with its assumptions about the coherence and continuity of the self, is amongst the fictions of integrity that it is the avowed business of deconstruction to put (and often enough to leave) in question. Here, at least with regard to Browning, deconstruction's gain may be literary criticism's loss. Browning certainly believed in the self, and for that very reason he was able to prize the diversity of its habits.[29] □

Tucker thus works from deconstructive premises but also concedes that in its most rigorous form this theory is not suitable for an analysis of Browning. The poet believed in the unity of the self and character psychology is central to his poetry, while deconstruction rejects the notion of the coherent self and sees character as an illusion created by language.

Tucker's take on Browning offers an explanation for the many ambiguities and unresolved tensions in the poet's work. Browning's anticlosural aesthetics also account for his obscurity, which

> ■ proceeds from a principled evasiveness that is utterly in keeping with his attitude toward form and his governing orientation toward the future. He makes his style slippery with the consistent purpose of avoiding any

structural or semantic enclosure that would dim the sense of the future with which he identifies his poetic mission.[30] □

Although the distinguishing feature of Tucker's influential book is its deconstructive approach, he does of course situate Browning's aesthetics in relation to Romantic concepts such as the centrality of the self discussed above. While Tucker identifies Browning's favouring of the incomplete and his related obscurity as anti-Romantic, David E. Latané considers this obscurity to be part of his Romantic inheritance. His approach, which offers a more pronounced combination of early nineteenth- and twentieth-century theories, also pays attention to the analogy between the author and the poet as evoked by Ryals.

## The Romantic Aesthetics of Difficulty

In 'Browning's *Sordello* and the Aesthetics of Difficulty' (1987), Latané acknowledges, like so many other critics, the central importance of *Sordello* for an understanding of Browning's poetics. However, he distinguishes himself by arguing not for the exceptional nature of this poem but for its conformity with a fashion among some authors during the 1830s for deliberately difficult literature. In line with Romantic aesthetics, these texts demand a high degree of creative participation from their reader:

> ■ The easiest way to force greater participation is through an increase in the complexity of style, thought, and figure. A corresponding decrease in the number of readers is made up by their quality. By the 1830s, paradoxically, a new orthodox view that great works must be difficult, obscure, neglected, and ridiculed is so widespread that some works written to this aesthetic [...] could become moderately popular. Such was not to be the case with Browning's poem, and the poem itself contains the best analysis of why this should be so.[31] □

Latané traces these elitist aesthetics which demand an active reader back to John Milton's (1608–74) address to his muse in *Paradise Lost* (1667), 'Still govern thou my song, / Urania, and fit audience find, though few' (Book VII, ll. 30–1). He considers their permutations in Romantic texts before focusing on *Sordello*. Unlike Yetman in his reading of *Sordello's* aesthetics and politics (see Chapter 1), Latané is primarily interested in the stylistic difficulties with which the reader is confronted. He draws on the reader-response theory of Wolfgang Iser (1926–2007) to analyse Browning's textual strategy in the poem. According to Iser, the literary work is the result of an interaction between the author and the reader. The author creates a text with 'gaps' or 'indeterminacies' of meaning, which the reader is left to fill. The reader is thus given a certain amount of freedom in the realisation of the text, but the meaning is not completely up to him/her.[32] Similarly, the Romantic aesthetics of difficulty value ambiguity but do not embrace radical indeterminacy.[33]

Latané cites, for instance, Browning's preface to *Paracelsus*, where the poet demands that his readers make an active effort to co-operate with the poet in the construction of meaning, using the metaphor of chasms rather than gaps:

■ It is certain, however, that a work like mine depends more immediately on the intelligence and sympathy of the reader for its success – indeed were my scenes stars it must be his co-operating fancy which, supplying all chasms, shall connect the scattered lights into one constellation – a Lyre or a Crown.[34] □

In *Sordello*, too, the protagonist compares the co-operation between author and reader to the intimate communication between brothers who almost understand each other without need for words:

■ How we attain to talk as brothers talk,
In half-words, call things by half-names
[...]
     'tis but brother's speech
We need, speech where an accent's change gives each
The other's soul – [V, 605–6, 615–7, 1840 version][35] □

Latané also discusses a statement by Browning which comes close to Iser's terminology. It appears in a letter to his publisher, written in 1856, when he was contemplating a more reader-friendly second edition of *Sordello*. Browning writes: 'I shall make it as easy as its nature admits, I believe – changing nothing and simply *writing in* the unwritten *every-other-line* which I stupidly left as an amusement for the reader to do – who, after all, is no writer, nor needs be.'[36] Latané explains:

■ What Browning, referring to *Sordello*, calls 'the unwritten every-other-line,' goes beyond what modern reader-response theory dubs 'blanks' or 'gaps.' Iser describes the communicative asymmetries between text and reader, noting that 'the blank is not a given, ontological fact, but is formed and modified by the imbalance ... between text and reader. Balance can only be attained if the gaps are filled, and so the constitutive blank is continually bombarded with projections' (*Act of Reading*, p. 167). As we read and reread *Sordello*, however, we find that the onslaught of readerly projectiles, while filling up one blank, rends the fabric of narration in another spot. Thus Browning's poem veers towards the status of *text*, in [Roland]

Barthes' sense of a subversive force opposed to generic taxonomies (the *work*). *Sordello* defeats any feeling on the reader's part of harmonious completion, not so much by maintaining an asymmetry between text and reader, as by continually, consciously reminding the reader that such fissures inevitably exist.[37] ☐

The reader has to fill so many gaps that the text is continually disintegrating. *Sordello*, Latané claims, goes beyond an illustration of Iser's theory and moves into the realm of the poststructuralist concept of the text, as proposed by Roland Barthes (1915–80), where meaning is never fixed. Via the route of reader-response theory, Latané thus arrives at a classification of Browning as anticipating a poststructuralist indeterminacy which brings him close to Tucker's position. Another analysis which suggests the poet's tendency towards poststructuralist aesthetics while situating him in relation to the Romantics – this time through his use of poetic voice – will conclude this chapter.

## Challenging the Romantic Personal Voice

Britta Martens' *Browning, Victorian Poetics and the Romantic Legacy: Challenging the Personal Voice* (2011) argues for Browning's role as a transitional figure in the history of poetry in that he creates unstable fragmented selves that foreshadow more modern poetry while still sharing the Romantics' belief in the self as the source of meaning, especially the self of the author. Browning's halfway position between Romanticism and poststructuralism is summarised thus:

> ■ While Barthes replaces the author as the generator of literary meaning with the reader, thus anticipating the preoccupations of reception theory and reader-response criticism, Browning [in the dramatic monologue] relinquishes part of his authorial control by erasing his voice from the text and calling for the reader's active participation in the constitution of meaning.
> [Here follows the quotation from the preface to *Paracelsus* cited in the previous section of this chapter.]
> Unlike Barthes, though, Browning still sees the author as contributing to the meaning and 'co-operating' with the reader, despite the absence of his voice. Another indicator of his Romantic roots is that he conceives of the reader as a single, solitary (male) reader and counterpart to the Romantic solitary genius of the author.[38] ☐

Although Browning still believes in the self of the poet as the source of meaning, he casts doubt over his own absolute perspective. The reader is therefore jolted out of a passive reading stance and made to question established assumptions about poetic voice and authority. The book focuses on the critically neglected poems in which Browning seems to speak in his own voice, such as the framing books of *The Ring and the Book* or 'One Word More' (1855). Instead of reading these – in line with Romantic self-expressive poetics – as straightforward statements of Browning's views, the study interprets them as dramatic confrontations with Romantic self-expression:

> ■ [W]hile they appear to adopt the personal voice of the self-expressive lyric, the majority of these poems are actually presented as dramatic addresses to a listener within the text or to the reader. [...] the resemblance to the dramatic monologue, with its potential to lay bare the speaker's internal conflicts, permits Browning to explore the tensions and contradictions in his attitude towards Romanticism. In the role of the *author*, he can take a detached look at himself as a quasi 'other' in the character of the *speaker* 'Browning', a dramatic version of his self whose ideas and behaviour need not fully correspond to those of the real Browning.[39] □

Browning uses the principles of the dramatic monologue with its distinction between author and speaker even in those poems which seem to be his self-expression in order to re-educate a Victorian readership whose poetic taste is still in the Romantic self-expressive mould. Reading between the lines and filling in semantic gaps, they are thus taught to become suspicious of the apparently authoritative authorial voice and are able to witness how Browning reflects on his own conflicting attitudes towards aspects of Romanticism. Instead of making explicit statements about his poetics in prefaces or essays, which he mostly avoided, Browning transfers the discussion of his poetics into the more ambiguous poetic text, combining theory with practice, and showing rather than telling his readers how to read his work:

> ■ [T]he hybrid form of a dramatic utterance by the poet himself means that Browning can enact the antagonism between the confessional lyric and the dramatic monologue in these poems rather than stating his disagreement with Romanticism dogmatically in a prose text. He thus invites his readers to consider the merits of his new poetics in practice. They are urged to become more critical of poetic conventions, to question the apparently reliable, sincere 'authorial' voice and the basic assumptions made by Romantic poetry.[40] □

The levels of engagement with Romanticism covered by the study include not just Browning's response to Romantic precursor texts (as discussed in this chapter and Chapter 1) but also his critical review of his own early Romantic taste and his dialogue with the still dominant 'derivations of Romantic aesthetics as they are embodied by contemporary poetic practice, audience expectations, the pressures of the literary market and criticism of his work, mainly in the "official" form of reviews but also in the shape of private criticism by his wife and friends'.[41]

Like Ryals, Latané and Martens do not apply ideas about reader participation and indeterminacy of meaning to the dramatic monologue, but such an application would have its merit. As Chapter 3 will show, the reader's activity in guessing what the speaker leaves unsaid is crucial to the dramatic monologue and plays a central role in critical readings of Browning's poems in the genre. Similarly, the space for interpretation which is created by the absence of an authoritative authorial voice is a major focus of critical attention. More than in the present chapter, where the similarities between nineteenth-century aesthetics and twentieth-century critical approaches were highlighted, we will see in Chapters 3 and 4 a tension between interpretations which apply twentieth-century theory to the dramatic monologue and readings which situate the dramatic monologue within its historical context.

Although Browning's early poems are not studied much these days, the first two chapters of this Guide have given some insight into how important their negotiations with a range of Romantic ideas are for understanding Browning's poetics and the more popular works of his mature period. As the next chapter will show, the poet's attitude towards the Romantic self-expressive lyric and the Romantic concept of the self is also crucial for many of the critics who explore the form and purpose of Browning's most famous genre.

CHAPTER THREE

# The Dramatic Monologue: Form and the Reader

Not only has Browning (together with Tennyson) been credited with inventing the dramatic monologue, the most important poetic genre of the Victorian period, his poems are also the main influence on the many dramatic monologues that were produced in the second half of the nineteenth century, and they are the prime texts on which definitions and analyses of this genre are based.[1] After some formal definitions of the genre by Ina Beth Sessions, Michael Mason, Alan Sinfield and Philip Drew, this chapter considers the most influential, reader-centred definition of the genre by Robert Langbaum, which most later critics use as a point of reference. This is followed by critiques of Langbaum's theory from three very different positions: E. Warwick Slinn's reading of the dramatic monologue as a process of creating a fictional identity, Ralph Rader's focus on the monologue's poetic form and Cynthia Scheinberg's feminist approach. Another two sections examine the dramatic monologue as a fictional act of communication. The first of these considers the importance of the audience both *of* the poem and *in* the poem in the work of John Maynard, Jennifer Wagner-Lawlor, Dorothy Mermin and Lee Erickson. The second presents analyses of the genre in terms of speech act theory by Cornelia D. Pearsall and Slinn.

## Defining the Genre

As A. Dwight Culler reminds us in his article about the genre, the term 'dramatic monologue' only began to be used over two decades after Browning and Tennyson had started to write dramatic monologues in the 1830s. Browning himself never used the term, although he did repeatedly label his poetry as 'dramatic', most famously in his 'Advertisement' to *Dramatic Lyrics* (1842), where he defines the collection as '"Dramatic pieces"; being, though often Lyric in expression, always

Dramatic in principle, and so many utterances of so many imaginary persons, not mine'.[2] 'Dramatic monologue' was first used in 1857 by George W. Thornbury (1828–76) to characterise a collection of his poems which were clearly influenced by Browning, and other poets and critics with a strong interest in Browning then adopted the term, applying it to a variety of poems with different formal features.[3] So unspecific was the use of the term that Isobel Armstrong (born 1937) even suggests that 'the "pure" dramatic monologue is an invention of the twentieth century'.[4]

Early- to mid-twentieth-century academic definitions of the genre tend to be based on a small corpus of poems by Browning (and, with varying degrees of complication, Tennyson). The rather limited choice of exemplary works raises the question as to whether these definitions can really claim to describe a universal genre or whether they should instead be seen as descriptions of poems by a single author. This flaw has been exposed by critics such as Armstrong, Cynthia Scheinberg and Glennis Byron, who argue for the role of Romantic women poets as the true founders of the genre and who have broadened the basis of exemplary texts to include many dramatic monologues by female poets.[5] Yet, since the interest of this Guide is Browning, the privileged position of his work in general definitions of the genre offers a rich landscape for exploration.

Early definitions of the dramatic monologue had a fairly strict focus on formal features and on the genre's origins with little interest in its effects and ideological implications. In her article 'The Dramatic Monologue' (1947), Ina Beth Sessions offered a classification of the genre into four subcategories exclusively based on Browning poems:[6]

### Sub-classifications of the Dramatic Monologue

| Perfect Example | Approximations | | |
| --- | --- | --- | --- |
| | Imperfect | Formal | Approximate |
| 1) Speaker<br>2) Audience<br>3) Occasion<br>4) Interplay between speaker and audience<br>5) Revelation of character<br>6) Dramatic action<br>7) Action taking place in the present | 1) Shifting of centre of interest from speaker; or,<br>2) Fading into indefiniteness of one or more of the last six Perfect characteristics | 1) Speaker<br>2) Audience<br>3) Occasion | 1) Speaker<br>2) Lacking one or more of the characteristics listed under the Formal or the Imperfect |

This rather mechanical taxonomy is a good starting point because it clarifies the genre's most obvious formal features and allows us to distinguish between formal variants, but it fails to capture the genre's purpose and what makes it attractive to the reader.

Michael Mason's 'Browning and the Dramatic Monologue' (1974) offers a similarly formal definition of the genre which stresses central aspects that Sessions overlooks, namely the separation between speaker and author, the linguistic realism of the utterance and the process through which character is revealed:

> ■ (1) The sort of dramatic monologue Browning wrote is a poem of which the versified part is devoted almost entirely to the imaginary utterance of some person other than the author. (2) There is a distinct attempt to reproduce the characteristics of actual speech, even in the unusual case where the utterance is supposed to have been written, or the form of the poem is that of simple lyric. (3) The utterance is used to do a job natural to extended speech, namely, to express a state of mind, disposition, attitude, or set of beliefs. It is not used to express action for its own sake, and, where it does express action, the interest is that this is a characteristic action for the speaker. (4) The state of mind, or whatever, is treated seriously, in the sense that it is given a full and fairly eloquent expression; it is not obviously discredited. (5) It matters for a full understanding of the text that the reader should take it as the utterance of some person other than the author, either because the interest is in the expression of a state of mind that is historically or culturally remote, or because there are ways in which the speaker betrays rather than consciously expresses aspects of this state of mind. In keeping with the spirit of (3) the speaker will not give conscious expression to more aspects of his state of mind than is plausible.[7] □

The revelation of character can therefore be said to be inadvertent: '[T]he reader has to gather more from the utterance than the supposed speaker is conscious of expressing. In a word, the treatment is ironical. The speaker *betrays* important aspects of his state of mind rather than *articulating* them.'[8] The innovative feature of Browning's monologues is, in Mason's view, that this discrediting of the speaker is not overtly comical.

The authorial intention that underlies this ironic betrayal of the speaker is to let readers approach the poem as they would normal, non-literary communication:

> ■ Doubtless it is by analogy with betrayals in ordinary intercourse that we know how to interpret the ironies Browning has inserted, but we cannot escape the consciousness of the author's activity in the matter. While we know that the speaker is not Robert Browning we do not forget that Robert Browning is the author. The idea that the speaker is 'other than the author' becomes peculiarly strengthened in such a case.[9] □

'The Bishop Orders His Tomb at Saint Praxed's Church' (1845) and 'My Last Duchess' (1842) illustrate the pleasure to be gained from reading the genre:

> ▪ When reading the bishop's utterance we recognize and applaud the representation of betrayal, rather than betrayal itself. We applaud it because of its deftness rather than its naturalism. We are satisfied by a piece of considerable virtuosity, as much as satisfied by having gauged the bishop's state of mind. [...] The response is a kind of delight, or glee, that any virtuoso performance gives, and, as with virtuoso performances, there is a close bond between the performer and the audience, a happy conspiracy of display on the one hand and applause on the other. This element of happy recognition of Browning the virtuoso seems to be a much larger part of a normal response to many of the dramatic monologues than is commonly allowed. For example, I believe we applaud the Duke's brief reference to his bronze Neptune at the end of 'My Last Duchess' [...] for its deft colloquialism and its appearance of historical authenticity well before we construe it as psychologically accurate. And the first feature I listed – the giving of virtually all the monologue's content through the speaker – now becomes more intelligible. The writer's adroit negotiation of this self-imposed obstacle will enhance the reader's pleased approval.[10] ▫

The reader's enjoyment of the poem derives from his/her appreciation of the poet's skill in revealing the speaker's true character although only the speaker's own voice is heard. Reader and poet are in allegiance, and the reader's attention seems to be focused less on the speaker than on the otherwise invisible poet.

The poet's position in relation to his poem is also of central interest to Alan Sinfield (born 1941) in his short book *Dramatic Monologue* (1977). He situates the dramatic monologue in relation to two other genres, the first-person poem in the poet's own voice and the third-person narrative of fiction:

> ▪ Dramatic monologue lurks provocatively between these two forms. The title, perhaps, and other hints as we go along indicate that the speaker is not the poet and hence has something to do with fiction; but the first-person mode makes an opposite claim for the real-life existence of the speaker on the reader's plane of actuality.[11] ▫

The dramatic monologue is a lie or a feint not only because it is a realistic utterance by a fictional speaker but also because it adopts the first-person lyric voice which is usually read as the poet's own.

> ▪ [T]he speaker is a convenient vehicle for the poet's opinions. We experience the 'I' of the poem as a character in his own right but at the same time sense

the author's voice through him. The consequence of the frequent choice of an actual historical figure – Fra Lippo Lippi ['Fra Lippo Lippi', 1855], for instance – also becomes apparent, for such a speaker has a mode of reality comparable with the poet's own but nevertheless teasingly at odds with it.[12] ☐

Despite the 'lie' of passing off the fictional speaker as a real-life person, the dramatic monologue can give us true insights into the poet's mind. This is because there are varying degrees of closeness between the poet and his speaker, ranging from a complete distance between them – for instance, Browning seems to have nothing in common with the mad homicidal speaker of 'Porphyria's Lover' (1836) – to the kind of speaker who is 'relatively unlocated in time and place so that there is little beyond the title, say, to remind us that it is not supposed to be the poet speaking'.[13] The poet's stance is thus not the same in all monologues, and in Sinfield's analysis it can be determined by the interpreter.

The poet's agency is not explicitly addressed in Philip Drew's *The Poetry of Browning: A Critical Introduction* (1970), but it is implicit in his analysis of how the process of reading is shaped by the text. Drew dissects the stages of the reading process, although he, too, starts off with a formulaic definition of the genre:

■ The typical form of one of Browning's dramatic monologues is a narrative (N) spoken by one person. From N we can infer one or more of the following:

   (i) the circumstances in which N is spoken,
  (ii) the preceding history of the speaker, especially the part that explains the occasion of N, and
 (iii) the character and motives of the speaker.

But these inferences are of two kinds:

 (A) those which the speaker realizes are apparent, and which he has presumably designed, and
 (B) those which the speaker has not designed, and which he presumably does not realize are apparent.[14] ☐

The reading process is divided into the stages of, first, completing the context of the utterance and, then, comparing, which can happen at three different levels:

■ (i) When a monologue is spoken by a historical character or by an invented character set in a specific period of history we are normally required to compare what is presented as a contemporary account with our own fuller knowledge. [*An Epistle Containing the Strange Medical Experience of Karshish, the Arab Physician* (1855)] is an obvious example.

(ii) More often the comparison is internal. That is, we compare N+A with N+A+B; in this way we measure the speaker's version of the case against what we have learned *from his own words* to be the truth. This to my mind is the central characteristic of the dramatic monologue as Browning developed it, that [...] the poet provides in a single poem a man's version of reality and the standards against which that version is to be tested.

(iii) Occasionally we are required, as in *Caliban upon Setebos* [1864], to compare the views put forward with our own. If there is no discrepancy then we must judge our own views as we judge those of the speaker: if there is a discrepancy then we must decide either that the speaker's arguments are false or that our own views are unsound. That is to say, the result of the monologue is to impose a fresh perspective on ideas which, for example, the reader has uncritically accepted.[15] ☐

The genre may thus invite the readers to engage in self-reflection about their own standards of judgment. Moreover, the readers' assessment of the speaker is complicated by the fact that they are only presented with the speaker's version of the story and therefore cannot access an unbiased or alternative version of it. Drew's and Mason's concern with the reader is a response to Robert Langbaum's analysis of the genre, which focuses on the effect the text has on the reader. It is now time to turn to this most influential of approaches to the dramatic monologue.

## Langbaum's Sympathy versus Judgment

*The Poetry of Experience: The Dramatic Monologue in Modern Literary Tradition* (1957) by Robert Langbaum (born 1924) is a key text in the rehabilitation of Victorian, and especially Browning's, poetry after the denigration of the Victorians by the modernists (see Introduction). Langbaum dismisses both the modernists' denial of their debt to nineteenth-century poetry and the common definition of the dramatic monologue as a rejection of the Romantic confessional style. Instead, he constructs a narrative of a historical continuation from Romanticism through Victorian poetry to the modern period.[16] The nineteenth and twentieth centuries both share a perception of the world as 'meaningless', he argues, a result of the eighteenth-century Enlightenment's questioning of traditional values and authorities (religion, social structures, the monarchy) and its attempt to replace these with scientific fact. In such an empiricist world which esteems above all objectively verifiable fact, values such as beauty and goodness are demoted to mere illusions.[17]

Contrary to modernist critics and poets, Langbaum does not see Romanticism as merely sentimentalist and driven by emotion. To him, it is an attempt to reconcile thought and emotion and thus an intellectual reaction to the new scientific world view. Romantic lyrics such as William Wordsworth's 'Tintern Abbey' (1798) or Samuel Taylor Coleridge's 'Frost at Midnight' (1798), which present the poet's response to landscape and which heighten both his perception of the external world and his self-knowledge, are what Langbaum calls 'poems of experience'. They are 'the attempt of modern man to reintegrate fact and value after having himself rejected, in the experience of the Enlightenment, the old values.'[18] The poetry of experience 'communicates not as truth but experience, making its circumstances ambiguously objective in order to make it emphatically someone's experience'.[19] Langbaum postulates that the Romantic poem of experience is 'both subjective and objective. The poet talks about himself by talking about an object; and he talks about an object by talking about himself'.[20] The Romantic lyric is like 'one side of a dialogue' by a speaker who lacks self-awareness, while the poet is compared to a playwright who 'only speaks through one of his characters'.[21] This description of the poem of experience recalls that of the dramatic monologue as discussed in the previous section of this chapter. Indeed, Langbaum concludes that the Romantic poem of experience is a new dramatic genre and that Browning and Tennyson needed to take it only one step further to develop what is now called the dramatic monologue.[22] Far from being diametrical opposites, as other critics claim, the Romantic lyric and the dramatic monologue are therefore separated by only a minimal difference.

Dismissing the formal, objective criteria of Sessions and others, Langbaum states that the dramatic monologue's appeal needs to be understood through a consideration of its 'effect, its *way* of meaning'.[23] In his analysis, the dramatic monologue works through a tension in the reader's mind between sympathy with and moral judgment of the speaker. Sympathy is part of the genre's Romantic inheritance. In the preface to the book's 1971 edition, Langbaum clarifies that his use of the term 'sympathy' must not be confused with colloquial usage. It

> ■ does not mean *love* or *approval*; it is a way of knowing, what I call romantic projectiveness, what the Germans call *Einfühlung*, what the psychologists call empathy. The difference between the dramatic monologue and other forms of dramatic literature is that the dramatic monologue does not allow moral judgment to determine the amount of sympathy we give to the speaker. We give him all our sympathy as a condition of reading the poem, since he is the only character there. The difference is that we split our sympathy from our moral judgment. The dramatic monologue is most effective when the speaker is reprehensible; for we are then most acutely aware

of the moral condemnation that is, not abolished, but temporarily split off from our sympathy. We take this excursion into sympathetic identification with the speaker in order to refresh and renew moral judgment.[24] ☐

Sympathy is thus in opposition to judgment but ultimately leads to a reflection on moral categories.

Langbaum's test case for this particularly pronounced tension between our sympathy and our condemnation is the simultaneously villainous and fascinating speaker of 'My Last Duchess'. Langbaum suggests that 'moral judgment does not figure importantly in our response to the duke, that we even identify ourselves with him' despite our knowledge that 'out of unreasonable jealousy [he] has had his last duchess put to death, and is now about to contract a second marriage for the sake of dowry'.[25] The duke's outrageousness is related to the form of his utterance, the fact that the person he tells about his murder of the first wife is the envoy with whom he is about to negotiate the marriage to the next wife:

> ■ What interests us more than the duke's wickedness is his immense attractiveness. His conviction of matchless superiority, his intelligence and bland amorality, his poise, his taste for art, his manners – high-handed aristocratic manners that break the ordinary rules and assert the duke's superiority when he is being most solicitous of the envoy, waiving their difference of rank ('Nay, we'll go / Together down, sir' [ll. 53–4]); these qualities overwhelm the envoy, causing him apparently to suspend judgment of the duke, for he raises no demur. The reader is no less overwhelmed. We suspend moral judgment because we prefer to participate in the duke's power and freedom, in his hard core of character fiercely loyal to itself. Moral judgment is in fact important as the thing to be suspended, as a measure of the price we pay for the privilege of appreciating to the full this extraordinary man.[26] ☐

The duke's unapologetic amorality and indifference to the envoy's likely judgment of his behaviour, his aesthetic sense which is stronger than a desire to hide his villainy, combined with the monologue form which obliges the reader to understand the speaker's perspective, lead to the reader's suspension of judgment in favour of sympathy.

Browning repeats the potent combination of villain and aesthete or powerful intellect in other famous monologues such as 'The Bishop Orders his Tomb', 'Bishop Blougram's Apology' (1855) or 'Mr Sludge, "The Medium"' (1864). Langbaum explains the appeal of these characters:

> ■ Arguments cannot make the case in the dramatic monologue but only passion, power, strength of will and intellect, just those existential virtues which are independent of logical and moral correctness and are therefore

best made out through sympathy and when clearly separated from, even opposed to, the other virtues.[27] ☐

The dramatic monologue's privileging of sympathy leaves the question of whether and how judgment gets established. Langbaum concedes that sometimes the poet's position is not clear, as evidenced by reviews of Browning's poems that disagreed over whether he approved of a certain speaker or not.[28] Stressing the historical setting of many monologues, Langbaum concludes that

> ■ judgment is largely psychologized and historicized. We adopt a man's point of view and the point of view of his age in order to judge him – which makes the judgment relative, limited in applicability to the particular conditions of the case. This is the kind of judgment we get in the dramatic monologue, which is for this reason an appropriate form for an empiricist and relativist age, an age which has come to consider value as an evolving thing dependent upon the changing individual and social requirements of the historical process. For such an age judgment can never be final [...][29] ☐

Like Drew, Langbaum contends that the speaker is judged in relation to the standards of his/her own historical period, but unlike Drew he does not state that the speaker is also judged in relation to the reader's own standards. Instead, the dramatic monologue reveals the relativity and unreliability of all judgment because it develops in a post-Enlightenment age when the belief in permanent values has been undermined. There are no longer fixed norms against which behaviour can be measured. We will see critics taking up this argument in the next chapter on the genre's cultural context, but now we will consider some main objections to Langbaum's theory.

## The Primacy of Language

This section and the following one present very differently based critiques of Langbaum's theory. Both E. Warwick Slinn (born 1943) and in the next section Ralph Rader point out that Langbaum seems to treat the dramatic monologue as though it were the utterance of a real person and that he consequently does not devote enough attention to the crucial role of the poet and the language that create the speaker.

Slinn's book, *Browning and the Fictions of Identity* (1982), challenges Langbaum's core argument that the dramatic monologue continues the tradition of the Romantic poem in that both create a close link between external reality and the experience of perceiving it, suggesting an identification of object and perceiving subject. In Slinn's view, Langbaum does not pay enough attention to the importance of irony in Browning's monologues; this 'undermine[s] his characters and so break[s] the bond of identification [between object and subject]. Thus he builds into his poems a challenge to the assumed continuity between experience and reality'.[30] Because the poet's irony calls into question the speaker's authority (unlike that of the Romantic speaker), we are directed to consider his subjectivity: '[I]n undermining the conceptual authority of the speaker in a monologue, irony emphasises his fallibility, his role as subject'.[31] Browning's dramatic monologue is therefore not, as Langbaum would have it, a way of avoiding the Romantics' problematic subjectivity and

> ■ an attempt to achieve an objectivity denied his Romantic predecessors. But Browning uses his personae to dramatise subjectivity, not to avoid it. If, as Langbaum says, 'the speaker directs his address outward in order to address himself, and makes an objective discovery in order to discover himself' (p. 200), then this is an entirely subjective process because caught in its own circularity. [...] far from coming to know themselves through self-objectification, as Langbaum claims (p. 25), they show through unconscious irony that they attain only the illusion of objectivity.[32] □

While the speaker of the dramatic monologue looks outside the self in the hope of attaining objectivity, the poem's irony makes the reader notice the speaker's subjectivity and self-delusion. The dramatic monologue therefore focuses on the illusions (or fictions of Slinn's book title) that the speaker creates through his/her speech.

Neither are the poet and the reader able to achieve objectivity, as one might think in a text that uses the distancing device of irony: 'Irony may enforce the author's detachment from his work, but at the same time it is the sign of his involvement in the shaping' of the poem.[33] The reader, too, is involved in the poem because the dramatic monologue depends on his/her interpretation of what the speaker says: 'The nature of the form requires the reader to make an interpretation of what is overtly another interpretation – the speaker's view of himself and his world – and the result of this interaction is both an illusory depth of reality and an illusory objectivity in the reader's level of action.'[34] As he/she can only access the poem's 'reality' through the mediating consciousness of the speaker, the reader is at two removes from it. In exposing the impossibility of attaining objectivity in any of the agents involved in the poem, Slinn concludes, Browning's poems anticipate the undermining of objectivity in post-modern literature.

It also follows from the focus on the speaker's subjectivity and how he/she constructs his/her self that judgment is far less important to the dramatic monologue than Langbaum suggests:

> [W]e are not involved in the speaker's subject, but in the speaker as subject. Consequently, making up our minds about the speaker's topic is also a subordinate task, part of a more central involvement in the whole process of his self-construction, part of the reader's absorption into the argumentative process, into the more unifying task of discerning relationships between perspectives and determining the limits of human ingenuity.[35]

The speaker's use of language forms his/her experience, or rather the fictions about the world and the speaker's self that he/she takes for experience. Browning's self-conscious use of language draws our attention to how the speaker creates this illusion. Thus his 'poems inevitably raise questions about the fictional dimension of human experience'.[36] Although Slinn rejects the view that Browning's poems are vehicles for any philosophy, their underlying suggestion that all human experience is an illusion can be considered a philosophical position and a challenge to the aesthetics of realism (see Chapter 5). This denial of an objective reality that can be accessed through experience of the world is also a tenet of deconstructive theory which Herbert Tucker applies to Browning's work (see Chapter 2).

Slinn's analysis therefore focuses on how ambiguous, self-conscious uses of language create the fictions of the speakers' identities. He draws on concepts from personality theory according to which the self creates his/her self-image through a dramatic act that puts him/her in relation to something external:

> Any active, perceiving subject depends for its existence on a relationship with an identifiable object, just as the subject of a sentence is defined through its function in relationship to a predicate. In dramatising themselves, the monologuists therefore make the self an object; then, through being 'experienced' in its making and in its acting, that dramatised self establishes in turn the impression of a self as the experiencing subject.[37]

Poetry, as the most self-referential use of literary language, and the communicative intention that characterises the dramatic monologue are particularly good means of displaying the psychological process of how a character creates his/her fictional identity.

This book partially anticipates the application of deconstructionist theory by Slinn in later works and by Tucker.[38] Both Tucker and Slinn interpret Browning's poetry, and especially the dramatic monologue, as exemplifying the undermining of representation which lies at the heart of Jacques Derrida's deconstructive theory. Their approach differs sharply from those discussed so far in that they reject as misguided essentialism the implicit assumption made by Langbaum and others that the speakers of dramatic monologues are (like) real persons, i.e. the erroneous belief that people and things have an underlying and unchanging 'essence' that makes them what they are. The deconstructionist reading argues for the primacy of language rather than the self: it is not the self that creates language but language that constitutes the self. In a footnote to his article 'From Monomania to Monologue: "St. Simeon Stylites" and the Rise of the Victorian Dramatic Monologue' (1984), Tucker states that '[t]he self of a dramatic monologue, after all, is the most elaborate illusion of the text, the product of a speech act and not its producer'.[39] As a result, Tucker suggests that any analysis of the dramatic monologue must concentrate on language 'to demonstrate how the imaginary selves of various dramatic monologues are made up in words, how they are textually and contextually constituted'.[40]

The main value of *Browning and the Fictions of Identity* lies in its challenge to Langbaum's general analysis of the genre. The two critics who will be covered in the next section engage more directly with Langbaum's dramatic monologue *par excellence*, 'My Last Duchess', as a starting point for their critique of his theory. While Ralph Rader stresses the artificial nature of a poem which seems to replicate the speech of real people, Cynthia Scheinberg's feminist reading questions Langbaum's assumptions about the values of the reader.

## Re-reading 'My Last Duchess'

In his article 'The Dramatic Monologue and Related Lyric Forms' (1976), Rader takes issue with Langbaum's statement that the message of the dramatic monologue may be open to interpretation and that the poet's assessment of his speaker may not be clear. On the contrary, these are poems 'whose meaning and relation to the real world are fixed by the immanent intention of the indwelling poet'.[41] The cause of Langbaum's misreading is that he treats the speaker of the dramatic monologue 'as if he were in effect a real person, as if he and the reader's response to him were independent of the poet's control', whereas the speaker is actually an artistic construct that has been devised by the poet's creative consciousness.[42]

Moreover, in Rader's reading, the duke reveals himself by design and not inadvertently as Langbaum claims:

▪ [I]f Browning's intention was to show the Duke as revealing himself by accident, [...] too much is left unexplained in terms of motive, in hints of sinister purpose, and in the Duke's pretense of kindness. Finally, there is a much narrower explanatory consideration which I think is nevertheless nearly decisive. If we require of a critical account that it strongly explain everything about a poem, then we must certainly ask an account of the 'Duchess' to explain why Browning chose to write the poem in iambic pentameter couplets and then concealed the rhymes by running on his lines. It is the very essence of couplets that their chime should be heard, yet here the poet deliberately muffles them. If we assume that Browning's intention is to show the Duke speaking inadvertently, the choice has no particular point and is perhaps even negative. But if we assume that the Duke speaks purposefully, we see that the couplets have a very definite function – to give a sense of submerged pattern running, like the Duke's hidden purpose, through the whole. Thus the particular conception of the form of the 'Duchess' developed here within the more general conception of the dramatic monologue form generates a precise explanation of the poem's most peculiar individual feature.[43] ☐

The tension between the purposeful patterning of the couplets and the hiding of this pattern through run-on lines can be read as a reflection of the speaker's clear purpose and his determination to hide this purpose. Given the complexity of the dramatic monologue and its psychological realism and closeness to prose discourse, it is easy to forget its status as poetry, but Rader shows how crucial this feature can be to an understanding of a specific poem or the genre as a whole.

Cynthia Scheinberg, in 'Recasting "sympathy and judgment": Amy Levy, Women Poets, and the Victorian Dramatic Monologue' (1997), takes a very different line of attack. She unmasks the underlying phallocentrism (male gender bias) of Langbaum's reading of 'My Last Duchess', which in her view is only possible from a man's perspective. The main intention of Scheinberg's article is to acknowledge the contribution made to the dramatic monologue genre by forgotten female authors. But she also offers an important challenge to Langbaum's assumptions about the reader's ability to identify with the monologist as evident in his analysis of 'My Last Duchess' quoted in the last section. Langbaum fails to acknowledge that

▪ a reader's capacity for sympathy is almost always linked to a reader's cultural, political, and gendered identity [...] Langbaum's theory assumes that, as a reading community, 'we' all share his ability to sympathize with the misogynist Duke and recognize, as Langbaum puts it, his 'immense attractiveness'; Langbaum makes a big leap, I think, when he assumes that this poem illustrates how every reader's sympathy can be suspended from all forms of moral judgment. [...]

What is ironic is that even though Langbaum argues that the dramatic monologue arises out of the Victorian suspicion of objective truth, Langbaum's move to generalize from his own reading practices assumes that all readers are like him, and so share a universal capacity to identify with the Duke's 'power and freedom.' Arguing that the dramatic monologue displays the Victorian poet's skepticism of objective truth, Langbaum constructs a mythic universal audience as the cornerstone of his own generic theory.[44] ☐

Langbaum's belief that all readers will judge the duke in the same way undermines his own thesis about the Victorian age as a relativist age which recognises that universal standards of judgment no longer exist.

Building on John Maynard's article 'Reading the Reader in Robert Browning's Dramatic Monologues' (1991), which will be discussed in the next section, Scheinberg then suggests that for a theory of the genre it is essential to take into consideration the individual reader's gender, class, ethnic and religious identity.[45] She explains how her own reading of 'My Last Duchess' is determined by her identity as a woman in a specific historical context:

■ I value this poem not for how it binds me to the Duke's rhetorical prowess, but rather for how Browning's poem makes any poetic sympathy/identification with the Duke impossible for a reader like me. My own positions as a woman, a feminist, and a scholar who was trained in the late eighties and early nineties have obviously influenced my reading: for me, this poem demonstrates Browning's insights as a proto-feminist. In such a reading, the genre becomes a way for Browning to alert readers that the 'truth' of the Duchess' life exists only in a series of verbal and pictorial transactions by men. Browning demonstrates to me how deeply women have been oppressed by male language, and by exploiting the form of the dramatic monologue, Browning becomes both a participant in and a critic of this artistic tradition. His poem – in my reading – does not split my sympathy from my moral judgment but rather reveals their contingency; my moral judgment of the duke's misogyny is exactly the reason that I do not identify with his 'power and freedom.' I understand his language, but this does not guarantee my recognition of his 'immense attractiveness.'[46] ☐

Rejecting Langbaum's tension between sympathy and judgment, Scheinberg sees them acting in harmony. Chapter 6 on gender relations will return to one of two problematic issues in Scheinberg's reading of the poem, her apparently contradictory statement that 'Browning becomes both a participant in and a critic of' the oppression of women by male language. The other problem here is that Scheinberg responds to the same elements of the duke's utterance as Langbaum but arrives at a completely different interpretation. This possibility to argue for such different interpretations of the poem would suggest that the reader's response is not a suitable criterion for defining the genre, but Scheinberg does not go that far. The next section will present two critics' reflections on this issue, which also relate the reader of the poem to the silent listener within the text, who in turn becomes the focus for two other critics.

## The Audiences of the Dramatic Monologue

In his essay 'Reading the Reader in Robert Browning's Dramatic Monologues' (1991), John Maynard tackles the problem of the endless possibilities of interpreting Browning's monologues, not only because so many different critical approaches can be applied to them but also because reader-response criticism suggests an infinite number of readings. Starting with the prototypes of the genre, 'Johannes Agricola in Meditation' and 'Porphyria's Lover' (both 1836) with their aggressively mad speakers, he sees Browning's dramatic monologue as a device for generating a reader response. 'Porphyria's Lover'

> ■ already has in effect two proto-listeners in the poem. There is the *very passive* listener [Porphyria], a true conversational target, a warning to make us shout out, of the ultimate consequences of letting ourselves be dominated by strong romantic voices. [The poem's final line] 'And yet God has not said a word!' is almost too heavy with provocations to the reader. God as listener raises the entire world of ethical response against the totalitarian solipsistic amorality of the speaker. It also tells us that *we* had better react and speak because the withdrawn God of the poem's world refuses to speak for us. If you will, it underlines the interpretative problem at the very beginning of the Browning monologue: God doesn't offer definitive reader responses and interpretations. In his silence, we will rush forward with our own interpretations. But if God won't, who will authorize the one standard meaning?[47] □

We are forced by the poem's form to perform the act of interpreting the speaker's utterance in lieu of the silent listener and to judge the speaker's ethics. This still means that there is a multiplicity of interpretations which invite the reader to reflect on his/her reading process and how it is determined, for instance, by his/her historical distance from the speaker.[48]

The relationship between the dramatic monologue's auditor and the reader is also the subject of Jennifer Wagner-Lawlor's article 'The Pragmatics of Silence, and the Figuration of the Reader in Browning's Dramatic Monologues' (1997), which draws on theories of silence from pragmatics, the field of linguistics that studies how context contributes to meaning. Linguists note that the absence of speech does not signify the absence of communication but that it has its own communicative value, although this value is ambiguous. Wagner-Lawlor's analysis therefore examines

> ■ how the pragmatic ambiguity of second-person silence in monologues highlights the tension between consensus and resistance. This tension is a central characteristic of the genre – what any dramatic monologue is 'really about' – because it clarifies the genre's ultimate irony: dramatic monologue ends up spotlighting the silent auditor precisely by effacing him/her in shadow.[49] ☐

There are crucial differences between the auditor and the reader. Firstly,

> ■ [w]hile the reader may be said to have 'chosen' to 'hear' a particular dramatic monologue, the textual listener often has not. The listener in the typical Browning monologue recognizes the speaker's superior position of power; given the latter's aggressive, sometimes even menacing nature, the apparent passivity of the silent listener seems at once the more remarkable, and yet the more understandable. [...]
> [...] the auditor is participating not in a voluntary or 'chosen' silence but in what linguists call 'imposed' silence, which Paolo Scarpi defines as occurring 'when one of the two [speakers] recognises the influence or supremacy of the other. . . . *Choice* and *imposition* can express respectively assertion and recognition of leadership.'[50] The imposed code of silence is grounded in fear, adds Scarpi, and while its pragmatic implication is 'consensus,' in actuality verbal communication has merely been 'suspended' by the intimidated listener.[51] ☐

We can think here of 'My Last Duchess', whose auditor, the envoy from the duke's prospective father-in-law, is a social inferior of the speaker, acting on the orders of his master and therefore not in a position to resist the duke. The duke may interpret the envoy's silence as assent, but the envoy is actually only withholding a response which may be positive or negative:

> ■ The position of the addressee is therefore ambiguous, and in the silence that maintains the ambiguity, the speaker can impose what meaning he will. [...] positively, silence can signal assent and favor; negatively, it signals dissent or disfavor.[52] ☐

The second difference between the fictional auditor and the reader is that

> ■ [w]hereas the auditor's silence may represent an involuntary consensus, the silence of the actual reader, who is forced to step out of the place of the noninterpretive auditor, may signify the opposite. This silence is the space of the open resistance of the will of the speaker by the interpretive will of the reader. In pragmatic terms, the reader (unlike, for example, either the 'next duchess''s envoy or the languid Lucrezia [in 'Andrea del Sarto', 1855]) may become 'impolite' in a manner that the textual listener, too intimidated or too acquiescent to challenge the speaker's superiority, dares not be.[53] □

Wagner-Lawlor uses 'My Last Duchess' to illustrate her point about the reader's resistance, focusing not on the 'official' auditor, the envoy, but on the portrait of the last duchess. The duchess suffers from an 'imposed silence' literally because she is dead, but in figurative terms she can be seen as an analogy for the reader. We have a strong sense of her presence 'Looking as if she were alive' (l. 2) and also of her silence and resistance to the duke which led to her death. Her portrait is

> ■ an ironic figuration of none other than the actual reader, who like the Duchess is a presence, 'alive' because s/he is ultimately beyond the control of the Duke's attempted rhetorical [...] tyranny; we, like the Duchess, are at once inside and outside the frame of the Duke's own verbal self-portrait. On the one hand, the will of the interpreting subject, provoked by the silence of the envoy and portrait alike, is constantly reanimated, as resistant to the Duke as that now monumentally indeterminate spot of joy [on the Duchess's cheek, l. 15]; on the other hand, the reader, like the Duchess, keeps the Duke alive, the dynamics of reading and interpretation in play.[54] □

The distance between reader and auditor, rather than their identification, and the reader's refusal to be dominated by the speaker is thus for Wagner-Lawlor a key defining feature of Browning's dramatic monologue.

Although focusing also on the silent auditor, Dorothy Mermin (born 1936), in *The Audience in the Poem: Five Victorian Poets* (1983), is more interested in how and what the speaker of the dramatic monologue communicates. As seen above, all of the formal definitions of the genre note the presence of an auditor as a key criterion but then fail to follow through on this point, as the genre's main purpose is seen as the revelation of the speaker's character.[55] By contrast, Mermin maintains that auditors are central to the genre, in that its main focus is not self-expression but the effect of the utterance on the auditor. The speaker's 'words are intended to have an immediate effect on his auditor – they are primarily instrumental rather than expressive – and both his utterance and the poem's meaning are significantly affected by the auditor's responses or refusal to respond'.[56] Mermin explains the inclusion of the auditor as a result of the Victorian poets' historical position, influenced by Romantic expressive theory but also anxious to be able to communicate with an audience so as not to become marginalised.[57] In an age when the novel predominates, these poems can explore 'how and to what effect one can speak publicly of imaginative visions and private feelings'.[58]

Turning to Browning, she proposes a neat categorisation of his work into three chronological phases. The first group, which includes poems from his 1842 and 1845 collections, focuses on the speaker's 'extraordinary freedom to speak', Mermin (1983), p. 48. In 'My Last Duchess' this 'is made manifest by the presence of the auditor':

> ■ We see the Duke's power in the envoy's silence, just as we see the weakness of the Spanish monk [in 'Soliloquy of the Spanish Cloister', 1842] and Porphyria's lover in the absence of an auditor. The monk mutters harmlessly to himself; Porphyria's lover, passive and voiceless in her presence, socially her inferior, murdered her in silence and belongs in a madhouse cell. Powerless, they speak freely but to no one.[59] □

While the poems in the first group require only 'passive acquiescence' from the auditor, the poems in the next group from *Men and Women* (1855), such as 'Andrea del Sarto' and 'Fra Lippo Lippi',

> ■ try to elicit the auditor's understanding and sympathy. Almost always, they fail.
>   Their failure reflects Browning's concern about his own relation to his readers. He wasn't sure either that he wanted to address an audience of dullards or that anyone would listen if he did. [...] with an auditor in the poem, the speaker has someone to talk to. Browning's theory of poetry [...] required responsive readers [...]. He was sure that the poet must be a teacher, with designs, however impalpable, on an audience. He often addressed his readers directly, arguing, explaining, questioning, joking, exhorting, and his painters and poets usually encounter or imagine groups of onlookers.[60] □

Andrea del Sarto speaks to his wife 'to keep Lucrezia sitting with him, not to tell her anything',[61] and of course he fails, since she leaves him at the end of the monologue to join her lover. Fra Lippo Lippi does not succeed in communicating his view of the world to the nightwatchmen he is addressing. Mermin's reading into the dramatic poems of Browning's concerns about his own failed act of literary communication is very different from other readings of the dramatic monologue that stress the poet's distance from his text.

The final and most complex group of poems, including texts like 'Mr Sludge, "The Medium"' and 'Bishop Blougram's Apology', presents speakers who are 'clever and disagreeable', drawing the reader's attention to the manipulation of language and the problem of relying on it to judge characters:

> ■ Though they try to ingratiate themselves with the auditor, they are predominantly hostile to him, defensive and aggressive by turns; their self-defense is largely attack. And finally, after saying much that is persuasive and true, they are revealed as disingenuous, and the reader is left with the problem of reconciling their lofty utterances to their low characters. [...]
>
> The auditor functions in these poems, then, not only to show the speakers' use of language for manipulative purposes, but to show how strangely and deceitfully they succeed. The poems demonstrate the mysterious disparity between what the speakers say and what they are, between what they intend and what they effect.[62] □

Mermin's progression towards the exposure of how speakers use their verbal medium is seductively neat but, like any schematic theory of artistic development that aspires to cover an author's entire career, it runs the risk of ignoring the complexity of earlier works.

In his book *Robert Browning: His Poetry and His Audiences* (1984), published only a year after Mermin's, Lee Erickson takes a very similar stance on the importance of Browning's textual auditors. Like Mermin, he rejects the definition of the dramatic monologue as merely the revelation of the speaker's character and the reduction of 'the speakers' audiences to emanations of speakers' personalities, when, in fact, those very audiences both affect and in some ways determine the speakers' selves'.[63] And, like Mermin, Erickson interprets the problematising of the communicative act in these poems as a reflection of Browning's own desire for recognition from his readers, a desire that was frustrated for a long time until he gained a modest fame in the 1880s. For Erickson, the whole of Browning's poetry needs to be understood in terms of his biography. Having been disappointed in his desire to relate to the wider public as a kind of self-sacrificing prophet with a political agenda in his early work, he finds an ideal loving audience in Elizabeth Barrett but loses this audience when she dies in 1861. Eventually, '[h]e comes to believe that man's only true audience is God and that one comes to know God only through the love of another'.[64]

Erickson explains his general approach to Browning's speakers as a way of understanding his poetics and psychology:

> ■ Contrary to his reader's expectations, Browning's poems do not begin with a self-sufficient ego that through its perception and expression orders and shapes experience, but instead with a speaker who is seeking form and a sense of self in the world. The drama of self-development, not the expression of an assured perspective, is the subject of his poetry. Moreover, this process of self-realization requires the active participation of others, for the speakers gain their self-consciousness by being recognized by their audiences. This poetic developed gradually during Browning's career and was grounded in Browning's own search for an audience and for a form that would allow him to express himself fully as a poet and as a man.[65] □

This dramatic self-constitution of the speaker through interaction with others is particularly obvious in the dramatic monologue, which is 'the drama of a speaker's search for the recognition of others that will give the speaker his or her sense of self'.[66]

Erickson's theoretical basis for this approach is derived from Georg Wilhelm Friedrich Hegel (1770–1831), who posits that the self can only constitute itself in relation to another self:

> ■ In *The Phenomenology of Mind* [1807] Hegel says, 'Self-consciousness exists in itself and for itself in that, and by the fact that it exists for another self-consciousness; that is to say, it *is* only by being acknowledged or "recognized."'[67] The dialectic of self and other reflected in Hegel's definition can help us understand the relationship between the speakers of Browning's dramatic monologues and their audiences and also allow us to read Browning's poems with a deep appreciation of their dramatic aspects and psychological intricacies. Further, in the light of a few of Hegel's remarks on romantic poetry in his *Aesthetics* [1835], one can see how this dialectic of self and other is worked out dramatically and symbolically within Browning's *Men and Women* in the form of the speakers' loving and being loved. One can see how Browning uses the dramatic monologue in *Men and Women* to show audiences making the speakers' image of themselves possible; how Robert's love for Elizabeth serves as an ideal form of this self-realization in the dedicatory poem 'One Word More'; and how the poems in the volume dramatically unveil the speakers' awareness of their audiences' shaping of their self-conscious selves.[68] □

In 'One Word More' (1855), where Browning claims to 'speak this once in [his] true person' (l. 137), he can express his self because the poem is a communication with his loving audience Elizabeth. By contrast, self-realisation fails if the other is not appropriately recognised, as in 'Porphyria's Lover', where the speaker is driven by a desire for domination rather than love and thus annihilates the other:

> ■ [I]n dramatizing the ethical consequences of man's finite self-consciousness and his dependence upon others for self-realization, Browning's poems imply that to project one's will and self upon another, as Porphyria's lover does with Porphyria, is an immoral act, an attempt to gratify the self in the way the master does in Hegel's master/slave relationship – by killing the other (the slave) and reducing it to nothingness.[69]
>
> [...] Browning's speakers [...] gain some measure of self-consciousness by confronting others, but must love another and be loved in order to become intimate with and know themselves. Yet given their inevitable human frailty and finitude, they can achieve only a limited self-consciousness which readers must fill out for themselves, partially, as Langbaum suggests, by mediating between the sympathy we feel for a speaker and the judgment we make of him or her,[70] and partially by remembering that Browning emphasizes man's incompleteness in relation to God's perfect fullness and man's inability to progress completely toward becoming one with God on earth.[71] □

In Erickson's view, Browning's speakers, however inadvertent their self-revelation, are conscious of how important it is for their constitution of self to be listened to by someone else. Browning's belief in man's limitations as opposed to God's perfection means that even his love poems tend to portray unsuccessful self-realisations. Chapter 6 on love and gender relations will return to this problem.

There is yet another linguistic theory that has been applied to the dramatic monologue, this time with a firm focus on the speaker of the monologue; this approach is illustrated by the two critics presented in the next section.

## Performativity

Both Cornelia D. J. Pearsall and E. Warwick Slinn have analysed the dramatic monologue as a performative act, drawing on the speech act theory of the philosopher of language J. L. Austin (1911–60). As Pearsall explains in *Tennyson's Rapture: Transformation in the Victorian Dramatic Monologue* (2008),

> ■ [i]n *How to Do Things with Words* [1962], Austin identifies the category of performative utterances, which accomplish an act by their enunciation. The marriage vow 'I do,' a statement that is a description but also an act, is the best-known example of this linguistic kind. With a performative utterance, according to Austin, 'the issuing of the utterance is the performing of an action.'[72] □

Both Pearsall and Slinn read dramatic monologues with their intention to communicate something to the silent listener as performative utterances in Austin's sense in that they 'articulate a speaker's goals, but the monologues themselves also come to perform these goals in the course of the monologue, by way of the monologue'.[73]

In Pearsall's essay 'The Dramatic Monologue' (2000), the starting point is, as for other critics, a disagreement with Langbaum, in this case his claim that 'the speakers never accomplish anything by their utterance, and seem to know from the start that they will not'.[74] Pearsall, by contrast, maintains that 'a major feature of this poetic genre is its assumption of rhetorical efficacy. Speakers desire to achieve some purpose, looking toward goals that they not only describe in the course of their monologues but also labor steadily to achieve through the medium of their monologues.'[75] Speakers may not necessarily achieve their aims, but their intention to use their utterance to have a particular effect is the key to understanding the genre. Pearsall's general term for the effect that speakers desire is 'transformation', which she describes thus:

> ■ [A] speaker seeks a host of transformations – of his or her circumstance, of his or her auditor, of his or her self, and possibly all these together – in the course of the monologue, and ultimately attains these, if they can be attained, by way of the monologue.[76] □

She then lists some concrete examples from Browning's and Tennyson's canon of famous monologues:

> ■ [M]ost speakers of dramatic monologues hold overt ambitions for some definite if occasionally indefinable result from their speaking. [...] the speaker of Browning's 'Soliloquy of the Spanish Cloister' (1842) seeks damnation of a colleague, while the speaker of Browning's '"Childe Roland to the Dark Tower Came"' (1855) seeks, of course, the tower. This list can continue, and include virtually every dramatic monologue by Tennyson or Browning, though in some cases the goals that help precipitate or sustain speech are less readily identifiable. This pattern in itself should prompt us to probe more deeply into the ways that dramatic monologists are all engaged in ordering, in arranging or dictating various aspects of their experience. Each speaker brings a complex of ambitions to his or her discursive moment. A dramatic monologue works actively to accomplish something for its speakers, perhaps something they are overtly seeking [...] but also something infinitely more subtle, some other kind of dramatic transformation of a situation or a self.[77] □

Both Slinn and Pearsall choose as a textual example 'The Bishop Orders His Tomb at Saint Praxed's Church' (1845), originally entitled 'The Tomb at Saint Praxed's'. They point out that the extension of the title in later editions, which includes the speaker and the labelling of his performative speech act as 'ordering', indicates the effect the monologist intends to have on his audience. Pearsall states:

> ■ [T]he revised specification of the speaker and his particular verbal activity points to the speaker's intention to attain his object, his own monument, by way of speech. Certainly, he also 'orders' his tomb in the sense of designing and imaginatively arranging all its components, from the building materials to the decorations at its base to its crowning effigy of himself. [...]
> In the course of his speaking, the Bishop's body begins to experience its own form of transubstantiation [i.e. the transformation of bread and wine into the body of Christ during the Eucharist], as he stretches his feet 'forth straight as stone can point' (88) and his vestments and bedclothes petrify 'Into great laps and folds of sculptor's-work' (90).[78] □

The bishop's desire to have his sumptuous tomb is explicitly stated in the appeal to his sons, which is his monologue, and although there is little doubt that his sons will ignore his wishes, the bishop's utterance in a sense accomplishes his transformation into an (imaginary) stone effigy.

In *Victorian Poetry as Cultural Critique: The Politics of Performative Language* (2003), Slinn undertakes a more extended and complex reading of the poem which focuses more on the use of poetry as a critique of cultural norms. Taking his cue from New Historicist critics like Jerome McGann (born 1937), he declares that the aim of his study is to 'show how poetry may enact a cultural critique through its self-conscious formalism, its foregrounding of just those language acts that many of the literary scholars most sympathetic to cultural critique have seemed least to take into account'.[79] Like Pearsall, Slinn points to Browning's revision of the poem's title to emphasise the speaker's performative act:

> ■ [T]he cultural observer might move away from the tomb as object and focus on the discursive processes through which that tomb is conceived.
> It is this crucial shift in focus that, I suggest, accompanies Browning's change in title. This focus on ordering emphasizes power – arrangement, control, structuring. It also foregrounds, through its poetic formalism, the discourses that produce a certain kind of consciousness – that peculiar consciousness which is untroubled by the interconnection of symbol and object, flesh and spirit, or life and death [...].[80] □

The use of poetic form emphasises the poem's message about the exertion of control through language. Like previous interpreters of the poem, Slinn places it in the context of Victorian Protestant criticism of Catholic doctrine, but instead of just reading it as ridiculing the Catholic belief in transubstantiation, he sees it as Browning's more earnest attempt to represent how a believer in transubstantiation perceives the world. The bishop's belief that he will literally lie on his tomb, which ignores the difference between his effigy (a symbol) and his body (the object represented), illustrates the confusion of symbol and the thing symbolised that lies at the heart of the doctrine of transubstantiation.

Unlike Pearsall, Slinn highlights the speaker's failures to effect a change, but these failures reveal to the reader the cultural processes in which he participates:

> ■ As a performative, the utterance apparently fails: the bishop's authority to order is undercut by his breaching of clerical law (he owns villas and stole the church's property), and his speech shows all the signs of failing to construct an authorizing audience (his sons, it seems, will not be persuaded or bribed: 'I know / Ye mark me not!' [ll. 62–3]). But the bishop's 'failures' may be less important as indicators of moral limitation or cultural incompetence than as a means of exposing the methods and assumptions that underlie his efforts to affirm power and identity. He attempts to act, to intervene on his own behalf in certain cultural processes, but any implicit failure to order – whether ordering the desired effigy or merely his own words – need not deny the nature of the process.[81] □

Slinn applies this to the bishop's fusion of his real body and its stone representation and his general confusion over literal and figurative language:

> ■ The bishop's literalized language can be read, for example, as a psychological response to the metaphysical and biblically proposed threat of impermanence: by concentrating on the physical details of his tomb he [with his Christian belief in eternal life] can reassure himself of an identifiable and personal continuity. It can also be read liturgically as an attempt to enact the promises of his faith. Then the poem performs an institutional critique, exposing the contradictions which need to be repressed in order to sustain the premises which underlie those promises.[82] □

Turning to the decorations on the projected tomb, which are an inappropriate mix of religious and Classical pagan figures, including sexually charged scenes, Slinn comments:

> ■ His aim seems to be to turn his life literally into an art object, to affirm the quality of his life through the aesthetic intensity of his experience and to produce his own effigy as the grand manifestation of order, status, and beauty. The tomb that he seeks to order thus functions as the introjected cultural object with which his subjectivity identifies. It is the central, dominating artifact of his utterance and the constitutive aim of his performative. Yet his sensual eclecticism becomes confused with his desire to manifest

social status through aesthetic effect, continually thwarting any attempt to conceive a harmonious whole or successful aesthetic product.[83] ☐

The tomb is meant to be a representation of how the bishop sees himself – as a powerful man of taste – but his sensuality undermines this self-image and its coherence.

Slinn finally examines the bishop's rivalry with 'old Gandolf', which permeates the whole of the monologue and reveals how the speaker operates in a male-dominated society. The poem offers

■ a sustained critique of patriarchal processes – critique in the sense of exposing ideological structures, not in the sense of transforming or subverting them. The bishop, for instance, acting through the motivations of his rivalry, exhibits all the features of the classical patriarchal subject: equating identity with mastery and the ability to order; exercising the power of ownership and economic negotiation; claiming both aesthetic power (knowing the value of stones for sculpture) and spiritual power (the ability to intercede with saints); sustaining the male gaze in watching Gandolf on his onion-stone – 'Put me where I may look at him!' (32) – in the ritual of the mass and in watching, potentially eternally, for Gandolf's return gaze; defining himself in terms of another male; and treating the woman as a subordinate other, as the means of providing sons, as the signifier of male status.[84] ☐

Slinn summarises how the poem's performative speech act exposes the workings of (Renaissance) culture through the three institutions of religion, art and patriarchy:

■ [B]y dramatizing this example of Renaissance politics, Browning illustrates the appropriations and structuring processes through which institutional discourses order our world. Here the combined processes of church, aestheticism, and patriarchy ensure that identity remains both phenomenal and male, tied to the sensuality and graphic tangibility of representation (signifiers/discourse) and to the competitive homosocial requirements of patriarchal ordering.[85] ☐

Both Slinn and Pearsall thus combine their analysis of the monologist's speech act with a consideration of how the poem participates in cultural debates. The next chapter considers criticism which is particularly interested in this cultural context of Browning's monologues and offers a variety of explanations for their emergence and form. In its focus on context it complements the present chapter's interest in the poem's nature as a communicative act. While the formalist definitions with which this chapter opened are not sufficient to appreciate the genre's impact and purpose, they are an important basis for understanding its workings. The rest of the chapter has shown how analyses of the same genre can diverge, depending on which aspect of the communicative process is taken as a starting point – the reader, the audience within the poem, the speaker or language as the source of meaning. All of these approaches make us reflect on how the dramatic monologue works and how the critical interpreter can read it. The next chapter will give us a better sense of how Victorian readers may have perceived the genre in relation to their own contemporary world and experience of literature.

CHAPTER FOUR

# The Dramatic Monologue: Causes and Context

Whereas the emphasis of the previous chapter was on the formal features of the dramatic monologue, on considerations of the genre as a communicative act and especially on Langbaum's generalised reading experience, this chapter focuses on the dramatic monologue within its historical and literary contexts. After a brief overview of suggestions for the dramatic monologue's generic predecessors, the second section of the chapter identifies those cultural and literary factors that led Browning and other Victorians to develop the genre. It covers Isobel Armstrong's influential concept of the 'Victorian double poem', J. Hillis Miller's interpretation of the genre as Browning's response to the Victorian Crisis of Faith, Loy D. Martin's Marxist reading and Britta Martens' analysis of the genre in relation to social changes and other prose genres. The third section focuses on research which positions the genre more specifically with regard to the developing discipline of psychology. Ekbert Faas, Michael Mason, Ellen O'Brien and Barry L. Popowich read the dramatic monologues about extreme mental states as applying ideas from contemporary psychiatry. Finally, Gregory Tate analyses Browning's portrayal of thought processes in relation to Victorian concepts of the human mind.

## Generic Predecessors

Many critics have investigated the reasons why Browning and other poets of the period developed the dramatic monologue. One approach to the question is to identify its generic predecessors. The most rigorous example of this is Benjamin Willis Fuson's *Browning and His English Predecessors in the Dramatic Monolog* [sic] (1948). In his search for poems which are not in the poet's own voice and which can therefore be seen as antecedents of the dramatic monologue, Fuson goes back as

67

far as the *Heroides*, epistolary poems in the voices of Greek and Roman mythological heroines by the Roman poet Ovid (43 BC to AD 17/18).[1] Taking the same broad definition of the genre, Alan Sinfield, in his *Dramatic Monologue* (1977), goes back even further, to the complaints in the voices of fictional speakers by the Greek pastoral poet Theocritus (third century BC).[2] A. Dwight Culler, in 'Monodrama and the Dramatic Monologue' (1975), considers the dramatic monologue as a development of the rhetorical exercise of prosopopoeia, in which a historical or imaginary character is impersonated, and which still featured in the education of nineteenth-century British boys.[3]

At the same time, Culler also argues for the debt of the dramatic monologue to the Romantic genre of the monodrama, a dramatic piece in a single voice, whose invention he credits to Jean-Jacques Rousseau (1712–78).[4] Other Romantic genres which can be argued to have facilitated the development of the dramatic monologue are the self-expressive lyric, which the dramatic monologue is seen either as rejecting and subverting or as developing (as in Langbaum's analysis in Chapter 3) and the lyrical drama, which is not intended to be acted on stage (see again Langbaum).[5] W. David Shaw, in *Origins of the Monologue: The Hidden God* (1999), adds another two Romantic sources to the list. Firstly, the conversation poems of Samuel Taylor Coleridge such as 'Frost at Midnight' (1798), with their addresses to real people, anticipate the silent auditor of the dramatic monologue, as they are 'poems which naturalize the ode and lyric by substituting, for formal apostrophes to the seasons, places, and natural phenomena, the dramatic monologue's vocatives of direct address to a person'.[6] Secondly, the concept of negative capability developed by John Keats (1795–1821), i.e. the poet's ability to be 'in uncertainties' and to impersonate other beings, is transformed by poets like Browning into the poet's impersonation of fictional or historical speakers in the dramatic monologue.[7] Shaw also suggests Browning's reading of the Socratic dialogues by Plato (424/423 to 348/347 BC) and their diverse uses of irony as an influence on different subcategories of his dramatic monologues.[8] All of these critics focus more on the formal features of the genre than on the motivations for developing them, whereas the next section considers the political (in the word's broadest sense) motivations that underlie Browning's development of these features.

## Why Browning Developed the Dramatic Monologue

In her important study *Victorian Poetry: Poetry, Poetics and Politics* (1993), which is so complex and wide-ranging that it does not lend itself readily to excerpting, Isobel Armstrong proposes politicised definitions of drama and the work of women poets of the 1820s as influences on

Browning's monologues.[9] A key concept which Armstrong presents in the book is that of the 'Victorian double poem', which may be a dramatic monologue but can also take other generic forms:

■ [Arthur] Schopenhauer [1788–1860] wrote of the lyric poet as uttering between two poles of feeling, between the pure undivided condition of unified selfhood and the needy, fracturing self-awareness of the interrogating consciousness.[...] The Victorian poet does not swing between these two forms of utterance but dramatises and objectifies their simultaneous existence. There is a kind of duplicity involved here, for the poet often invites the simple reading by presenting a poem as lyric expression as the perceiving subject speaks. Mariana's lament [in Tennyson's 'Mariana' (1830)] or Fra Lippo Lippi's ['Fra Lippo Lippi', 1855] apologetics are expressions, indeed, composed in an expressive form. But in a feat of recomposition and externalisation the poem turns its expressive utterance around so that it becomes the opposite of itself, not only the *subject's* utterance but the *object* of analysis and critique. It is, as it were, reclassified as drama in the act of being literal lyric expression. To re-order lyric expression as drama is to give it a new content and to introduce the possibility of interrogation and critique.[10] □

A dramatic monologue is both a subjective poem in the Romantic tradition because it seems to be in a single lyric voice and a poem which critically analyses subjectivity from an objective distance because the voice is that of a dramatic speaker. We are back to the discussions in Chapter 1 over whether Browning's poetry is either objective like drama or both subjective and objective at the same time. The poem's objective element, which acknowledges the heterogeneity of the 'interrogating consciousness' and which opens the possibilities of critiquing aspects of the poet's contemporary culture, is the more exciting element in the double poem. Values and assumptions made by the speaker can be called into question because the objective presentation invites the reader to consider them from a critical distance.

Armstrong's emphasis on objectivity, which is also so pronounced in Browning's interest in the objective poet in the *Essay on Shelley* (1852), derives from a consideration of the dramatic monologue's context which goes beyond the domain of literature and takes into account the broader culture. One key change in Victorian culture is the Crisis of Faith, the waning of belief, mainly among members of the middle class, in orthodox Christianity and the account of creation in the Book of Genesis, brought about primarily by scientific discoveries and biblical scholarship (see also Chapter 7). J. Hillis Miller (born 1928), in *The Disappearance of God: Five Nineteenth-Century Writers* (1963), reads the dramatic monologue as Browning's way of coming to terms with the Crisis of Faith. He starts from the premise that since the nineteenth century we no longer feel the presence of God in the world due to 'a whole set of changes, both spiritual and material [which] happened more or less simultaneously [...] the rise of science and technology: industrialization, the increasing predominance of the middle class, the gradual breakdown of the old hierarchical class structure, the building of great cities'.[11] In the spiritual domain this corresponds to 'a gradual dissipation of the medieval symbolism of participation', for instance in the Protestant understanding of the Eucharist as not the literal transubstantiation of Christ into bread and wine but a symbolic act recording the absence of God.[12] The medieval symbolism has been replaced by subjectivism, which makes the individual's consciousness the starting point of all experience. This focus on the self leads to a sense of alienation, made worse by the emergence of historicism, which replaces the certainty of objective, divinely imparted facts with 'an assumption of the relativity of any particular culture'.[13]

Browning is one of the Victorian authors who feel the disappearance of God:

> ■ He finds that God has withdrawn from the world, or at any rate from his own heart and mind. The two discoveries are really the same. He is entirely on his own *because* God is not present in his soul. God seems to be operating everywhere else in the world, as an immanent force directing the development of life and justifying it. But when Browning turns inside himself, where the presence of God should be most close and intimate, he finds – nothing but himself. When he tries to go outside, and to embrace the God who seems to be manifest in the world, he sickens at last on the dead gulf of himself. This leads to a complete reversal of his original boisterous conviction that his 'fierce energy' was the very presence of God working in his soul. Now he finds that he knows nothing whatsoever about God.[14] □

Browning does see the presence of God in the external world, but not in the most important place, his own soul.

The dramatic monologue, in which the poet goes beyond his own self to impersonate other characters, allows him to reconnect with the divine that is outside but not inside him:

> ■ The decision to write dramatic monologues is Browning's way of dealing with his own existential problem. Other men seem to have a single germ of life which can be fulfilled in a single mode of existence. He alone must find some way to indulge all feelings equally, to hear all sides of life. [...] Though Browning cannot ape God's infinitude, there is one way in which he can approach God's fullness, and that is through a certain kind of poetry. The direct way to God has failed. Now Browning must turn to the peripheral way, not the way up, but the way around. He must enter in patient humility the lives of the multitude of men and women who make up the world, and he must re-create these lives in his poems.[15] □

Browning's way of reconnecting with God is to recreate the infinite variety of creation through inhabiting different dramatic characters. However, Browning's dilemma runs deeper. He discovers that his self is not just emptied of God but also suffers from an absence of selfhood:

> ■ [I]n Browning's day, and in England, the idea of the indeterminacy of selfhood was a scandalous notion, contrary to the traditional British conviction that each man has a substantial inner core of self. [...] Browning's excessive desire for privacy, as well as his decision to write dramatic monologues, may be not so much an attempt to hide the positive facts of his private life as an attempt to keep hidden his secret failure to have the kind of definitive, solid self he sees in other people, and feels it is normal to have. [...]
> If we turn to Browning's poetry to find a revelation of what he 'really' believes we find ourselves bewildered by a profusion of apparently contradictory assertions, and Browning would affirm that even the poems which seem the most personal are just as dramatic and imaginary as any of the others. Many of the opinions and attitudes which seem most peculiarly Browning's own are put in the mouths of 'villains' [...].[16] □

Miller rejects here a common biographical explanation for Browning's choice of the dramatic monologue, his dislike of personal revelations in the public text; he suggests instead that Browning lacks identity, and this is a condition which, according to Miller, is not acceptable in Browning's society. Because Browning has no identity, his poetry cannot be used as a way of discovering his ideas. Even his apparently personal poems give no access to his self. If none of these poems give access to Browning's ideas, it is therefore paradoxical that Miller writes an entire chapter in which he claims to deduce from the poetry what Browning thinks about God and the world. In his methodology, he even contradicts his last point in the above quotation: when he quotes from Browning's poetry, he usually does not give the poem's title but only its page number in his edition of Browning's complete works. He thus makes no distinction between those poems which are dramatic and do not purport to represent the author's ideas and those that might be expressions of his personal opinions. Instead, Miller's method of citation suggests that everything that is said in Browning's poetry can be attributed to the poet.

While Miller finds the impetus for Browning's monologues in the contemporary climate of religious doubt, Loy D. Martin, in *Browning's Dramatic Monologues and the Post-Romantic Subject* (1985), offers a purely secular explanation. In a theoretical *tour de force*, his study seems to draw on more or less every theoretical paradigm that had currency during the hey-day of theory in the 1980s, including the psychoanalysis of Jacques

Lacan (1901–81), the concept of the semiotic by Julia Kristeva (born 1941), the dialogism of Mikhail Bakhtin (1895–1975), socio-linguistics, stylistics, biographical criticism and cybernetics, but above all Marxism, on which we will focus here. Martin subscribes to the conviction of Karl Marx (1818–83) that material conditions determine ideology, which in turn shapes cultural consciousness and cultural forms such as literary genres. Like Miller, Martin stresses the relevance of nineteenth-century industrialisation and urbanisation and especially the rise of capitalism and its effects on the individual and the artist. He contrasts the Victorians' response to these conditions with that of their Romantic predecessors, suggesting that Victorian poets share the sense of alienation from the self and others that can already be traced in Romantic poetry. Yet unlike the Romantics, who strive to recover a lost unity with nature or society, the Victorians are ambiguous about this sense of alienation. On the one hand, they only use the established devices of closure and unity ironically in order to undermine them; on the other hand, speakers like Browning's monologists desire a connection with others.[17] Browning's desire for connection is evident, for instance, in the open-endedness of the dramatic monologue, which often starts *in medias res*, as if in the middle of a conversation, looking both back to previous events and forward to events that will occur after the utterance has ended. At the level of language, the simultaneous autonomy and connection with others can be seen in the combination of poetic language with the recreation of colloquial speech and also in the fact that his dramatic monologues convey the personalities of the individual speakers while at the same time being unmistakably in Browning's personal style.

Browning is, according to Martin, particularly interested in how the alienated individual is constituted through language:

■ [T]he individual speakers of the poems furnish hypothetical centers of being-in-language. But the language in which they have their being always fuses them with that which is outside themselves – other persons, other times, other cultures. The dramatic monologue, more perhaps than any other literary form, challenges the immense prestige of the Cartesian dualism of the self and the other. While it exclusively displays the unique individual, it allows him or her to exist only as an indissoluble part of something that is not himself or herself and thereby lays siege to the sovereignty of the *Cogito* as a basis for subjectivity.[18] □

Browning goes against a bedrock of Western philosophy, the idea of René Descartes (1596–1650) that the existence of the thinking subject, the *Cogito*, is the foundation of all knowledge of reality. Instead, the dramatic monologue presents the self in context and as part of a whole shared with others (the silent auditor, a particular historical context, a language shared with others). A discussion of 'Pictor Ignotus' (1845) in Chapter 5 will demonstrate how Martin applies his ideas to Browning's representation of the artist as caught between a desire for artistic autonomy and the need to relate to others as represented by the changing demands of the art market.

Another article that situates the dramatic monologue in its cultural context is Britta Martens' 'Dramatic Monologue, Detective Fiction and the Search for Meaning' (2011), which combines this angle with a narratological analysis of the genre. The article's starting point is the resemblance between the reading processes of the dramatic monologue and detective fiction in that both genres rely 'on the withholding of information and their stimulation of the reader's desire to find this information and thus establish meaning'.[19] The reader of detective fiction mirrors the detective trying to reconstruct the hidden story that led up to the crime. The reader of the dramatic monologue also pieces together past events, although with the ultimate aim not of reconstructing a coherent chain of events but of understanding hidden traits of the speaker's psychology. Moreover, the criminal and the monologist can both be seen as analogous to an author. While criminals plot

■ first their crimes, and then false stories of their crimes by eliminating clues or planting false ones which initially lead the investigator(s) and the reader to construct a logical, but wrong, plot [, monologists] construct stories or representations of the world that they want their auditor(s) to adopt. The readers, however, suspect this to be biased and subjective, which leads them to scrutinize the speakers' utterances for different stories.[20] □

Both criminals and monologists 'lose control of the story they construct and inadvertently reveal their true character/actions. Of course, criminals practice deception consciously' whereas monologists deceive themselves, wanting to believe in their own stories.[21]

More important than this difference between the criminal's and the monologist's consciousness is the divergence in the theories of knowledge that underlie both genres: '[T]he relativist dramatic monologue clearly challenges the belief in absolute meaning, while the classic detective formula depicts the problematic process of arriving at an apparently unambiguous truth.'[22] Going along with Langbaum's reading of the dramatic monologue as a symptom of an age of relativism that has lost the belief in absolute meaning (see Chapter 3), Martens reads both genres not only as critiquing the Romantic literature of subjectivity but also as reflecting a new middle-class society where the law and rationality are beginning to replace religion and a rigid class structure as the sources of cultural authority. Yet while the classic detective formula seems to reinforce the new ideology by using the detective's rationality to expose transgressors against social order and make them subject to the law, the dramatic monologue is more complex and does not provide this reassuring certainty that order will eventually prevail. Outcomes range from official punishment (e.g. Guido in *The Ring and the Book* (1868–69)) to avoidance of it (the duke in 'My Last Duchess' (1842)) or, in many cases, to unclear consequences for the speaker ('The Laboratory' (1844)).[23] The reader is thus either obliged to guess what will happen to Browning's transgressive monologists after they have finished speaking or he/she is confronted with different historical settings which demonstrate that social norms and laws are not eternally fixed.

Finally, the article suggests that the dramatic monologue's ambiguous relationship with social order may be a debt to the mode of the Gothic, where the drive to re-establish order is complicated by the fact that moral norms are undermined by evil representatives of social authorities (i.e. aristocrats and/or clerics). Examples of Gothic aristocratic villains obsessed with social status and controlling their passive wives are again the Duke of Ferrara and Guido in *The Ring and the Book*, as well as the speaker of 'A Forgiveness' (1876). Browning's immoral Catholic clerics (the Bishop of Saint Praxed, Bishop Blougram, Fra Lippo Lippi, the adulterous monk in 'A Forgiveness' or the scheming confessor in 'The Confessional' (1845)) are reminiscent of the Gothic novel's villainous monks and clerics. Moreover, 'Browning also draws on the claustrophobic enclosed spaces of the Gothic: Renaissance palazzos, the laboratory with its reminiscence of [Mary Shelley's] *Frankenstein* [1818], and the woman's metaphorical imprisonment in the work of art, as in the portrait of the last duchess'.[24] This critique of historically distanced aristocratic and clerical misuses of authority articulates Browning's radical political and Protestant stance (see Hawlin's work discussed in Chapter 7).

Whereas Miller, Martin and Martens read Browning's dramatic monologues as motivated by very broad cultural contexts, there is another notable approach to contextual criticism which is much more specific. It explains his development of the genre and especially its first two published specimens, 'Porphyria's Lover' and 'Johannes Agricola in Meditation' (both 1836), as Browning's response to contemporary developments in the medical discipline of psychiatry and the evolving discourse about mental illness.

## The Rise of Psychology

'Porphyria's Lover' and 'Johannes Agricola in Meditation' (1836) were labelled by their author as madmen through the 'Madhouse Cells' title under which the poems were joined in publications after 1842, although Browning omitted the joint title when republishing the poems from 1863 onwards. These two speakers are not Browning's only monologists whose sanity is in doubt. The speakers of other famous poems, such as 'My Last Duchess' and 'The Laboratory', can also be considered to be mad. The same applies to Tennyson's first work in the genre, 'St Simeon Stylites' (1842), and to later monologues by Dante Gabriel Rossetti (1828–82) such as 'A Last Confession' (1870). Browning's fascination with madness is also evident in his long poem *Red Cotton Night-Cap Country* (1873) and in his interest in the poet Christopher Smart (1722–71), who wrote his most celebrated poetry while in an asylum and who features in Browning's collection *Parleyings With Certain People of Importance in Their Day* (1887).

Critical attention to Browning's interest in madness began with Michael Mason's essay 'Browning and the Dramatic Monologue' (1974) (see also Chapter 3).[25] Mason identified two contemporary sources for 'Porphyria's Lover': a text entitled 'Extracts from Gosschen's Diary' published in *Blackwood's Magazine* in 1818, which pretends to be the memoir of a German priest reporting on his encounter with a mad murderer in his prison cell who shares key characteristics with Browning's speaker; and the poem 'Marcian Colonna' (1820) by Browning's friend Bryan Procter (1787–1874), which presents a madman sitting by the corpse of his murdered mistress. Mason argues that while the two sources present the madmen's insanity as wholly irrational frenzy, Browning portrays his mad characters as following a rational logic, albeit a logic which starts from false premises. This concept of madness, Mason suggests, is influenced by contemporary changes in psychiatric theory. The period saw a shift towards an emphasis on the objective observation of lunatics and a more humane treatment of them, a substitution of mere physical restraint with 'moral management' of the patient, which assumes that he/she is not wholly devoid of rationality. Psychiatrists developed a number of related concepts of 'rational lunacy' or 'moral insanity' which assumed that 'a lunatic may be disordered in his behaviour and, supposedly, in the impulses that prompt his behaviour' but 'his intellectual powers are quite unimpaired, in particular he suffers from no delusions about the external world'.[26] Mason concludes that 'Porphyria's Lover' is Browning's attempt to portray such a case of rational lunacy where the lunatic is aware of his surroundings and acts in a rational way but reasons on the basis of the false assumption that his lover wants to die.

In *Retreat into the Mind: Victorian Poetry and the Rise of Psychiatry* (1988), Ekbert Faas (born 1938) conducts a more in-depth study of the dramatic monologue's relationship with the developing mental sciences, surveying the period's literature about psychology and the interest of psychologists in the dramatic monologue.[27] Faas can muster no evidence of Browning's direct contact with discourses about psychology. Instead, he relates his poetry to the investigation of psychic processes in Romantic poetry and in the literary analysis of Shakespeare's characters. Relying very much on contemporary reviews of Browning's work, he argues that the poet transferred the hidden self-analysis that he had practised in *Pauline* (1833) to a more objective and safely distanced observation of fictional characters in the dramatic monologue.

Faas' cautious connection between Browning and the contemporary discourse about mental illness contrasts with a more assertive but much more specific connection made by Barry L. Popowich in his article 'Porphyria is Madness' (1999). He suggests that 'Porphyria's Lover' is named after the delusional madness porphyria (named for its purple discolouring of the patient's urine) whose most famous sufferer was King George III (1738–1820). Although he cannot cite any sources from the 1830s which connect purple urine with the violent madness shown by Browning's speaker, Popowich suggests that the poet, whose interest in medicine is indicated by his attendance at medical lectures in 1829, might have heard about or even seen sufferers from the condition in London asylums.[28] The texts by Mason, Faas and Popowich show the inherent difficulties of this kind of historical research: the analogies between Browning's poetry and the contextual sources are plausible, but in the absence of factual proof that the poet read certain sources, there always remains a degree of conjecture in the analysis.

A more recent study which revisits the subject is *Crime in Verse: The Poetics of Murder in the Victorian Era* (2008) by Ellen L. O'Brien (born 1970). The book examines how poetry intervenes in the Victorian debate about crime, mainly in the genres of the popular ballad and in the dramatic monologue. As part of this analysis, which draws on the approach to Victorian poetry as a means of cultural critique taken by Armstrong and Slinn, O'Brien situates 'Porphyria's Lover', 'My Last Duchess', 'The Laboratory' and Rossetti's 'A Last Confession' in relation to the competing discourses of the law and the mental sciences. Going beyond the other three critics covered in this section who cite medical writings of the time, she also considers medico-legal documents which discuss the concept of criminal lunacy and sources about insanity defences in murder trials. The defence pleas of criminals as 'not guilty on the ground of insanity', O'Brien argues, blurred the distinction between responsible criminality and insanity and thus 'frustrated collective desires to define murder and punish killers and pitted the authority of medical experts against the fears of a concerned citizenry and the traditions of learned jurists'.[29] Poets participated in this process and 'exploit[ed] the curiosity and confusion surrounding these anxieties [about the definitions of crime and madness] to simultaneously aestheticize and politicize murder'.[30]

In O'Brien's analysis, Browning's readers are faced with the dilemma of deciding whether his three monologists need to be judged as morally responsible criminals or according to the medical categories of irresponsible insanity. 'Porphyria's Lover' might be read as a study in moral insanity, i.e. a 'perversion of natural feeling without any remarkable disorder or defect of the intellect'.[31] However, the speaker demonstrates both the emotional chaos that defines moral insanity and the cool reasoning that defines responsible criminality, as succinctly illustrated in these lines:

■         at last I knew
Porphyria worshipped me: surprise
Made my heart swell, and still it grew
While I debated what to do. [ll. 32–5] ☐

On this O'Brien comments:

■ The character's presumptions about Porphyria's worshipful sentiments, his use of the word 'surprise,' and his swelling heart suggest the category of moral insanity as a disease that arises out of emotional excess and irresistible impulse. The character's internal debate, however, reproduces the problems inherent in separating responsible criminals from irresponsible lunatics. That the speaker 'debated,' and that he recollects a process of debating, insinuates intellectual clarity and willful agency.[32] ☐

'My Last Duchess' is a possible case of monomania, insanity which is restricted to a single subject while the intellectual powers are not affected in other areas. The duke exhibits two key characteristics of the monomaniac, excessive self-love and a fixation with a single subject, his wife. He can be diagnosed more specifically as a case of 'misanthropical monomania', in that he believes himself to be the object of secret hatred and plots, O'Brien (2008), p. 137. Yet at the same time, his mastery of language (which he plays down) and his ability to combine an art tour and a marriage negotiation show his rational agency and self-control. Moreover, in his Renaissance context there is no need for madness to explain his act since his murder of the duchess would have been legal if she had indeed committed adultery. '[T]he intentionally murderous but apparently monomaniacal Duke hovers between Renaissance and Victorian understandings of murder.'[33]

Finally, 'The Laboratory' is a possible candidate for mania, i.e. 'raving madness, in which the understanding is generally deranged'.[34] O'Brien argues that the poem's end-stopped rhyming couplets and the metrical irregularities 'establish a sense of manic speed and energy'[35] and that the speaker 'makes some illogical statements which suggest irrationality.

But at the same time her premeditation and the use of poison through the chemist indicate deliberate criminal intent. As in 'My Last Duchess', the cultural context in which love affairs are not mere affairs of the heart but serious power struggles for social survival at court offers a rational motivation for her deed. The poem thus also appeals to Victorian ideas about the corruption of aristocrats during the *ancien régime*, the absolutist political and social system that existed in France before the 1789 revolution.

In sum, O'Brien argues for these poems as ways of making the reader reflect on the difficulty of defining and judging behaviour as either criminal or mad and more broadly on epistemology, or how we attain knowledge of meaning in general. Because Browning's murderers can be situated 'outside the realm of judicial accountability', the poems 'withhold the comforts of moral resolution', mirroring the 'ethical impasse that accompanied the medicolegal debates of the mid-Victorian period'.[36] The playful aesthetic form of poetry is thus used as a means of formulating an ethically serious political critique, calling into question key Victorian ideas about morality, legality, gender and knowledge.

In the most recent contribution to research on the intersection between poetry and psychology, Gregory Tate shifts the critical perspective from the focus on extreme psychological states to a consideration of introspective poetry. In *The Poet's Mind: The Psychology of Victorian Poetry 1830–1870* (2012), he examines 'how poets responded to the broad intellectual shift in Victorian Britain towards an understanding of the mind as an analysable and embodied thing'.[37] He demonstrates how Victorian poets draw on the discourse of the evolving discipline of psychology in their use of the Romantics' associationist theory (which conceptualises mental activity as a succession of related ideas originating in sense experience) and newer physiological theories of the mind (which take account of the brain as a physical entity). This is further complicated by the recourse to the religious idea of the metaphysical soul. Tate scrutinises how poets 'search for languages and forms that will allow them both to express mental processes and to analyse the mind, to break it down and study it as a combination of physical, psychological, and spiritual impulses'.[38]

Browning features in two of Tate's chronological chapters. The first argues that Browning's and Tennyson's poetry of the 1830s is torn between the notion of a traditional metaphysical soul and more modern physicalist theories of the mind. In *Pauline* and *Sordello* (1840), Tate asserts, Browning's hesitation between physical and metaphysical concepts of the mind is apparent in his uses of binaries such as 'head' and 'heart'.[39] In *Sordello,* Tate identifies the binaries of 'thought and perception, of flawed intellection and felt intuition [as] a structuring concern'.⁴⁰ He concludes that Browning's struggle to reconcile the conception of the mind as both a physical, mutable entity and a metaphysical soul accounts for the obscure style of *Sordello*: 'The pervasive obscurity and linguistic intricacy of the poem suggest that the only way Browning saw to fit the infinity of his soul to the finite systems of thought and language was to use a syntax and style so difficult as to verge on impenetrability.'⁴¹

Tate returns to Browning in his final chapter about the dramatic monologue sequence *The Ring and the Book*. Although key sections of the poem, especially the monologues by the Pope and Browning himself, still adhere to a metaphysical model of the mind, the recourse to the physiological model is the poem's striking feature, making it a high point in the use of poetry as a means of psychological exploration. Tate reads the poem's favourable critical reception as evidence that Victorian literary taste had adapted from the Romantic expressive ideal to the idea of poetry as the analysis of an individual's psychology.⁴² Browning's own earlier work and its influence on other poetry, Tate contends, is key to this change in taste.

Tate identifies the problem of expressing and understanding thought as a central concern of *The Ring and the Book*, tracing in the poem the influence of contemporary writings about thought as a physiological process that Browning probably read, such as the 1865 article 'The Heart and the Brain' by George Henry Lewes (1817–78):⁴³ Tate illustrates how Browning

> ■ describes the psychological processes of his speakers as physical motions. The truth about the events surrounding the murders, he says, must be reached
>
> > Not by the very sense and sight indeed –
> > (Which take at best imperfect cognizance,
> > Since, how heart moves brain, and how both move hand,
> > What mortal ever in entirety saw?) (I, 826–9)
>
> In these lines psychology is hidden within corporeal interiority. Its physical location is not restricted to the nervous system: here, as in his earlier reference to the 'high-blooded' brain [I, 37 and I, 88], Browning follows Lewes in claiming that the heart exerts an influence on the organ of thought.⁴⁴ □

Thought is here conceived not as the cause of a physical act, but as the result of a physical influence from the heart. Representations of the mind which borrow from Victorian discourses about thought as an 'unwilled physiological process' can be found throughout the poem.⁴⁵ The poem's villain, Guido Franceschini, at times uses this concept of psychology in his defence:

> ■ Guido tries to have it both ways, arguing that he is an autonomous agent, that his acts are directly informed by willed thoughts, while also claiming that he is driven by psycho-physiological motors beyond his control. This is evident in his account of the murders in his first monologue, during which he relates how he was finally moved to act after days of deliberation:
>
>> I started up – 'Some end must be!' At once,
>> Silence: then, scratching like a death-watch-tick,
>> Slowly within my brain was syllabled,
>> 'One more concession, one decisive way
>> And but one, to determine thee the truth,–
>> This way, in fine, I whisper in thy ear:
>> Now doubt, anon decide, thereupon act!' (V, 1612–18)
>
> On the one hand these lines present thought as an active process that leads immediately to Guido's subsequent act. Guido stages his thinking as recordable speech, sounding within the brain and initiating a process of determined decision-making that in turn instigates action. This sense is reinforced by his squeezing the cohesive operation of thinking ('now doubt, anon decide') and acting into a single line, and by his repetition of the verbs two lines later in his assertion that 'I doubt, I will decide, then act' (V, 1620). On the other hand Guido implies that he has to be told what to do: the speech in his brain is not straightforwardly his own, as indicated by the passive construction of 'was syllabled', by the 'death-watch-tick' which suggests that he is suffering from a sort of neurological infestation, and by the use of 'I' to denote a separate subjectivity in line 1617.[46] □

Guido simultaneously presents his actions as driven by a conscious decision and the result of an involuntary physical impulse, which relieves him of the responsibility for murder. Tate's scrutiny of the way Guido analyses the mechanisms of his own mental processes could beneficially be applied to Browning's other dramatic monologues, as a way of elucidating what is arguably the poet's central interest. As Oscar Wilde (1854–1900) succinctly observed, 'it was not thought that fascinated him, but rather the processes by which thought moves'.[47]

This chapter has gone beyond the dramatic monologue's formal features and the poem as a communicative act to interpretations which try to fathom the historical contexts and various cultural debates in which Browning participated through his poetry. These approaches allow us to get closer to understanding why Browning wrote and how his poetry appeals to readers past and present. The criticism situating his dramatic monologue in its wider social environment and in relation to non-literary discourses such as medicine and the law suggests the cultural significance of the genre. As the genre most closely associated with Browning, the dramatic monologue will continue to occupy a prominent place in the chapters of this Guide that follow. In the next chapter on Browning's aesthetics, the genre's role in defining his concept of art comes under scrutiny. We will see how critics deal with the problem of reading poems as expressions of the author's aesthetics although his voice is, of course, absent from the text.

CHAPTER FIVE

# Aesthetics: Realism and the Grotesque

Apart from his two essays discussed in Chapter 1 and some prefaces to earlier works, Browning was reluctant to spell out his aesthetics. However, there are a number of poems that can be said to convey his views on poetry and art in general. This chapter presents criticism which attempts to explicate Browning's aesthetics by drawing on his poetry. It opens with a consideration of Browning's realism, which is perhaps the most striking and unpoetic feature of his work. Descriptions of his poetry as realism by Walter Bagehot and John Woolford are contrasted with E. Warwick Slinn's more fundamental questioning of realist aesthetics. Browning's realism is frequently described as a consequence of his interest in the grotesque, and this issue is covered in the next section. Browning's grotesque is judged very differently – negatively by his early critics Bagehot and George Santayana, and much more sympathetically and analytically by the modern scholars Woolford and Isobel Armstrong. Another section focuses on Browning's famous painter poems, which not only express conflicting views on pictorial art but are also read as veiled discussion of Browning's poetics. Here, as in the previous section, we can see Browning participating in contemporary debates about aesthetics which also have important political and religious dimensions. These aspects are revealed by David DeLaura's analysis, whereas Laurence Lerner tries to account for contradictions in the aesthetic statements in different painter poems. Finally, the chapter also gives insights into other ways of reading the painter poems, focusing on a psychoanalytical reading championed by Harold Bloom and refuted by Lerner and a Marxist reading by Loy D. Martin.

## Realism

Oscar Wilde, in his characteristically witty style, once described Browning in terms with which many Victorian critics would have agreed. He called him not a poet but 'the most supreme writer of fiction', whose only contemporary rival was George Meredith (1828–1909) in his novels: 'Meredith is a prose Browning and so is Browning. He used poetry as a medium for writing in prose.'¹ Wilde put his finger on a resemblance between Browning's poetry and the realist literary mode which prevailed in the nineteenth-century novel. This manifests itself in various aspects of Browning's work, such as the poems' contemporary or historical settings, depictions of material detail, the range of convincingly real characters and the realistic situations in which they find themselves, the scrutiny of the characters' psychology, and the recreation of spoken language with all its roughness and ugliness (as far as this is possible in metrical poetry). Examples of all of these features can easily be found throughout the corpus of Browning's work. 'Fra Lippo Lippi' (1855), for instance, presents a fictional, yet realistically detailed, situation in the life of the painter Filippo Lippi (ca. 1406–69) and recreates the historical setting of fifteenth-century Florence. Its speaker discusses not just his realist aesthetics as a painter (see below) but also taboo subjects such as sexuality which transgress against the traditional decorum of poetry, and he uses coarse language and swear words. Throughout the remainder of this section, the focus will be on how critics assess Browning's choice to adopt the mode of realism and on the aesthetics or intentions which underlie this choice.

Like Wilde, Browning's contemporary critics mostly condemned his realism and thus showed that their own aesthetic standards were informed by more traditional ideas of poetry as a medium in which (beautiful) general ideals rather than (ugly) individualised realities should be represented. Walter Bagehot (1826–77) is better known for his writings about politics and economics, but he also wrote literary reviews, including the essay 'Wordsworth, Tennyson, and Browning; or, Pure, Ornate, and Grotesque Art in English Poetry' (1864), to which we will return in the next section on the grotesque. The essay attacks Browning's poetry but acknowledges his realism:

■ He has applied a hard strong intellect to real life; he has applied the same intellect to the problems of his age. He has striven to know what it *is*: he has endeavoured not to be cheated by counterfeits, not to be infatuated with illusions.[2] □

By contrast, from a twenty-first-century critical perspective, John Woolford, in *Robert Browning* (2007), offers an explanation of the aesthetics that motivated the poet to write in the realistic mode. He opens by quoting paratextual comments by Browning himself which suggest a notion of realism in the nineteenth-century positivist sense. For instance, Browning writes to his friend Julia Wedgwood (1833–1913), who had complained about the ugly realism of *The Ring and the Book* (1868–69):

> ■ [T]he business has been, as I specify, to explain *fact* – and the fact is what you see and, worse, are to see. The question with me has never been, 'Could not one, by changing the factors, work out the sum to better result?' but declare and prove the actual result, and there an end. Before I die, I hope to purely invent something, – here my pride was concerned to invent nothing: the minutest circumstance that denotes character is *true*: the black is so much – the white, no more.[3] □

These remarks and similar ones suggest Browning was driven by a moral mission to convey the truth. This seems borne out by the many uses of the terms 'true' and 'fact' and their derivatives in Browning's work, which Woolford compares to the much less frequent use in the work of other Victorian poets. Yet rather than classifying Browning's aesthetics as the poetic equivalent of the positivist intention to present objectively verifiable facts that underlies the contemporary realist novel, Woolford argues that Browning's realism is indebted to a poetic predecessor, William Wordsworth. He cites passages from Wordsworth's 'Preface' to *Lyrical Ballads* (1800), in which Wordsworth rejects the conventionalised language of poetic decorum in favour of an attempt to realistically represent the spoken language of common people in his poetry. However, Woolford contends that the next literary generation misread Wordsworth as positing a scientific, empirical concept of truth:

> ■ Wordsworth makes it very clear that what he means by *truth* is absolutely not 'matter of fact, or Science' [...] but there can be no doubt that his Victorian successors synthesized his linguistic realism with the growing contemporary cultural pre-eminence of empirical, positivist factuality. [...] This was natural enough in a period when the theological account of the universe was being overtaken and superseded by the scientific, but when this displacement was attended not with complacency, but usually with doubt, occasionally terror and often a certain amount of guilt.[5] □

Woolford examines the following passage from 'Fra Lippo Lippi' to show how the poem's concept of 'truth' points beyond the scientific towards a religious 'truth':

> ■ However, you're my man, you've seen the world
> – The beauty and the wonder and the power,
> The shapes of things, their colours, lights and shades,
> Changes, surprises, – and God made it all!
> – For what? Do you feel thankful, ay or no
> For this fair town's face, yonder river's line,
> The mountain round it and the sky above,

> Much more the figures of man, woman, child,
> These are the frame to? What's it all about?
> To be passed over, despised? or dwelt upon,
> Wondered at? oh, this last of course! – you say.
> But why not do as well as say – paint these
> Just as they are, careless what comes of it?
> God's works – paint any one, and count it crime
> To let a truth slip. ['Fra Lippo Lippi', ll. 282–96] ☐

Woolford explains:

> ■ Thus Fra Lippo Lippi, in Browning's poem, repudiates the anti-realism of medieval theology, but assigns his own realism to the domain, not of scientific naturalism, but religious attention taken in a more refined [...] sense. [...] The word *truth* in the final line compounds the ideas of, first, lyrical integrity in the object and, secondly, accuracy in its representation: both are the conditions for a religiously inspired contemplation of the external world and the human spectacle.[6] ☐

In Woolford's analysis, Browning adopts the pantheism of Romantics like Wordsworth, the belief that every part of the outer world is not just a product of divine creation but is itself divine. This means that, for Browning, objects in themselves are sacred, and this explains his strong interest in physical objects.[7]

Having documented the (differently motivated) fascination with physical objects in the Victorian novel, Woolford demonstrates through this example from 'Mr Sludge "the Medium"' (1864) how the similar centrality of physical details in Browning's poetry is used to characterise the speaker:

> ■ May I sit, sir? This dear old table, now!
> Please, sir, a parting egg-nogg and cigar!
> I've been so happy with you! Nice stuffed chairs,
> And sympathetic sideboards; what an end
> To all the instructive evenings! (It's alight.) ['Mr Sludge "the Medium"', ll. 76–80] ☐

Woolford draws the reader's attention to

> ■ the bracketed final sentence, with its intimation that even a speaker's confession of crime [...] must be negotiated within a world of familiar objects and banal actions. This is, however, more than just scene-setting. Physicality, the world of objects, are at the forefront of Sludge's mind, and the poem has begun with a physical attack upon him by his patron, Hiram H. Horsefall, registered by cries and stylized choking: 'Aie – aie – aie!/

Please, sir! your thumbs are through my windpipe, sir!/ Ch-ch!' (ll. 16–18). What is most visible, though, is the immense irony on which the poem is erected: that Sludge, who as a medium claims to have and give access to spiritual existence, is actually a materialist for whom 'sideboards' and 'eggnogg', not to mention 'dollars, V-notes, and so forth' (l. 100) apparently represent the ultimate reality. Thus Sludge's vision of heaven simply duplicates the contents (and gratifications) of quotidian reality: 'Bacon advises, Shakespeare writes you songs,/ And Mary Queen of Scots embraces you' (ll. 1408–9).

It was Browning's interest in this kind of material(ism), no doubt, that led to the objection most articulately put forward by Walter Bagehot and George Santayana, that Browning exhibited 'failure in rationality and the indifference to perfection' – that his conception of *truth* was a degraded, antispiritual one.[8] □

As the next section will show, Woolford, like Bagehot and Santayana, ultimately explains Browning's realism as a consequence of the poet's interest in the grotesque. But before we turn to this issue, it is worth balancing the apparently so obvious characterisation of Browning as a realist with an approach which questions not only this classification of Browning but also realism as such. E. Warwick Slinn in *Browning and the Fictions of Identity* (1982) does not deny Browning's skill in recreating conversational speech but suggests that the aesthetics of realism are an illusion:

■ We are faced with the paradox that Browning's mimetic method challenges the assumptions of mimetic art. Through dramatising men thinking about the world, he imitates a process which transforms, and it is more often than not the transformation which is paraded as reality by his characters. The elements of artifice in a Browning monologue mean therefore that it is less a slice-of-life than a contrived representation of the contrivance in human reality. Browning employs the illusion of a person speaking in order to suggest the illusion in human understanding; the point is not only to portray experience but also to question it, and he does this by indicating the linguistic artifice which underlies all speech. While spontaneous conversation reinforces a commonplace realism, there is another paradoxical sense in which it undermines the illusion: in the way that temporal progression is constantly impeded. Elliptical, heavily parenthetical sentences tend to break the pattern of normal syntax with its forward movement and so divert attention from ends to process. Consequently, although there is a necessary overall temporal dimension to a monologue, since that is how everyday experience occurs, there is little intermediate temporal or narrative impetus, and in so far as syntactic interruption draws attention to itself, it minimises the referential aspect of the language, depreciating the realism and encouraging a sense of the artifice in human expression.[9] □

Browning's poetry exposes the fiction that the literary mode of realism can truly represent life. This is firstly because the poems, in which we hear only the voice of the biased speakers, focus on the way they want the world to be rather than on the world as it is. This is a reminder of the illusion or self-deception to which we are all prone and raises wider questions about the reliability of personal experience as a way of understanding the world. Secondly, the highly structured poetic language of the dramatic monologue is one of artifice which again makes us aware of the artifice in the everyday use of language. Browning's frequent use of disrupted sentence structure, while making the poem sound more like spontaneous speech, makes the reader aware of the process of constructing the sentences instead of making us forget about the language and treating it as a transparent medium that gives access to reality, which is the ambition of realism.

## The Grotesque

The more traditional way of assessing the heightened awareness of language that is created by Browning's 'ugly', unpoetic style is to describe it as a manifestation of the grotesque. J. Hillis Miller, in *The Disappearance of God* (1963), offers a neat summary of the formal features that create Browning's grotesque style:

■ Grotesque metaphor, ugly words heavy with consonants, stuttering alliteration, strong active verbs, breathless rhythm, onomatopoeia, images of rank smells, rough textures, and of things fleshy, viscous, sticky, nubbly, slimy, shaggy, sharp, crawling, thorny, or prickly – all these work together in Browning's verse to create an effect of unparalleled thickness, harshness, and roughness.[10] □

The term 'grotesque' was first associated with Browning's poetry in Walter Bagehot's essay 'Wordsworth, Tennyson, and Browning; or, Pure, Ornate, and Grotesque Art in English Poetry' (1864), as cited above. Here Bagehot defines Browning's grotesque poetry in contradistinction to pure poetry, exemplified by William Wordsworth, and to ornate poetry, exemplified by Alfred Tennyson. Pure and ornate art 'paint the types of literature in as good perfection as they can', though the latter is inferior in that it 'uses undue disguises and unreal enchantments':

■ But grotesque art does just the contrary. It takes the type, so to say, *in difficulties*. It gives a representation of it in its minimum development, amid the circumstances least favourable to it, just while it is struggling with obstacles, just where it is encumbered with incongruities. It deals,

to use the language of science, not with normal types but with abnormal specimens; to use the language of old philosophy, not with what nature is striving to be, but with what by some lapse she has happened to become.
  This art works by contrasts. It enables you to see, it makes you see, the perfect type by painting the opposite deviation. It shows you what ought to be by what ought not to be, when complete, it reminds you of the perfect image, by showing you the distorted and imperfect image.[11] ☐

Bagehot's reference to scientific 'types' suggests the influence of evolutionary biology, popularised most famously but not exclusively by *On the Origin of Species* (1859) by Charles Darwin (1809–82). But underlying this is a concept of art which distinguishes between abstract ideal types and their real, less perfect manifestations, a distinction which goes back as far as Plato. Bagehot can only conceive of art which aims to make the reader aware of the ideal, even if in Browning's case this happens through the portrayal of its opposite.

This is still a fairly neutral account of Browning's technique, but Bagehot then moves on to explain why he objects to it. Firstly, again in line with traditional and contemporary Victorian taste, he expects art to be pleasing to its audience, unlike Browning's ugly subjects such as the irreligious speaker of 'Caliban upon Setebos' (1864), 'a nasty creature'.[12] Browning's difficult and ugly style which makes his poetry hard to appreciate is a further cause for criticism.

Bagehot summarises the conflict between the defence of Browning's grotesque style as a form of realism and his own idealism thus:

■ Mr. Browning possibly, and some of the worst of Mr. Browning's admirers certainly, will say that these grotesque objects exist in real life, and therefore they ought to be, at least may be, described in art. But though pleasure is not the end of poetry, pleasing is a condition of poetry. An exceptional monstrosity of horrid ugliness cannot be made pleasing, except it be made to suggest – to recall – the perfection, the beauty, from which it is a deviation. Perhaps in extreme cases no art is equal to this; but then such self-imposed problems should not be worked by the artist; these out-of-the-way and detestable subjects should be let alone by him. It is rather characteristic of Mr. Browning to neglect this rule. He is the most of a realist, and the least of an idealist of any poet we know.[13] ☐

Bagehot's deprecating analysis of Browning's poetry as anti-idealist is echoed by the philosopher George Santayana in his essay 'The Poetry of Barbarism' (1900). As can be expected from a professional philosopher, he is primarily interested in Browning's ethics. He situates himself in opposition to the late nineteenth-century admirers of Browning as a religious and philosophical sage (see Introduction). While Bagehot shows appreciation for Browning's intellect although it demands too much of the average reader, Santayana dismisses the poet as irrational and lacking a desire for perfection – deficiencies that make him an uncivilised barbarian:

> ■ [W]e are in the presence of a barbaric genius, of a truncated imagination, of a thought and an art ill-digested, of a volcanic eruption that tosses itself quite blindly and ineffectually into the sky [...] one may notice in Browning many superficial signs of that deepest of all failures, the failure in rationality and the indifference to perfection.[14] □

Moreover, Santayana perceives a correspondence between Browning's rough style and his ethics which lacks 'nobility':

> ■ He has no sustained nobility of style. He affects with the reader a confidential and vulgar manner, so as to be more sincere and to feel more at home [...] We get in these tricks of manner a taste of that essential vulgarity, that indifference to purity and distinction, which is latent but pervasive in all the products of his mind. The same disdain of perfection which appears in his ethics appears here in his verse, and impairs its beauty by allowing it to remain too often obscure, affected, and grotesque.[15] □

The terms 'nobility' and 'vulgarity' imply that Santayana makes a class-based judgment of Browning's grotesque art. Purity and perfection are aristocratic; the grotesque is vulgar in the etymological sense of the Latin 'vulgus' meaning 'the common people'. This develops Bagehot's remark that Browning appeals to the 'half educated' reader.[16]

Such an analysis of the grotesque in political terms can be traced back to the first use of 'grotesque' in relation to art in general in volume 3 of *The Stones of Venice* (1853) by the influential art critic John Ruskin (1819–1900). Ruskin commends the grotesque as the artistic expression of ordinary working men, and its roughness is due to their lack of education which hampers their artistic execution. The grotesque is one of the manifestations of Gothic art and architecture. Ruskin favours the Gothic period over the preceding classical style, which he associates with the absolute rule of feudal societies, as a kind of democratisation of art. The Gothic with its many individualised ornaments allows the individual workman to express himself rather than just execute the design of the architect.[17] Two modern critics, John Woolford and Isobel Armstrong, have developed Ruskin's ideas in their application to Browning.

The main argument of Woolford's 2007 book *Robert Browning*, which has already been discussed in the previous section, is that the grotesque is key to Browning's aesthetics. Woolford points to Browning's inferior social background in comparison to other poets. His origins as a man who had not inherited wealth and whose religious non-conformism barred him from attending the universities of Oxford and Cambridge can be seen as inclining him towards a more democratic poetics as expressed through the grotesque. Woolford sees the Victorian grotesque as replacing the Romantic pursuit of the sublime, the celebration of the immeasurably grand and noble, whose terrifying effect leads to a (spiritual) elevation of the perceiver's mind, as in the Romantic representation of sublime natural scenery such as mountains, ravines, torrents, and so on. He contrasts the 'fetishisation of power' in the sublime with the grotesque as a symptom of the rise of liberal democracy in the Victorian period, which calls into question the veneration of power.[18] Woolford illustrates this point with a passage from 'Caliban Upon Setebos':

> ■              Ha! The wind
> Shoulders the pillared dust, death's house o' the move,
> And fast invading fires begin! White blaze –
> A tree's head snaps – and there, there, there, there, there,
> His thunder follows! Fool to gibe at Him!
> Lo! 'Lieth flat and loveth Setebos!
> 'Maketh his teeth meet through his upper lip,
> Will let those quails fly, will not eat this month
> One little mess of whelks, so he may 'scape! ['Caliban upon Setebos', ll. 287–95] □

In this passage with its grotesque language and physical details, Caliban interprets the sublime storm as a threat from his god Setebos and chooses to submit to this god in order to be spared punishment. Woolford calls this scene 'an episode of *degraded* religious terror induced by the natural sublime':

> ■ During this passage into the grotesque, the sublime loses its spiritual and moral authority: the subtitle of 'Caliban', 'Natural Theology on the Island', indicates that this was precisely Browning's intention. Caliban's superstitious terror marks the end-point of constantly renewed attempts during the eighteenth and nineteenth centuries to derive religious ideas and authority from the sublime by making God its ontological source.[19] □

The poem could be seen as a kind of parody of the Romantic poetry which precedes Browning and which reads sublime nature as a proof of the divine. Through the grotesque Caliban and his imagined god Setebos we see the mechanism of how a mind full of terror invests nature with meaning and interprets it as a manifestation of the divine.

Woolford does a more directly political reading of the grotesque in 'The Patriot' (1855), whose speaker contrasts a past walk through Brescia in Lombardy, when he was cheered as a hero by the crowds, with his present solitary walk through the city on his way to the scaffold. Woolford concentrates on the poem's striking

> ■ contrasts of imagery. The speaker's triumphal entry is described in terms of the solemn perceptual disorientation of sublime experience ('The house-roofs seemed to heave and sway / The church-spires flamed, such flags they had... The air broke into a mist with bells,/ The old walls rocked with the crowds and cries' [ll. 2–3, 6–7]); his downfall is accompanied by grim tokens of the grotesque (*a palsied few* [l. 17]), in particular the stoic pathos of
>
>> I go in the rain, and, more than needs,
>> A rope cuts both my wrists behind,
>> And I think, by the feel, my forehead bleeds ['The Patriot', ll. 21–3]
>
> The speaker is reduced to an afflicted body enclosed by and enclosing an impoverished, despairing subjectivity groping its way phenomenologically (*by the feel*) to the site of its extinction. This combination of features illustrates the close association between the grotesque and realism in Victorian poetics: reality presents as a stunted deformation of ecstatic visions proclaimed by the sublime of idealism [...][20] □

Again, the lofty sublime is replaced by the painful physicality of the grotesque, and implicitly the sublime vision is revealed to be an illusion while the grotesque represents reality. We can see here how Browning opposes the idealism of the Romantic sublime and why supporters of idealist aesthetics like Bagehot and Santayana could not appreciate Browning's work.

'The Patriot' seems to be inspired by the changing fortunes of Arnold of Brescia (ca. 1090–1155), a cleric who called on the Church to renounce worldly possessions. He was initially welcomed as a political reformer but eventually executed on the orders of the Pope. Yet, as Woolford points out, Browning removed specific details of this historical source, such as the cause which the speaker espoused and the reason for his turn of fortune – i.e. was it his own fault or was he betrayed by others? This and the subtitle, 'An Old Story', give the poem a more general relevance as an ironic comment on betrayed leader figures.[21]

Woolford proposes two explanations for this interest in leaders who are betrayed or betray their followers, and these are related to Browning's own politics. Browning started out as a Radical, espousing the radical change of society by revolutionary means, but he later turned to the more moderate position of a liberalism supporting gradual, non-violent change. Browning's fascination with fallen leaders in 'The Patriot' and elsewhere in his work (for example, in the dramas *The Return of the Druses* [1843] and *A Soul's Tragedy* [1846] or *Prince Hohenstiel-Schwangau* [1871]) may be a denunciation of 'the corruption induced by power in those who usurp it even in a good cause. Browning clearly had in mind the example of, for instance [Maximilien de] Robespierre [1758–94] and Napoleon [Bonaparte, 1769–1821], leaders who started out as proponents of the French revolutionary cause but (arguably) ended up betraying it.'[22] Browning might thus be taking a radical principled stance vis-à-vis leaders who abandon radical ideas. Alternatively, poems like 'The Patriot' may be a veiled way of dealing with his own guilt at having betrayed the cause of radicalism for a more moderate politics.[23] The continuing recourse to the grotesque throughout his work would then be an indicator of his continued radicalism and subversiveness, even if only hidden at an aesthetic level.

Woolford's close reading of Browning's grotesque partially builds on Isobel Armstrong's essay 'Browning and the "Grotesque" Style' (1969) and her multi-author study *Victorian Poetry: Poetry, Poetics and Politics* (1993), which places Browning in a broader cultural context. Her chapter 'Browning in the 1850s and after: New experiments in radical poetry and the Grotesque' argues for the grotesque as one of the ways of articulating a politically radical cultural critique (see Chapter 4), a critique most famously expressed by Ruskin as discussed in the previous section of this chapter.[24] Armstrong reads Browning as engaged in a complex dialogue with Ruskin throughout a number of poems from the 1850s. The poem which Ruskin himself singled out as the poetic equivalent of his art criticism will serve us as an example of Armstrong's analysis. In volume 4 of *Modern Painters* (1856), Ruskin acknowledged that 'The Bishop Orders His Tomb at Saint Praxed's Church' (1845) anticipates the assessment of Renaissance culture in his own, more widely read, art criticism:

■ I know no other piece of modern English, prose or poetry, in which there is so much told, as in these lines, of the Renaissance spirit, – its worldliness, inconsistency, pride, hypocrisy, ignorance of itself, love of art, of luxury, and of good Latin. It is nearly all that I said of the central Renaissance in thirty pages of the *Stones of Venice* put into as many lines, Browning's being also the antecedent work.[25] □

Armstrong explains where exactly Ruskin seems to see the parallel between the two works:

■ Those 'thirty pages' are presumably the account of the decadence of the Grotesque with the emergence of Renaissance luxury in the last volume of *The Stones of Venice* (1853), where the pursuit of pleasure and family aggrandisement has subordinated work, and the degenerate Grotesque art of the culture which plays 'inordinately' has displaced the 'noble' Grotesque. [...] Thus in associating Browning with the politics of the Grotesque Ruskin was connecting him with the reconfiguration of a radical aesthetic which was going on round his own work, and acknowledging that this alignment was not necessarily one which involved direct influence but belonged to a formation of common ideas and analyses.[26] ☐

Ruskin sees Browning as subscribing to the same radical political agenda as himself, distinguishing between a 'noble' grotesque associated with his idea of the Gothic which allows the individual workman to express himself and the 'degenerate' grotesque which is about hedonism and self-aggrandisement.

Armstrong then analyses how the grotesque works in 'The Bishop Orders His Tomb'. The poem is

■ based on a typical Grotesque procedure – the distorted perspective of restricted vision. The dying Bishop, surrounded by 'nephews', can only think of his magnificent tomb from the perspective of someone lying on it, just as he is lying on his deathbed. The irony is that from this position looking outwards into the church one could see precisely what a spectator in front of it could not see – but one would have to be dead, or one of the stone effigies on the tomb, to do so. The violent power of the gaze, a greedy appropriation of the aesthetic and the sexual, and a complete failure to imagine or comprehend death are conveyed through the limited comprehension of the gaze itself. The monologue combines [...] what seem to be two incompatible and incongruous propensities, an extreme intellectual and epistemological sophistication and an extreme commitment to the voracious power of anarchic, libidinal emotion and desire. [...] A fantastic, ludic, intellectual complexity and the raw intensity of disruptive libido are not perhaps compatible with one another but they live together as elements of the Grotesque in Ruskin's analysis as the related forms in which the oppressed consciousness both responds to and resists its condition.[27] ☐

Armstrong defines Browning's grotesque literary technique here as visual distortion: firstly, in the physical sense, the speaker imagines the view his future stone effigy will have of the church, ignoring the fact that the effigy is only a representation of him; and secondly, at a figurative level, the perception of the otherwise intelligent and sophisticated bishop is limited by his sensuality, his decadent aesthetic sense and his inability to conceptualise death (in the way he as a Christian should do). The bishop's strange combination of intellectual sophistication with sexual and material desire corresponds to Ruskin's definition of the grotesque, oppressed individual.

Armstrong and Woolford are not the only critics who interpret Browning's apparently apolitical poems as encoding the poet's political beliefs. We will return to this political Browning in Chapter 7 with a consideration of how Browning's choice to set poems in earlier periods allows him to comment obliquely on politics past and present.

Armstrong and Woolford are also not alone in situating Browning in relation to contemporary art criticism. As the next section will show, his poems about Renaissance painters, in which the keen amateur sculptor Browning demonstrates his familiarity with art history, have led critics to scrutinise his aesthetics within his cultural context.

## The Painter Poems

Browning was famously reluctant to discuss his poetics directly, but his dramatic monologues by painters and his poems about paintings – above all 'Pictor Ignotus' (1845), 'Fra Lippo Lippi', 'Andrea del Sarto' and 'Old Pictures in Florence' (all 1855) – are often read as indirect expressions of his aesthetics. They both give an insight into Browning's views on the historical development of pictorial art and allow us to establish parallels with the principles of his own poetics.

It is well known that an important source for the painter poems was the biographical work *Lives of the Most Eminent Painters, Sculptors, and Architects* (1550) by Giorgio Vasari (1511–74), who was himself a painter and architect. Critical editions of Browning's work point the reader to the aspects of this text that Browning adopted or adapted from Vasari. However, Browning not only engages with this Renaissance assessment of his painters, as seen in the previous section, he also participates in nineteenth-century debates about the respective value of artistic eras and particular painters.

David J. DeLaura, in 'The Context of Browning's Painter Poems' (1980), focuses on such a debate in which art criticism is closely linked to religion. According to DeLaura, Browning's painter poems must be read in the context of nineteenth-century British attitudes towards Catholicism. For historical reasons, going back to Henry VIII's split from the Catholic Church and his foundation of a Protestant state church, British Protestants often did not appreciate early religious art with its depiction of Catholic subjects such as saints or the Madonna. Yet during the 1830s–1850s, the Catholic Revival in Britain saw the gradual gaining of political rights by Catholics, the re-establishment of Catholic bishops and the argument by a faction of the Church of England, the Oxford Movement, for a reorientation towards Catholic theology.

Part of this re-engagement with Catholic values was the response to the art historical work *De la poésie chrétienne* (*The Poetry of Christian Art*, 1836) by the conservative French Catholic Alexis François Rio (1797–1874). Rio proposed a re-assessment of High Renaissance art (1490s–1527) and the medieval painting which preceded it. Rio's measure of an artwork's value was its ability to have a spiritual impact on the viewer,

# AESTHETICS: REALISM AND THE GROTESQUE  95

its capacity to inspire the viewer to prayer or religious contemplation. Hence the paintings of the medieval period, which were technically less accomplished than those of the celebrated Renaissance masters, were to be judged on their spiritual value. Moreover, Rio also diagnosed a change in aesthetics which took place over the fifteenth century, as art gradually abandoned idealised depictions and spiritual exaltation in favour of 'naturalism' and 'paganism'. Rio blamed the banking and political dynasty of the Medici family who ruled Florence for this degradation of art into fleshly realism.[28] Cosimo de Medici (1389–1464) is of course the patron from whose house Fra Lippo Lippi (i.e. Filippo Lippi) escapes in Browning's poem, and Lippo with his naturalist style of representation and inability to adhere to his monastic vow of chastity is singled out by Rio as responsible for the onset of this new phase of decadence.[29] Despite their Catholic ideological underpinning, Rio's ideas informed British non-Catholic art critics like Ruskin, and Browning with his keen interest in Italian art had opportunities to encounter second-hand versions of this reading of the Renaissance even before Rio's book was translated into English in 1854. DeLaura suggests that the Protestant dissenter Browning, whose anti-Catholicism shines through other poems like 'The Bishop Orders His Tomb' or 'Bishop Blougram's Apology' (1855), and who shared the established view of the sixteenth century as a high point in art, nevertheless drew inspiration from Rio as a point of reference in opposition to whom he could formulate his own ideas.[30]

The position opposing Rio's neo-Catholicism is represented by Charles Kingsley (1819–75), whose views DeLaura proposes as a source for Browning's defence of realism in 'Fra Lippo Lippi'. In texts like his polemical novels *Yeast* (1848) and *Alton Locke* (1850), Kingsley opposed Rio's Catholic aesthetics with a 'Protestant aesthetic of realism'[31] which promoted the portrayal of the realistic particular over the ideal and which also criticised the hostility to sexuality in Rio's aesthetics – a hostility evident in Rio's condemnation of Lippo's immoral lifestyle and use of his mistresses as models for paintings of saints.

DeLaura reads 'Fra Lippo Lippi' as Browning's response to Rio's attack on this painter, focusing on the speech by the prior of Lippo's convent. The prior rebukes the monks who admire Lippo's realism (ll. 175–237) and advises Lippo to 'Paint the soul, never mind the legs and arms' (l. 193):

> ■ In fact, only the elaborate case made by Rio himself can, I suggest, account for the various polemical elements of the poem. [...] Rio had treated Lippo as of central importance in his historical scheme, calling him the 'famous monk, ... who by his naturalism contributed more than any other artist to corrupt the Florentine school' (pp. 347–48).[32] Browning

would have noted with special interest Rio's acknowledgment that 'living nature' was 'almost the sole object of [Lippo's] study and his worship' (p. 89). Nevertheless, despite Lippo's use of 'the good side of naturalism; namely, force and intensity of expression, and particularly ... the introduction of landscape back-grounds,' he is blamable for 'having sown the first seeds of decadence,' degrading the 'type' of his madonnas and saints by using his mistresses and introducing his contemporaries into biblical scenes (pp. 91, 89, 77). In short, 'It's art's decline, my son!' ['Fra Lippo Lippi', l. 233][33] □

The prior's speech is hence a parodic version of Rio's ideas. DeLaura then shows how Browning's refutation of Rio's/the prior's position echoes Kingsley:

■ Taking up the challenge that Browning saw in [...] Rio's [...] 'idealist' or supernaturalist view that the 'supreme beauty' is to be found 'in something beyond the visible,' 'Fra Lippo Lippi' asserts something like the opposite.
In response to the current theory, the poem dramatizes the most emphatically naturalistic side of Kingsley's Protestant counteraesthetic of 'the universal symbolism and dignity of matter, whether in man or nature' (*Yeast*, Ch. xv), and uses terms strikingly like Kingsley's own. The Carmelite painter [Lippo] is content to depict 'simple beauty and nought else' ('about the best thing God invents') and to paint the shapes of things 'Just as they are, careless of what comes of it,' 'and count it crime / To let a truth slip' (ll. 217–18, 294–96). These lines give us a less 'philosophical' version of Kingsley's 'stern regard for fact' (*Locke*, p. 74) and his call for artists with a 'patient, reverent faith in Nature as they see her,' who know that the ideal is only to be 'found and left where God has put it, and where alone it can be represented, in actual ... phenomena' (*Yeast*, Ch. xv).[34] □

The naturalism of both Kingsley and Browning's Lippo has a 'distinctly *sexual* basis', DeLaura observes, as is obvious in Lippo's many references to sexuality throughout the poem and his admission 'I'm a beast, I know.' (l. 270) But this does not mean that their realism does not aspire to a spiritual dimension.[35]

DeLaura summarises the difference between Rio, on the one hand, and Browning and Kingsley, on the other:

■ Whereas the Rio school conceived of the arts as direct instruments of Christian theology, or as vehicles of pious emotion, [...] Kingsley and Browning, like other mid-Victorian liberal Protestants, wanted God to be evident in the world, in its vitality and abundance. In this new vitalistic natural theology, that extra layer of soft and 'passive' Catholic devotionalism could be put aside in favor of the more 'masculine' and active manifestations of mundane human striving and appetency [i.e. desire]. [...] Many Victorians wished to be assured that they could gain the spiritual benefits of the older culture simply by participating in the heady activity of the new acquisitive and sensate culture. 'Fra Lippo Lippi' is an important document in the mid-century attempt to reconcile soul and flesh, old idealism and new naturalism, without quite giving up the traditional theological framework.[36] ☐

In DeLaura's analysis, Browning's Lippo is not a mere sensualist but represents a genuine attempt to reconcile an appreciation of the real world with spirituality because the physical world is a manifestation of the divine. He is, moreover, not just representative of Browning's position but of a wider section of Victorian society.

Laurence Lerner, in 'Browning's Painters' (2006), broadens the critical perspective from DeLaura's primary focus on 'Fra Lippo Lippi' to a consideration of several painter poems. He tries to explain the contradiction between what seems to be a clear endorsement of realist aesthetics in 'Fra Lippo Lippi' and the reverse statement about the respective merits of the body and the soul in 'Old Pictures in Florence'. The former poem portrays the medieval religious painting recommended by the prior as lifeless and needing liberation through the realistic representation of the human body by painters of the next artistic era, the Renaissance; the latter, spoken by a Victorian speaker who may be Browning himself, praises medieval painting despite its unnaturalistic style because it captures the 'soul' of its subject and thus represents a progression in comparison to the perfection of the ancient Greek art that preceded it.

The explanation that these two poems reflect a change in Browning's aesthetics over time has to be discounted since both 'Fra Lippo Lippi' and 'Old Pictures in Florence' were first published together in *Men and Women* in 1855. Lerner summarises the contrasting aesthetics of the two poems:

■ In *Fra Lippo Lippi* medieval painters painted the soul because they were stiff and static, and art had not yet found its liberation through Lippi's brilliance in painting the body; whereas in *Old Pictures in Florence* they paint the soul as a sign of progress and liberation: it is through them that 'growth came' [l. 113]. They do not represent a stiffness the great Renaissance masters had to reject, but they are the elder brothers from whom the later painters derive. 'Old and New are fellows' (l. 62).[37] ☐

While Fra Lippo Lippi praises the naturalistic representation of real people in Renaissance painting as superior to the preceding formulaic medieval painting which was claimed to be a more spiritual representation of 'soul', the speaker of 'Old Pictures in Florence' celebrates the medieval painters who manage to capture the soul of their subjects because they reject the sterile perfection of ancient Greek art.

This obvious contradiction is not surprising, Lerner argues, given that Browning presents views by different dramatic characters, not those of a consistent character or even himself. Moreover,

> ■ [i]f we think of the history of art as more like the history of humanity than the history of opinion, then two apparently contradictory interpretations could be two different ways of cutting through the multifariousness. We need only think about the word 'renaissance': if what was being reborn was classical civilization, then ancient Greek art was not something to be pushed aside, but a stimulus to rebirth: and if – as can be plausibly argued – the Renaissance was a typically medieval movement, then the stimulus of ancient art was always there. I do not think it possible to exempt Browning from an inconsistency in his terminology – painting the soul can hardly be both a sign of progress and a sign of conservatism – but once we cease to see history as regular progress, we can expect to see the contrary pull of soul and of body occurring at any time.[38] □

Although he does not spell this out, Lerner seems to account for this paradox by establishing an implicit parallel with Browning's theory of the history of poetry in the *Essay on Shelley* (1852) as one of dialectic alternation between the opposed modes of objective and subjective art (see Chapter 1).

Another dramatic monologue that invites comparisons between its artist-speaker and Browning himself is 'Andrea del Sarto', the painter poem that has elicited the strongest critical disagreements. Andrea del Sarto (1486–1530) was, as the poem's subtitle informs us, 'Called "The Faultless Painter"'. Yet, despite the technical perfection of his work, he is only an inferior artist because, as he admits in the poem, he lacks the 'soul' of the great Renaissance masters which Browning praises in 'Old Pictures in Florence'. Andrea himself considers the cause of his artistic failure to lie in his unhappy relationship with his unfaithful wife, muse and addressee in the poem, Lucrezia, whom he nevertheless tries to stop from leaving to meet her 'cousin', i.e. her lover. The connection between the speaker's frustrated emotional relationship and his professional identity has attracted various psychoanalytical readings. For Harold Bloom, the poem is, in line with his anxiety theory discussed in Chapter 1, another exploration of the theme of belatedness, though in a more limited aspect than in the argument covered in Chapter 1. Andrea suffers from 'an anxiety of representation, or a fear of forbidden meanings', a Freudian fear of the return of the repressed:

> ■ Recall that Freud's notion of repression speaks of an unconsciously *purposeful* forgetting, and remind yourself also that what Browning could never bear was a sense of *purposelessness*. It is purposelessness that haunts

> Childe Roland [...] Browning's great fear, purposelessness, was related to the single quality that had moved and impressed him most in Shelley: the remorseless purposefulness of the Poet in *Alastor*, of Prometheus, and of Shelley himself questing for death in *Adonais*. Andrea, as an artist, is the absolute antithesis of the absolute idealist Shelley, and so Andrea is a representation of profound Browningesque anxiety.
>
> But how is this an anxiety of representation? We enter again the dubious area of *belatedness*, which Browning is reluctant to represent, but is too strong and authentic a poet to avoid. Though Andrea uses another vocabulary, a defensively evasive one, to express his relationship to Michelangelo, Raphael, and Leonardo [da Vinci], he suffers the burden of the latecomer. His [wife] Lucrezia is the emblem of his belatedness, his planned excuse for his failure in strength, which he accurately diagnoses as a failure in will. And he ends in deliberate belatedness, and in his perverse need to be cuckolded [...].³⁹ ☐

In Bloom's view, Andrea's acceptance of, indeed his unconscious desire for, sexual betrayal is a symptom of a more hidden artistic problem. His lack of artistic purpose is a projection of Browning's own repressed fear that he may not have the purposefulness he associates with Shelley's poetry. Thus we are back to a variant of Bloom's anxiety of influence theory according to which Browning worries that he is not able to live up to the model of his superior predecessor Shelley, here represented by the great Renaissance painters (who are actually Andrea's contemporaries rather than predecessors).

Lerner's essay is again helpful here in that it both summarises and critiques psychoanalytical readings like Bloom's:

> ■ Andrea tells Lucrezia that her inadequacy as a wife is responsible for his not having reached the greatness of Raphael and Michelangelo, and the modern critic who sees this as evidence against Andrea will almost inevitably propose that it is his unconscious wish to fail as an artist that binds him to Lucrezia – and in Bloom's case, go on to psychoanalyse Browning himself. To interpret the poem in this way would free us from the suspicion of blaming things on the woman (as Vasari certainly does in the first version of his *Life*, which is very contemptuous of Lucrezia); Andrea then becomes a simple example of projection, externalizing an internal inhibition and investing in Lucrezia a weakness that actually belongs to him. [...] The problem with this is the problem with all psychoanalytic interpretations, that it seems to deny the existence of any causation outside the self. A world [...] in which faithless spouses are helping to fulfil some unconscious wish to fail on the part of their partner is [...] a convenient world for adulterers. [...] the psychoanalytic reading is not generated by the poem, it is imported into our reading by our allegiance to psychoanalytic theory.⁴⁰ ☐

Psychoanalysis is, in Lerner's view, a short-sighted approach because it only searches for the causes of traumas within the speaker's psyche, discounting external causation.

Although Lerner distances himself from Bloom's biographical perspective, his reading shows some overlaps with Bloom's in that both diagnose the root cause of Andrea's dissatisfaction as lying within his art rather than his relationship with his wife. Yet in Lerner's view, the cause is merely that diagnosed by Andrea himself: his inability to combine technical perfection with 'soul'. Lerner focuses on the passage in which Andrea compares his own soulless perfection with, on the one hand, Raphael (1483–1520), who is a truly great master although his representation of an arm may be imperfect, and on the other hand, twenty inferior painters who lack skill but who share Raphael's spirituality (ll. 68–119):

■ What is the relationship between the aspirations of the twenty inferior painters whose works drop groundward and the inspiration of Raphael, who gets the arm wrong but has all the play, the insight, and the stretch? [...] Raphael's genius (to accept Browning's example) was that the spiritual striving of those who cannot paint well finds its way into his work. 'A man's reach should exceed his grasp', says Andrea in the most famous line of the poem (l. 97). Andrea has skill, the twenty such have spiritual striving, only Raphael has both.[41] □

Taking a very different approach from Bloom and Lerner, but also focusing on Browning's portrayal of the frustrated artist, Loy D. Martin, in *Browning's Dramatic Monologues and the Post-Romantic Subject* (1985), proposes a Marxist reading of 'Pictor Ignotus' ('Painter Unknown', 1845). Martin distances himself from previous readings of 'Pictor Ignotus' which see it as an ironic portrayal of a failed artist who lacks the courage and imagination to produce innovative work. Instead, Martin advances a Marxist reading of the poem as depicting the dilemma which the alienated artist faces as a result of his conflicting urges, on the one hand, to express his individual artistic identity and, on the other hand, to submit to the demands of the art market. This poem about a sixteenth-century painter whose name is unknown because his personal style is not sufficiently distinctive to differentiate his work from that of contemporaries also addresses the situation of the nineteenth-century poet. At a time when literature becomes increasingly commercialised, the artist becomes alienated from his work like the contemporary factory worker in the Marxist analysis of capitalism: 'Browning's poem foregrounds the incompatibility between maintaining the integrity of the self and submitting that self to the exchange values of trade.'[42]

The speaker opens with the statement: 'I could have painted pictures like that youth's / Ye praise so' (ll. 1–2). He explains that he deliberately chose not to follow the youth's example although he does not lack the requisite technical ability. The youth is probably Raphael, whose new, more realistic style of painting made him famous and replaced the traditional symbolic style of painting stock religious scenes as still practised by the speaker. It is clear from the way the speaker discusses his own paintings that he closely identifies his work with his self, to the extent that it is ambiguous whether 'My face' (l. 34) refers to his own face or a face he has painted.

Yet while he personally values this expression of his identity in his work, his fate is – in line with Marxist theory – determined by the material conditions of the market. He cannot, within the context of a changing art market in the sixteenth century, expect the whole public to share his values:

■ In the Quattrocento [i.e. the fifteenth century], the 'consumer' for a painter's work was indeed relatively individual and homogeneous in nature. Paintings were produced on commission, and the contracts that set the painters to work typically stipulated in advance much of what the painting was to depict and even exactly what materials were to be used. [...] Such security of communication requires, of course, a stable code, and that code, for Quattrocento painters, was the code of symbolic religious painting, the language of 'Virgin, Babe and Saint' [l. 60]. By contrast, the code of emerging realist conventions, while still perhaps allegorical and abstract, is nevertheless relatively indeterminate. [...] This is the form of the modern or bourgeois market, where an artisan like a painter must risk his own appraisal of what the public wants by completing his work previous to any commitment to purchase it. [...] His success will depend on his correctly predicting the relations between signifier and signified that will strike his public as natural.[43] □

Painters before this period could work in the certainty that their work would be universally appreciated because the only consumer of art was a Church whose taste was uniform. The subjects and style of painting were agreed in advance and the painter produced his commissioned works in the safe knowledge of getting paid for them. By contrast, new consumers have now entered the market in the form of private individuals, and artists have to take the risk of producing uncommissioned works in the hope that these will find buyers. Paradoxically, the new mode of realism would suggest that there should be an objective standard and common consensus over what is good art since the painting is a naturalistic representation of the subject depicted, but this ideology clashes with a free-market system which caters for the divergent tastes of different individuals. In short, Browning's speaker realises that 'the realist code demands a predictable consensus that the free market precludes'.[44]

The speaker is trapped in another paradox that results from the material conditions of the new art market: if the painter abandoned the stereotypical representation of 'Virgin, Babe and Saint' and expressed his individual identity in his paintings, he would make a name for himself and no longer be a 'pictor ignotus'. He would assert his identity, yet at the same time he would experience alienation because his valued works would turn into market commodities, decorative 'garniture and household-stuff' ('Pictor Ignotus', l. 51) subject to the casual value judgments of consumers.[45]

In order not to undergo this degrading alienation through commercialisation, the speaker chooses not to express his individuality in paintings and to continue in the now outdated symbolic style of painting which keeps him in the position of the unindividualised, unknown painter and consists in a 'dead language that can only be repeated endlessly without hope of response'.[46] In Martin's view, the poem documents rather than judges the painter's decision: 'Browning offers not clear preference between the polarities of his choice. Instead, he presents the speaker in a literary form that denies the homogeneity of the subject.'[47] The dramatic monologue presents an individualised speaker, but as an unknown painter he lacks a distinct identity.

This also has implications for the genre's use of realism. The poem articulates a critique of realism since the speaker exposes what he considers its flaws. Moreover, Browning's own use of realism here is problematic.

> ■ The choice of the unknown painter is only a meaningful choice from within the position that the monologue refuses. For the artist who creates the monologue itself, the literary style of realism appears only in order to be defamiliarized. The speech itself seems realistic because it is the common idiom of nineteenth-century English conversation. But its very naturalness alienates it from the sixteenth-century Italian subject that it pretends to represent. [...] The dramatic monologue is, in the fullest and most conscious sense, the product alienated from its producer.[48] □

The poem is a realistic representation of a verbal utterance, but at the same time it is not realistic because it recreates the way Browning's contemporaries would speak and not the way a sixteenth-century Italian would. Martin's analysis of 'Pictor Ignotus' thus offers not just a fresh perspective on Browning's views about the artist's role but also presents a Browning who is highly conscious of the literary mode that he has chosen.

This chapter has explored key features that make Browning stand out from the more conventional poetry of the Victorian era, notably his realism and his grotesque. We have seen how critics have tried to account for these characteristics by tracing them not merely to the predictable parallel with the contemporary realist novel but to more complex considerations of the poet's political convictions and his broader aesthetics. The Browning who emerges from these interpretations is a poet who is intensely engaged in contemporary and historical debates not just about politics but also about art and religion. The next chapter will consider the poet's contribution to another major cultural debate of his time, the role of women and gender relations. On this subject, too, we will see that the stance taken by his poetry is interwoven with Browning's aesthetics, politics and religion. Here especially, the absence of the poet's voice from the text opens up a wide field of debate over Browning's own views on gender issues.

# CHAPTER SIX

# Love and Gender Relations

The fact that Browning called what is now his most famous collection *Men and Women* (1855) is an indication of how central issues of gender are to his poetry. The role of women is indeed key to many of his best-known poems. Moreover, the genre of the dramatic monologue, which allows male poets to adopt the voices of female speakers, gives Browning ample opportunity to explore his perception, as it were, of the woman's perspective. It is therefore not surprising that Browning's work has received a level of attention from feminist critics that is often only accorded to female authors.

This chapter presents the most important evaluations of his portrayal of both women and men, of gender relations and his concept of love. The first section examines the intertextual relations between Browning and the most influential (female) poet for him, his wife Elizabeth Barrett Browning. A brief insight into biographical readings of his love poetry by Betty Miller, William Clyde DeVane and Daniel Karlin is followed by Corinne Davies' discussion of specific poems by Robert as influenced by or echoing Elizabeth's poetics. Contrasting with these interpretations is Nina Auerbach's thesis that a patriarchal Browning tried to dominate Elizabeth through his poetry. Criticism by Karlin and Isobel Armstrong in the next section offers explanations for the frequent representation of unhappy love relationships in Browning's poetry.

The chapter then turns to the most contentious aspect of gender relations in Browning, the critical disagreement over whether his representations of suffering females make him a defender or a critic of patriarchy. While Joseph Bristow and U. C. Knoepflmacher see Browning, in different degrees, as willing but unable to abandon a male perspective, other critics present him as resolutely feminist: Ann Brady and Susan Brown read *The Ring and the Book* as a feminist text; Penelope Gay focuses on the entrapment of Browning's women; and Shifra Hochberg, Catherine Maxwell and Ernest Fontana uncover the hidden empowerment of women in poems where a male artist or art collector apparently dominates the female model.

To balance the emphasis on women in the chapter, the penultimate section is devoted to Browning's portrayal of masculinity, covering criticism by Michael Ackerman, Herbert Sussman and Evgenia Sifaki, who all argue for his awareness of how men struggle to conform to gender expectations. Finally, a completely different motivation for Browning's preoccupation with love is explored by William Whitla and Jochen Haug in a section which interprets this preoccupation as an expression of his belief in the Christian dogma of the Incarnation of the divine through the human body of Christ.

## Intertextual Dialogues with Elizabeth Barrett Browning

Despite Browning's protestations that his poetry was completely detached from his personality, a substantial body of criticism traces the impact on his poetry of his personal experiences, especially his relationship with his wife. Predictably, such readings of his work can be found in biographies, one example being the Freudian analysis by Betty Miller which sees him as moving from an Oedipal mother-fixation into a submissive relationship with Elizabeth (see Chapter 1) before he tires of her and she dies just in time to save his myth of their happy union. For Miller, the fact that unhappy love poems in Browning's work outweigh those about happy lovers is an indicator of his marital disillusionment.[1]

Another much discussed issue is the projection of his personal experience with Elizabeth onto his art and vice versa, as illustrated by the plot of *The Ring and the Book* (1868–69). In the poem, the triangular relationship between the priest Caponsacchi, the mistreated wife Pompilia and her cruel husband Guido is compared to the legend of St George. In turn, this chivalric rescue of the victimised female is read as mirroring Browning's interpretation of his secret courtship and elopement with Elizabeth: St George / Caponsacchi / Browning rescues the maiden in distress / the abused wife Pompilia / the invalid Elizabeth from the dragon / the oppressive husband Guido / Elizabeth's tyrannical father who did not allow his children to marry.[2] The thesis that Browning diverged from the evidence in his historical sources in order to make art imitate his life is taken one step further by William Clyde DeVane, who proposes that Browning's interpretation of his own love story was itself shaped by art. Pointing to an engraving of Perseus' rescue of Andromeda from a sea monster which hung above Browning's writing desk in his parental home, DeVane states that it was this Greek equivalent of the St George legend which gave Browning the idea to see his own experience in terms of this literary pattern.[3]

All of these biographical readings of the poetry, appealing though they may be, should be taken with caution as they rely on varying degrees of conjecture about the poet's private motives and ideas. A more detailed study of Browning's self-conceptualisation as a poet in relation to Elizabeth (and vice versa), which is based on much more compelling evidence from both poets' own paratext, is *The Courtship of Robert Browning and Elizabeth Barrett* (1985) by Daniel Karlin (born 1953), to which we will return in the next section.[4] The study documents Browning's self-portrayal in the couple's courtship correspondence as a dramatic poet in opposition to Elizabeth's lyrical and subjective genius, and also his insistence on her poetic superiority as illustrated by his request that she correct his drafts. Elizabeth did indeed try to remedy his syntactical obscurity and to smooth out his rough metre – changes which Browning eagerly adopted in the first published text but intriguingly undid in editions after her death.

Going beyond Elizabeth's stylistic influence on Robert's work as discussed by Karlin, a number of critics have examined links between poems by the two Brownings, focusing on intertextual relations between literary texts rather than on the slippery subject of personal relations between the two private individuals. These critics are helpfully reviewed in Corinne Davies and Marjorie Stone's '"Singing Song for Song": The Brownings "in the Poetic Relation"' (2006). In their chapter, which takes the form of an exchange of letters, Davies and Stone stress the poets' mutual influence, their role as each other's prime audience and their collaboration. Davies, for instance, points out the 'textual interchanges' in early works, such as Elizabeth's 'The Romaunt of the Page' (1839) and Robert's 'The Flight of the Duchess' (1844), a poem which she critiqued and revised in their courtship correspondence at his request. For Davies, the parallels between these poems prove the couple's shared concerns with genre and gender. The ballad-romance

■ provided them with a conventional literary site, ripe for revision, on which to play out their notions of social and sexual politics – which they acted out in their own flight to Italy. The thematic similarities in these two poems are striking. Both deal with the attempt to fashion a proper, gentle, silent wife by her male counterpart, whether medieval knight, duke, or Victorian husband. In both ballads the figure of clothing is used to interrogate socially encoded sexual difference. In 'The Romaunt of the Page' EBB's female protagonist cross-dresses as a page, only to 'unman' herself in a tragic moment of defiance and self-recognition before she embraces death. In 'The Flight of the Duchess' RB satirically strips the masculine disguise (i.e. 'unmans' it) from the Moldavian court to reveal the lifelessness of an outdated pseudochivalric patriarchy. EBB's representation, in her cross-dressing heroine, of the transgressing of social, sexual, and generic archetypes is literal, whereas RB's is metaphorical. Yet in both poems strong women triumph over outmoded systems of chivalry, cut the bonds of femininity, and escape the subservience demanded by the husband.[5] ☐

Robert hence replicates Elizabeth's more literal defiance of traditional gender roles (ironically in the genre of the ballad-romance which traditionally reinforces these roles). Elizabeth's poem was published in the popular gift-book annual *Finden's Tableaux of the Affections*, and Davies suggests that, having published unpopular long poems in the 1830s, Robert learned from Elizabeth how to use the popular ballad-romance in order to get an audience for his subversive critique of contemporary genre and gender stereotypes:

■ In turning to the same form in 'The Flight of the Duchess' he similarly undercuts its conventions. The result is a very humorous parody of the fetishizing of history and medievalism in Victorian pseudoballads, combined with a political message on the 'woman question'.[6] ☐

Contrasting with critics who see the Brownings' reciprocal influence as nourishing and mutually beneficial, some feminist critics of Barrett Browning argue that Robert's influence on his wife's work was a negative one and that there was a struggle for power, also reflected in their poetry, within the apparently so happy and romantic marriage of the poets. The most extreme version of this position is the article 'Robert Browning's Last Word' (1984) by Nina Auerbach (born 1943). She argues that Robert's artistic rivalry with his more successful wife was given more space for expression after her death, notably in the epic ambitions of *The Ring and the Book* rivalling the epic claims of Elizabeth's *Aurora Leigh* (1854):

■ Once the worst had happened – Elizabeth's death and the loss of his Italian exile – Robert freed himself to transplant her material and her legend into his own poetic territory. During her life, she had regarded his fascination for the Old Yellow Book [the source of *The Ring and the Book*] with some horror [...]; when he melded its violence and intrigue into *The Ring and the Book*, he must at last have known she was dead. To be safe, though, he killed her again. His absorption of Elizabeth's iconography – particularly the glorification of Marian Erle in *Aurora Leigh* as a holy twin of the supreme woman poet who personifies her age – resurrects his sainted wife in order to butcher her in the person of Pompilia. His most radical butchery is spiritual. *The Ring and the Book* erodes Elizabeth Barrett Browning's cherished systems of salvation, a devastation over which he makes her preside in the attenuated person of 'Lyric Love.'[7] ☐

According to Auerbach, Robert transforms Elizabeth's secondary heroine Marian Erle, a working-class girl who is brutally raped but survives with her child in a happy community with the poet-heroine Aurora, into his heroine Pompilia, the mistreated wife and mother who is killed by her husband. Moreover, in invoking Elizabeth as his muse, his 'Lyric Love' in the framing books of *The Ring and the Book*, he gives the impression that she sanctions the transformation of the empowered woman who survives rape into the passive, dying victim Pompilia.

The representation of Elizabeth as an angelic, unearthly being contrasts sharply with the vigorous and physical metaphors of breasts and blood which Elizabeth uses in *Aurora Leigh* (V, 213–22) to state that the subject of her poetry is contemporary life. By contrast here again, Browning forces her to be associated with a subject from the past which she herself repudiates through *Aurora Leigh*'s championing of a poetry reflecting its own age:

■ Since [Lyric Love] is 'half angel and half bird,' [I, 1391] she has no breasts and little blood to speak of; since 'heaven [is her] home,' [I, 1414] she has evaporated helplessly out of her age, passing from cynosure to spectator, forced to gaze on a bloody past she cannot affect. [...] Now, Elizabeth herself is relegated to ghostliness, while Robert reanimates the seventeenth century in all its confused vitality. The woman who claimed to embody her age has been pushed into a past more remote than Italy's, forced to become the Muse of a tale she never would have told.[8] □

Another token of Robert's attempt to disempower Elizabeth is, in Auerbach's view, Pompilia's lack of voice. This claim seems odd, given that she is the speaker of the central monologue, Book VII, in *The Ring and the Book*, but Auerbach here refers to Browning's decision to go against the evidence of his source and make his literary heroine illiterate, which hampers her ability to request help and to leave a record of herself to her son as she is dying: 'It may be Robert Browning's ultimate victory over his celebrated wife that he robs Pompilia of a public voice.'[9]

Pompilia's illiteracy allows the patriarchal poet Browning to cast himself as a saviour figure who gives the voiceless woman a voice through his poem:

■ *The Ring and the Book* is ruthless in insisting that if the saving poet had not descended to give Pompilia his own versatile voice, she would have been forever unheard. Elizabeth Barrett Browning's 'unscrupulously epic' [*Aurora Leigh* V, 214] claims for absolute authority in her age are in *The Ring and the Book* suppressed with loving brutality. The story of Pompilia, who is perfect in whiteness and exemplifies truth, suggests that a woman speaks with purity only by dying unheard.

Having survived a poet who made epic claims for herself, Robert Browning perpetuated her voice by turning it into his own; he 'married' Elizabeth Barrett one more time when he appropriated her after her death, weaving her declarations into the corrosive fabric of his dramatic monologues.[10] □

Browning thus appropriates – albeit lovingly – both Pompilia's and Elizabeth's voice. By turning his wife into a character in his own work, and the type of character she would have despised, he achieves complete dominance over her. As we will see in the section about Browning's representation of women, Auerbach's feminist attack represents a minority position and is outweighed by many interpretations which praise him as a feminist. But before we turn to this issue, we will take a broader look at the representation of love relationships in Browning's poetry, and in particular the prevalence of poems about unhappy lovers.

## Unhappy Lovers

Browning's love poems are among the most popular of his oeuvre. On closer inspection, however, it is striking how many of these poems deal with problematic, strained and sometimes even sadistic relationships. Daniel Karlin, in a chapter about 'Love and Marriage' in his joint book with John Woolford, *Robert Browning* (1995), points out the preponderance of unhappy love poems in Browning's two main collections: in *Men and Women* (1855) the ratio of unhappy to happy poems is more than four to one, and in *Dramatis Personae* (1864) six poems out of twenty are about love, with only the shortest of them presenting a happy relationship. Karlin examines the causes for these unfulfilled relationships and diagnoses a deeper problem that Browning finds in the human condition:

> ■ [I]f we look at the circumstances which govern these poems, one factor recurs: a wrongness in the nature of things, a flaw or gap, a refusal to communicate or fit, of which the failure of particular lovers to find fulfilment is only an instance. As the speaker in 'By the Fire-Side' [1855] puts it:
>
> If you join two lives, there is oft a scar,
> They are one and one, with a shadowy third;
> One near one is too far. (ll. 228–30)
>
> In this rare instance the join is perfect: the 'bar' between the lovers is 'broken', and they are 'mixed at last / In spite of the mortal screen' (ll. 233–5). Another, and disturbing, form of this perfect union occurs in 'Love Among the Ruins' [1855], where the lovers 'rush' together and 'extinguish sight and speech / Each on each' (ll. 71–2). Most of Browning's lovers never manage even this violent overcoming. Their language is filled with images of frustration and thwarted desire. 'Yet one thing, one, in my soul's full scope, / Either I missed or itself missed me', says the speaker of 'Evelyn Hope' ([1855] ll. 45–6). 'Where does the fault lie? what the core / Of the wound, since wound must be?' asks the speaker of 'Two in the

Campagna' ([1855] ll. 39–40). His assurance that 'wound *must* be' is shared by Andrea del Sarto: 'In this world, who can do a thing, will not – / And who would do it, cannot, I perceive' ([1855] ll. 136–7). [...]
   What these speakers cannot reconcile is a gap between the ideal and the actual.[11] □

Browning writes in an intellectual tradition based on the antagonism of binary pairs, including the ideal versus the actual. For him love is an ideal, and the reality of the two human lovers cannot, or can only rarely, live up to the ideal of perfect union. As Karlin observes, this overcoming of the lovers' separation despite their devotion to each other is most likely to happen in physical union or non-verbal communication, as in 'Love Among the Ruins', suggesting that Browning is also acutely aware of the limits of his own medium.

In *The Courtship of Robert Browning and Elizabeth Barrett* (1985), Karlin considers in more detail the preoccupation with the verbal communication of feeling that is shared by the lover and the artist. He identifies three core principles that underlie Browning's philosophy:

■ First, there is a fundamental and unbridgeable gap between the conception of something, and its execution or expression. Poems, for example, are conceived in 'moments' of timeless perfection, but are written in the 'real time' of language. Second, and following from this, language is the human and fallible instrument of a divine and perfect inspiration. 'God is the perfect poet,' says a character in Browning's early poem *Paracelsus* [1835], 'Who in his person acts his own creations' [II, 601–2]. Human beings, in a version of Original Sin, are cursed with the necessity of using an external medium to convey their 'own creations'. Their inspirations may be divine, but their productions are human, and therefore flawed, damaged, corrupt. Third, [...] the two preceding principles can be applied to any form of creative process, whether in art or life. Hence Browning's intense interest in painters and musicians; hence, too, his interest in bishops and politicians, grammarians and doctors, spiritualists and alchemists. For they, too, are trying to create or express or accomplish something – a work of art, a political system, a vision. And, of course, lovers – in a sense the ultimate artists in Browning's work – who attempt to 'realize', in the medium of the flesh, the ideal communion of their souls.[12] □

Browning's many portrayals of creative individuals as well as frustrated love relationships reflect his general suspicion of the flawed medium that is language, which cannot adequately express the feelings the lovers seek to convey. This suspicion has a religious base in his belief in man's sinful fallibility as opposed to God's unique status as the perfect communicator, as stated in the first verse of the Gospel of St John, 'the Word was God'. Even the intimate communication between lovers cannot achieve the proximity of conception and expression that is God's privilege. If it is briefly achieved, as in 'Two in the Campagna', 'the good minute goes' (l. 50) and we are left with the unfulfilled longing of the poem's closing lines: 'Infinite passion, and the pain / Of finite hearts that yearn' (ll. 59–60).

In 'Browning and the Victorian Poetry of Sexual Love' (1974), Isobel Armstrong also reflects on the preponderance of negatively portrayed love relationships in Browning's work. Like Karlin, she sees the perfect union of the lovers as a myth rather than an achievable reality. In her view, this disenchanted perspective on love is due to Browning's essentially ironic attitude towards romanticised ideas about love. This attitude also has to be understood as part of his challenge to Romanticism's belief in stable identity:

> ■ Browning's love poetry is about the tragic solipsism and privacy of love, with its corollary in fantasy and morbid erotic feeling. It examines and erodes the great human myth of continuing love, and the high Romantic myth of a continuing, stable identity with which it supports itself, exploring the wilful strains and conflations of past with present selves that go into the creating of a belief in continuity and stability. [...] these love lyrics are self-undermining, swerving into a counter-movement of irony against passion, or into passion against mockery. They twist and turn in order to display the complicatedness and vulnerability of any *beliefs* about loving, any formulations about feeling. If in the end they return to and celebrate the great Romantic myths, they only do so at the cost of an immense agnostic undermining of them.[13] □

As examples of this 'tragic solipsism' of love, Armstrong cites 'Love Among the Ruins' where the lovers try to place their relationship 'in an extra-historical, extra-social emptiness',[14] and poems such as 'A Lovers' Quarrel', 'Mesmerism', 'Evelyn Hope' and 'Any Wife to Any Husband' (all 1855) where the lovers are, or fantasise about being, in enclosed, sequestered spaces.

Karlin offers yet another perspective that accounts for Browning's focus on the negative aspects of love. In his book on the various forms of hatred in Browning's poetry, *Browning's Hatreds* (1993), he observes that love in Browning can easily turn into hate. Moreover, Browning challenges the traditional Christian associations of love with creativity and of hate with sterility. Karlin's exemplary passage is one from the love poem to Barrett Browning, 'One Word More' (1855, ll. 32–49), in which the Renaissance poet Dante Alighieri (1265–1321) is portrayed as drawing an angel to express his love for his muse Beatrice with the same pen with which he writes the most hate-fuelled representations of sinners in the *Inferno*, the first book of his epic, *The Divine Comedy*.

In 'Dante, who loved well because he hated' (l. 42), the ability to love is a result of the ability to hate. These diametrically opposite emotions turn out to be derived from the same source, with the conventionally uncreative hate begetting, surprisingly, a great poem as well as love.

Karlin traces a similar collapse of the love-hate dichotomy in other poems, suggesting that this is the most basic example of Browning's habitual calling into question of established binary opposites. A case in point is 'A Forgiveness' (1876), whose speaker suggests his wife might have admitted her adultery to him because she was 'hungry for my hate ... Eager to end an irksome lie, and taste / Our tingling true relation, hate embraced / By hate one naked moment' (ll. 62–6):

> ■ This 'one naked moment' is no different in kind from the 'moment, one and infinite' of the lovers in 'By the Fire-Side'. It turns out, as the speaker of 'A Forgiveness' later realizes, that this was not what his wife had in mind at all: but he speaks truer than he knows, because hatred is indeed, in this instance, the mouthpiece of love.[15] □

Although his wife initially declares 'I love him as I hate you' (l. 79), she later admits that this hate had been a lie, provoked by her husband's neglect of her. Therefore, 'the hatred she expressed was the inverse image of her desire for him'.[16] Now the speaker realises

> ■ that it was love masked as hate, and not hate masked as love, which motivated her actions. The hierarchy of love over hate reasserts itself, and allows the woman, in turn, to 'rise / High by how many a grade!' (ll. 361–2) in the speaker's estimation: his former contempt for her gives way to hatred, and hatred (after he has killed her) to love.[17] □

Unlike in the passage from 'One Word More', love here engenders hate, or rather the pretence of hate, and the two protagonists oscillate between the two opposed emotions. 'A Forgiveness' is just one of a group of Browning poems which represent the suffering of women at the hands of strong patriarchal figures. Establishing Browning's ideological stance in relation to patriarchy is a major concern of his critics, as the next section will show.

## Patriarchal Poet or Feminist?

There is a general acknowledgement by critics that Browning is a poet unafraid of writing about sexuality (within the limits of Victorian decorum of course) and about the social position of women. Yet there are strong disagreements over whether Browning's own position on sexuality and women is a traditional patriarchal one or whether he can be classed as a feminist. Broadly siding with Nina Auerbach's critique of Browning as patriarchal (see above), though more sympathetic, Joseph Bristow asserts in his introductory book *Robert Browning* (1991) that the poet was unable to abandon a male perspective, even though he acknowledges that as a political liberal and egalitarian Browning was striving to overcome the traditional emphasis on the difference between the sexes:

■ Where sexuality is concerned, Victorian poets take risks, and Browning is one of the most adventurous. On the face of it his views on relations between the sexes are liberal-minded and egalitarian. For him sexual acts bear no shame. They are a source of celebration for he views heterosexual love as one of God's greatest gifts to men and women. So he urges its revelation, not concealment. Everyone should be able to recognise the attraction between men and women, he argues. But [...] in championing the spirit of individualism and equal partnership in love, Browning has his masculine biases. Masculinity and femininity – which he recognised as determined opposites – are continuously in conflict with his firm commitment to the liberal subject: a free, independent and ostensibly ungendered being.[18] □

If we picture the critics of Browning's gender relations as situated on a spectrum stretching from Browning the defender of patriarchy to Browning the feminist, U. C. Knoepflmacher's article 'Projection and the Female Other: Romanticism, Browning, and the Victorian Dramatic Monologue' (1984) represents a further step towards the latter pole. He sees Browning as both participant in and critic of the objectification of women by male poets and men in general. Knoepflmacher considers Browning through the Romantic theme of the quest for the female epipsyche, i.e. the poet's / character's desire to fuse with his counterpart of the opposite sex that complements him. Despite their declared desire to find an epipsyche, Knoepflmacher suggests that the Romantics actually silence or replace the female epipsyche, turning her into a mere projection of the poet's male self. Browning inherits this temptation to dominate the epipsyche, but he is also able to ironise it. In his dramatic monologues, unlike in his earlier lyrics and dramatic romances, '[i]ncompleteness is far more prominent than the fusion of complementary selves'.[19] In poems like 'Porphyria's Lover' (1836), 'My Last Duchess' (1842), 'Andrea del Sarto', 'The Bishop Orders His Tomb' (1845) and even 'Fra Lippo Lippi' (1855)

■ Browning parodied his own male desire to flatten women into the 'fixed' and immoveable Andromedas of graphic art [...].
'Porphyria's Lover' and 'My Last Duchess' [...] feed on the very incompletion they depict. They still render the appropriation of a Female Other who is portrayed as elusive and silent; at the same time, however, they

introduce a critical distance that was absent in the lyrics and the dramatic romances. Removed as either lyricist or narrator, Browning now ironizes the act of projection by which a devouring male ego reduces that Female Other into nothingness. Animations of a process of deanimation, these monologues thus self-consciously mock the poet's very own enterprise. Though an ironist, the poet also acts as abettor and accomplice, for he too flattens a female anima into a mere image, a representation, an object of art.

Still, if the Browning who animates the pathological windings of the Lover's and the Duke's minds ostensibly partakes of their suppression of the Female Other, he actually maneuvers the reader into becoming that suppressed Other's chief ally.[20] ☐

The speakers of 'Porphyria's Lover' and 'My Last Duchess', who appropriate the Female Other by killing her, are extreme versions of Browning's own search for the ideal epipsyche – exemplified, as discussed above, by his casting of Elizabeth Barrett as his idealised Andromeda. Yet despite Browning's complicity with the suppression of the Female Other, his poetry is redeemed because the self-critical poet also moves the reader of such monologues to side with the suppressed woman.

Contrasting with the earlier 'My Last Duchess' and 'Porphyria's Lover', Browning's mature monologues restore the woman's agency and resist the male's attempt at projection:

> ■ Even when dead or silenced, however, Browning's later incarnations of the Female Other continue to confound the male's attempts at mental possession. The fair 'she' appropriated by that other art collector, the Bishop of St. Praxed's (a church named, significantly enough, after a female martyr) will find avengers in her sons. In 'Andrea del Sarto' Lucrezia enacts the inconstancy that Porphyria's Lover had feared. But her behavior defiles her would-be possessor more than herself. She is an unchaste Cynthia [the Greek moon goddess] whom he must share with others: 'My face, my moon, my everybody's moon' (l. 29). Her mobility sets in relief the impotence of this 'half-man.' [cf. l. 140] Although Andrea would, like Porphyria's Lover, dearly want to restrain the woman's movements, he can only paralyze himself. His self-loathing strangles his very dream of artistic immortality in a New Jerusalem where he, as the elect decorator of a fourth great wall, might join Leonardo, Raphael, and Michelangelo, 'the three first without a wife' (l. 264). Sadly, he realizes that he remains walled in by the mental prison that Lucrezia can flee.[21] ☐

Browning's poetry thus eventually seems to tip in favour of the woman who, as in Lucrezia's case, outwits the male who would dominate her. Challenging Nina Auerbach's reading of the *Ring and the Book* (discussed above), Knoepflmacher considers Pompilia the most notable case of a female who is empowered despite her death.

This reading of the poem within a feminist frame is taken further by two critics, Ann Brady and Susan Brown. Brady, in *Pompilia: A Feminist Reading* (1988), celebrates *The Ring and the Book* as a feminist text which attacks not just the seventeenth-century Italian church and society but also Victorian culture and religion. The poem

■ reveals how completely aware he is of the sexual cynicism emanating from the core of a patriarchal society. He forthrightly addresses these issues with their destructive effects on women, and exposes them to an equally patriarchal society in his own Victorian England [...] *The Ring and the Book* is not only a powerfully incisive feminist judgment on the androcentric mores of patriarchy, and on its concomitant subjugation of women; it goes farther, judging and rejecting as an idol the god made by man in man's image: the god who devised, upholds, and enforces the laws of men, and severely punishes those who question him. [...]
Since the focus of *The Ring and the Book* is on the victim, Browning thereby has created a perfect vehicle for examining the attitudes and traditions of an ascendantly male culture supported by the patriarchal church so opposed to the *caritas* [charity] enjoined by Christ. The poet's insights into this androcentric culture and its institutions, particularly marriage, exude from every page.[22] □

Browning with his strong commitment to Christian values does not attack Christianity as such, but exposes how its patriarchal power structures lead the church to abandon the most important Christian principle of charity. In both seventeenth-century Italy and nineteenth-century Britain, religious and civil institutions are closely interwoven, most importantly for the poem through marriage. In both societies, man and wife are in the eyes of the law one person, and Guido even has the legal right to kill his adulterous wife. Pompilia turns in vain to representatives of church and state to protect her, only to discover that these authorities sanction her husband's abuse of her.

Brady concludes that the contrast between patriarchal misogyny and the promotion of womankind as the true embodiment of Christian love is the poem's key message:

■ Pompilia Comparini, who comes across the pages of the Old Yellow Book as an unfortunate, faceless victim, Browning has transformed into a brave, self-directed young woman. Chained by the helplessness society devised for wives, she seeks help from that society and finds none. Ultimately she finds her rescuer outside the structures. Pompilia flees her husband with the aid of a priest who, by all expectations, should have urged her to remain and accept 'the proper lot of women.' She loves Caponsacchi without desiring physical consummation – loves in a way that culturally redefines *love* as *caritas*.[23] □

Susan Brown, in '"Pompilia": The Woman (in) Question' (1996), expands on Brady's reading of *The Ring and the Book* as a feminist critique of Victorian patriarchy, comparing Pompilia's situation to that of Victorian women helpless in the face of domestic violence. Yet she detects greater intricacy than Brady in both Pompilia and her creator. As Brown points out, both feminist and non-feminist critics of the poem agree that Pompilia is a passive victim; but given the generic conventions of the dramatic monologue, according to which the speaker should not be trusted and his / her motives must be scrutinised, Brown calls into question the 'straight' reading of Pompilia as naïve and utterly truthful:

> ■ Pompilia is on trial, and she knows it. Her narrative works, as many have observed, to exonerate Caponsacchi, but she also speaks on her own behalf. The narrator in *The Ring and the Book* says that it was thought she took so miraculously long to die 'Just that Pompilia might defend herself' (1.1080). [...] Although Pompilia is not testifying in a court of law as Guido is in his first monologue, according to Book I she does have a body of listeners, which includes the nuns who are caring for her, as well as 'leech and man of law' (1.1087). A defense also suggests persuasive rhetorical strategy, which Pompilia's monologue amply exhibits. Her defense is so effective that generations of critics have believed it implicitly. One instance of a common rhetorical strategy in Pompilia's defense is her refusal to specify the acts of abuse committed by Guido, claiming in places amnesia – 'All since [her marriage] is one blank' (1. 583) – and in places a reluctance to incriminate him.[24] □

While Brown does not doubt the suffering of Pompilia at the hands of her husband, she argues that the apparently so artless seventeen-year-old girl uses language just as shrewdly as other monologists. Thus she omits the specifics of her physical abuses from her narrative, so that the reader/listener has to imagine Guido's cruelties.

The characterisation of Pompilia as passive is also undermined because, contrary to what she claims, she did not suffer abuse without resistance but solicited the help of several figures of authority. Moreover, Brown's analysis shows how the poem, and especially Caponsacchi's account of the moment when Guido caught up with Caponsacchi and Pompilia in their flight, undermines the Andromeda/St George romance pattern that is imposed on their plot: Pompilia now appears not as the passive Andromeda but as active, brandishing a sword against her husband, while Caponsacchi turns out to be passive and to fall short of the model of the chivalric rescuer. Pompilia's strategy of presenting herself as a passive victim in order to justify her active resistance to patriarchy, Brown suggests, parallels the rhetorical strategy of Victorian feminists. She summarises the social message of *The Ring and the Book*, asserting that the Victorian Woman Question has an impact on both the poem's theme and its play with the romance genre:

■ On the level of narrative, *The Ring and the Book* addresses the position of a disenfranchised wife, battered and sexually abused by a husband whose rights are buttressed by Church and State alike. Despite her cultural and political disenfranchisement, Pompilia defies those powers, and although her bid for freedom fails, her husband is brought to justice for his murderous insistence that she is a piece of property rather than a person. Furthermore, the poem's exploration of the viability of romance as an emancipatory form creates a parodic rescue plot driven by female rather than male agency. Pompilia's agency functions as a narrative subtext which is obfuscated by the discourse of female passivity which she deploys to construct her defense. This discourse, like the other discourses in the poem, is emphatically cultural rather than natural, and traceable to the position of the speaker in a particular location in the social nexus at a specific historical moment. To insist on Pompilia's agency, then, is to redefine agency not as a fixed category but as the product of particular social and linguistic parameters – in this case, paradoxically, the construction of woman through the discourse of female passivity.[25] □

Browning thus exposes a patriarchal culture in which women are expected to be passive by creating a female character who cleverly uses this expectation to manipulate her audience to her advantage.

Also taking a feminist stance, Penelope Gay's 'Desire and the Female Voice in Browning's *Men and Women* and *Dramatis Personae*' (1989) reads Browning's poems in female voices as texts which draw the reader's attention to the oppressive nature of Victorian patriarchy, 'which denies them a voice'.[26] Gay sees these female characters as caught in the conventions of their contemporary culture. Even if they do speak, they are unable to speak of female sexual desire. They are forced into the passive role of the Victorian 'Angel in the House' (as celebrated by Coventry Patmore [1823–96] in his poem of that title [1854]) whose happiness is defined entirely by the man's sexual enjoyment. Gay cites 'By the Fire-Side' with its sexually charged account of a happy relationship (see e.g. stanzas x–xiii) as a poem in which female sexuality is acknowledged, but concedes that even here the woman is passive:

■ 'By the Fireside' is a daring and beautiful poem in its willingness to speak of the importance of sexual desire and its fulfilment in a love-relationship. But the woman in it is a silent partner, or, at best, an answerer 'prompt as rhyme' [stanza xxiv] to the male initiative and endeavour.[27] □

Gay analyses a number of poems with similar scenarios:

> ■ The women who speak, silently, to their husbands, in 'A Woman's Last Word', 'Any Wife to Any Husband', and 'In a Year' [all 1855] speak, not of their desire, but in classic Victorian fashion, of their fear of loss of their husband's desire. The irony implicit in the dramatic stance of 'A Woman's Last Word' has only recently been appreciated,[28] as feminist criticism re-educates our reading prejudices [...] The woman recognizes that she is in a prison constructed by the patriarchal order, to which she has willingly acquiesced for social and emotional survival: if she speaks, 'contends' [cf. l. 1], then her words are 'wild' [l. 5], uncivilized, and will loose a 'creature stalking' [l. 9] into a system which has been in place since the formulations of the Book of Genesis. One of the neatest ironical points in this 'Woman's Last Word' is the use of oxymoron: the patriarchal system is one in which 'truth is false' [cf. l. 13] to the powerful 'thee' whom she addresses. When she speaks of 'Eve and I' [l. 20] – all women – losing their Edens, she indicates the ruling view that Paradise is not lost as long as you have a man around: a man who quite unprotestingly allows himself to be addressed as 'god' [l. 21], indeed, prayed to in stanzas vii–viii.[29] □

The speaker of the poem is ironically aware of her entrapment in patriarchy, yet she cannot free herself from a social role that is so deeply rooted in her culture, going back as far as the first book of the Bible.

Gay asserts that even Browning's male lovers are not at ease with these culturally imposed gender relations:

> ■ The image of the eternally questing and unsatisfied male which haunts Browning's poems of love – 'Love in a Life', 'Mesmerism' [both 1855] are strikingly erotic examples – suggests that the patriarchal system of sexual relations is finally unsatisfactory for men also. 'Two in the Campagna' is the most poetically complex exploration of this perception. The sacramental love, both physical and spiritual, so confidently evoked in 'By the Fireside', is here proved an illusion: body and soul remain separate; 'passion', as a natural force, is indeed 'infinite', but cannot soothe 'the pain of finite hearts that yearn' [cf. ll. 59-60]. *Post coitum triste.* [After sexual union one is sad.][30] □

In a society where women are not allowed to be men's equals and to enjoy their sexuality but are instead restricted to being idealised, spiritual creatures, Browning's ideal of both spiritual and physical union remains unattainable.

In another feminist reading, Shifra Hochberg opposes the interpretation of 'My Last Duchess' which sees the duchess' portrait as evidence of men's dominance over women. Instead, she argues that the portrait can be read as a 'countertext' to the text of the duke's monologue in that it reveals female self-empowerment and encodes desire, in the dual sense of sexual desire and the desire for power.³¹ Like the portrait itself, which is concealed by a curtain, Hochberg argues that the poem hides a subversive discourse about female power through art that rivals the Duke's patriarchal view of her:

■ [A]lthough the portrait appears to be authorized as a male cultural construct, it represents in actuality, the Duke's misprision [...] of the Duchess, a misreading that ultimately deconstructs his phallocratic interpretation of her. I would like to suggest that although the patriarchal text of the Duke appears to be defining the Duchess by displacing her material body onto the portrait, as central theme of both his monologue and the painting, *she* defines him.³² □

Hochberg focuses on the pictorial representation of the duchess in both the portrait and the duke's monologue as an indicator of her 'countertextual resistance':

■ The portrait, we are told, is arrestingly lifelike, the Duchess' offensive gaze and 'spot of joy' [ll. 14-15] rendered so realistically that their mimetic purity startles all those who view her 'pictured countenance' [l. 7]. I suggest that the joined lips of the smile which so angered the Duke of Ferrara are synecdochal representations of female sexuality, of the other, unnameable parts of the female lower anatomy,[...] and that the 'spot of joy' is a Victorian code for female *jouissance* as sexual arousal, pleasure, and, equally important, as Sandra Gilbert defines it, 'a virtually metaphysical fulfilment of desire'.[33] Synecdoche here is not only the fragmentation of the female body, [...] but is a *displacement* of the whole onto the part. Thus it mirrors the displacement of desire onto the portrait, which then becomes a more potent – because immortalized – recontextualisation of female erotic and creative power. The portrait, hence, not only emblematizes the attempted repression and fragmentation of female desire, but signifies, simultaneously, a [...] displacement of libidinal energy from the original object of desire onto another.³⁴ □

The portrait thus both represses and expresses the woman's sexual desire. This self-expression is linked to the power of art which is ultimately stronger than the instruments of patriarchy that are at the duke's disposal:

■ Woman perpetuating herself and her desire through the unchanging, timeless medium of art not only forms an alternative to male self-perpetuation through progeny and the history of a 'nine-hundred-years-old name' (33) handed down patrilineally from father to son, but symbolizes the function of art itself for the poet. The Duchess' portrait thus represents an escape into art, a relocation of female erotic energy which is associated with the eternal, creative vitality of art. In this medium it can continue to assert the opposing 'otherness' of female desire. Thus the Duke both kills and, simultaneously, eternally empowers the Duchess.[35] ☐

Catherine Maxwell's chapter on Browning in *The Female Sublime from Milton to Swinburne* (2001) is another text examining Browning's treatment of gender relations through art. Balancing the critical interest in Browning's allusions to the Perseus and Andromeda myth (see above), she is struck by his recurrent variations on the myth of Pygmalion, who, out of disgust for real women, creates a sculpture of his ideal woman, falls in love with her and is pitied by Venus, who makes his statue come alive:

■ Browning lays bare the misogyny of Ovid's Pygmalion, for whom no living woman is good enough. His poems show how male subjects, threatened by woman's independent spirit, replace her with statues, pictures, prostheses, corpses, which seem to them more than acceptable substitutes for the real thing. Browning's male speakers typically invert Ovid's myth, reducing a woman, even through her death, to a composition of their own creating. They desire feminine simulacra, static art-objects, whose fixed value will reflect their self-estimation. Yet these attempts are always equivocally presented as, time and time again, Browning shows us their fatuity. We see exposed the confusion of values that allows these speakers their justifications. But not only is the error of judgement made plain; increasingly, as he explores the myth, Browning reveals how the speaker's plan goes askew. The female subject consistently eludes her captor, unmasks the poverty of his suppositions, or returns to haunt him. Allied spectres of memory and history cloud his presentations, while intermittent moments of vision and the recognition of the repressed disturb the reader's apprehensions. Art-objects cannot be fixed any more than human beings; contexts can change them, and no artist or owner can control the divergent responses they may arouse in the viewer.[36] ☐

Browning's Pygmalions who ultimately fail to subjugate the desired female include not only the Duke of Ferrara, Porphyria's lover and Andrea del Sarto, but also the speaker of *Pauline* (1833), the sculptor Jules in *Pippa Passes* (1841) and the painter Francesco Romanelli in 'Beatrice Signorini' (1889).

An incisive analysis of the latter poem is Ernest Fontana's 'Browning's "Beatrice Signorini" as Portrait Poem' (1999). Fontana argues that in contrast to the earlier 'My Last Duchess', and more like 'Andrea del Sarto', 'Beatrice Signorini' redresses the power relations between the genders:

■ [I]nstead of demonstrating ironically the male impulse to dominate and control living female beauty by objectifying it into art, Browning's last portrait poem demonstrates the impotence and inability of the male artist to control and dominate successfully living female beauty.[37] ☐

Fontana points out that Artemisia Gentileschi and Francesco Romanelli see their joint painting, in which she paints the floral frame and he the woman at its centre, in different ways: for her, it is a collaboration of equals, whereas for Romanelli, who chooses to paint Gentileschi rather than his wife Beatrice Signorini, it is a way of dominating Gentileschi, a compensation for his inability to possess her sexually. Yet eventually his attempt to dominate both women fails:

> ■ Romanelli's attempt to dominate Gentileschi by transforming her into a visual simulacrum is subverted by his wife, who destroys the image, thereby freeing Romanelli from both his fetish and his fixation with the elusive and indomitable Gentileschi. Freed from his fantasies of sexual domination, the libertine Romanelli suddenly sees his wife with both renewed desire and gratitude. Beatrice by her action achieves a 'statuesque' (319) presence; for a moment she becomes a work of art by destroying one.[38] □

In destroying her husband's fetish, Beatrice

> ■ not only frees him [...] from his obsession, but more importantly frees the reader from the morbid homosocial politics of Browning's earliest portrait poem, 'My Last Duchess,' that of two living male spectators sharing in a moment of intimacy a hitherto veiled and secreted portrait of a dead female. Here the female subject is not dead, nor the privileged spectator male and acquiescent. [...]
> 
> Because of his wife's destruction of both his one 'masterpiece' and of his impulse towards sexual mastery, he is presented as having achieved the singular good fortune of a happy life. 'Beatrice Signorini' is thus unique among portrait poems / narratives in that it ends with a tone of achieved domesticity rather than one of tortured Gothic neurosis and pathology. It, in effect, 'sanitizes' the genre as Browning, near the end of his life, seems to exorcise the ghost of one of his most powerful early monologues.[39] □

In making the chastised Romanelli a happier man than his earlier self, the poet seems to encode a clear message about his ideal balanced gender relations.

Fontana's remarks on 'My Last Duchess' draw attention to the character of Browning's men and relations between men which can be overlooked as critics focus on the portrayal of women and the interaction between the two genders. The next section presents criticism which redresses this critical imbalance by considering Browning's presentation of masculinity. The first of these texts also takes up Fontana's reference to the Gothic as a genre through which gender issues are thematised.

## Masculinities

While feminist critics of Browning tend to work with a clear opposition between female victims and male oppressors, Michael Ackerman proposes a reading of Browning's males as both villains and victims. In 'Monstrous Men: Violence and Masculinity in Robert Browning's *The Ring and the Book*' (2007), he considers Browning's villains through a definition of the Gothic as a genre which exposes the difficulties of embodying a strong male identity rather than its straightforward hegemony:

■ Robert Browning's poetic investigations into the abnormal psyche created a coterie of terrifying male figures, and his experiments in the Gothic almost always emphasize men as generators of fear, men who are violent (often towards women), and men who struggle to interpret the cultural codes for regulating and maintaining masculine identity. As his troupe of Gothic villains respond violently to moments of personal and cultural crisis they reveal a nexus of Gothic tropes that interrogate the terrifying technology of masculine subjectivity. [...]
  The terrorizing activities of many of Browning's male characters are rooted in their own sense of terror at the thought of being emasculated men, seemingly unable to produce the fear necessary in the domestic realm to completely control the woman who is held captive there. Abjected from the patriarchal social structures that provide them with an illusory stable self, these characters murder the women in an attempt to reassert their place in the system of patriarchal authority that rejected them. This rejection, and the concomitant loss of identity, leads to the violent reassertion of authority in a bid to reappropriate their shattered sense of a proper masculine self.[40] □

In *The Ring and the Book,* Guido Franceschini is emasculated because he does not initially manage to dominate his resistant wife, although the law gives him the right to maim and even kill her with impunity. Once this weakness has been publicly exposed through Pompilia's flight to Rome, he tries to reassert his lost authority by killing Pompilia and her parents. Yet his two monologues highlight his failure rather than his success at imposing his male authority on his wife:

■ His line of argument is that he should be allowed the brutal murders of his wife and her family because he restrained himself so long when they clearly deserved worse treatment. Guido is correct, of course, that neither church nor state would have charged him if he had privately dealt in such a violent manner with Pompilia. His defense becomes, however, an inadvertent confession revealing his emasculated state within his own house. The fact that he was not violent enough at home, that he was unable to produce [...] a level of fear necessary to control his wife, proves this lack of 'mastery.' In this sense, the patriarchal powers of the state and church, designed to establish and maintain masculine domestic authority, potentially emasculate the men subject to their authority. This is particularly true of Guido, who must consistently rely on help from the archbishop and the governor to try and control Pompilia.[41] ☐

In Ackerman's view, *The Ring and the Book* is thus another Gothic text which reveals the fragility of actual masculine identity as it struggles to live up to the myth of a violently dominant masculinity.

The difficulties of Browning's male characters in conforming to concepts of masculinity are also the subject of Herbert Sussman's analysis. In *Victorian Masculinities: Manhood and Masculine Poetics in Early Victorian Literature and Art* (1995), he considers Browning as part of his wider study of the social construction of Victorian manliness. Sussman explains that Browning subscribed to a contemporary bourgeois concept of manhood which measured manliness according to a man's performance in the commercial world, 'where manhood marked as aggressive energy and commercial success was tested against other men'.[42] This middle-class ideal of 'entrepreneurial manhood' was problematic for Victorian male poets, as 'this definition of male identity conflicted with the ideal of the poet based on a romantic model in many ways constructed to oppose the new formation of bourgeois man. This romantic model valorized isolation from the commercial or male sphere, emotive openness and imaginative inwardness, passivity, and even the drive toward dissolution and death'.[43] Browning is one of the early Victorian male poets who try to define a masculine poetic which revises the romantic, feminine idea of poetry and draws instead on the aggressive commercial and sexual energy of bourgeois entrepreneurial manhood. His artist poems 'represent the project and problematics of forging a masculine poetic that would ground the manliness of the poet in the normative values of bourgeois masculinity'.[44]

Sussman focuses in particular on Browning's interest in monasticism as a countermodel to entrepreneurial manhood:

■ In ways that resonate with his criticism of the puritanism of his own time, he codes in the limit case of monastic celibacy the ways that repression of male sexuality leads to voyeurism and to the murder of women, to the distortion of male art through mimetic failure, and to aestheticism as a fetishizing of the art object that substitutes for the natural flow of male sexual energy.[45] ☐

This unmanly fetishising aestheticism is best illustrated by Browning's two art lovers, the Duke of Ferrara, who prefers contemplating the artistic representations of his last duchess and his bronze of Neptune taming a seahorse to real bodies, and the (officially) celibate speaker of 'The Bishop Orders His Tomb', who transfers his forbidden sexual energy to the art object that is his projected tomb.[46] Similarly, in 'Soliloquy of the Spanish Cloister' (1842), Browning 'equates male chastity with male madness' as 'the speaker exemplifies the average sensual man turned monstrous when natural energy is distorted by sexual repression, an intimation of what Lippo might have become had he remained within the cloister'.[47] By contrast, Fra Lippo Lippi is

> ■ the exemplar of the manly artist. In this figure of the robustly heterosexual monk painting religiously powerful work while in the employ of the exemplary mercantile patron [the banker Cosimo de Medici], Browning dramatizes a valorized constellation of male sexual energy, artistic potency, commercial success, and moralized art that seems to reconcile artistic achievement with bourgeois manhood.[48] □

Sussman interprets Lippo's realistic style as a manifestation of his bourgeois manhood:

> ■ For Browning, the rise of realism is identified not only with the rise of the market, but also of the phallus. [...] Lippo's repudiation of a symbolic for a realistic art is conflated with his movement from monastic celibacy to sexual liberation represented as a movement from the unnatural to the natural: 'You should not take a fellow eight years old / And make him swear to never kiss the girls' (lines 224–25). Mimetically accurate art is thus marked as a manly style, the inevitable effect of removing unnatural restrictions on male sexual potency.[49] □

Although a monk, Lippo has kept his virility. Yet Sussman disputes the common critical reading of Lippo as Browning's ideal successful artist, and he also questions the Victorian ideal of bourgeois masculinity empowered by capitalism. Pointing to Lippo's dependence on his commercial patron and his reliance on commodified sex through the brothel, and also to Andrea del Sarto's suffering within bourgeois marriage, he suggests that these factors create new constraints for male energy.[50]

Broadly agreeing with Sussman's analysis, Evgenia Sifaki examines Browning's attitude towards the common Victorian association of heroic manliness with imperialism. In 'Masculinity, Heroism, and the Empire: Robert Browning's "Clive" and Other Victorian Re-Constructions of the Story of Robert Clive' (2009), she argues that Browning's 1880 poem about Robert Clive (1725–74), the British military leader whom the Victorians celebrated as a national hero, undermines dominant values.

Unlike the other texts that Sifaki considers, the poem refuses to subscribe to the common glorification of colonialism through an association with adventure, exposing instead the greed of the colonial enterprise. It focuses on an early episode in Clive's life when he refuses to pay a fellow officer to whom he had lost money at cards but who had cheated. The cheat has the opportunity to kill Clive but offers to spare his life if he withdraws his accusation of cheating. When Clive refuses, the other lets him live, concluding that he must be mad.

While other Victorian texts read this episode as evidence of Clive's bravery, Browning's poem interprets the behaviour as moral weakness, since his Clive refuses to comply because he fears the public disgrace if he had lived and been considered a liar. Clive thus appears as another Browning character trapped by the expectations associated with masculinity, while the speaker redefines the concept of true heroism as Christian self-discipline. He

> ■ discredit[s] Clive's code of honour altogether, naming it 'desperation, madness' (l. 226) and 'a rush against God's face' (l. 228).[...] For the speaker, Clive's priorities, in which fear of disgrace overcomes the fear of death, are a form of mental deficiency, the incapacity to endure pain, a failure in insightfulness, and a lack of a sinner's self-awareness. [...]
>
> Indeed, in Browning's poem the speaker's whole case against Clive's conduct relies on an argument for manly self-discipline and control. He locates and emphasises Clive's essentially 'unmanly' attributes – his lacking in self-restraint and the incapacity to endure pain – which he represents as Christian precepts.[51] □

Clive's later years as a degraded opium addict and the speaker's own alcoholism reinforce this undermining of Victorian colonial heroism. Sifaki concludes:

> ■ Browning's text does not allow for any potentially positive correlation of what Sussman has called a successful masculinisation process and the practices of colonialism. Rather, it intimates the opposite: that the experience and politics of colonialism may have caused Clive's tragic ending as well as the speaker's unhappy situation. Furthermore, the poem can be read as a 'staging' of an inquiry about ideas such as fear and its relation to courage and heroism, honourable conduct, rightful violence, justice, etc., while ironically suspending the concluding answers to the questions raised. It avoids identifying explicitly with any one 'politically correct' position, but it turns tacit assumptions, such as the ideal of heroic manhood and the civilising mission of the imperialist project, into questions, registers a crisis of Victorian masculinity, and exposes the problematic interlocking of certain – typical of the age – formations of the masculine with imperial politics.[52] □

The three analysts of Browning's representation of masculinity covered here present him as a critic of traditional gender roles and thus support the feminist readings of his female characters as challenging patriarchal values. Yet the poet's modern views on gender do not preclude a commitment to traditional values. As the final section will show, his strong interest in the theme of love can be attributed to his religious convictions, notably in relation to the New Testament doctrine of the Incarnation. Contrasting starkly with the rest of this chapter, this approach to Browning's work uncouples the issue of gender from the theme of love.

## Divine Love: The Incarnation

The central doctrine of Christianity is the Incarnation of God in Jesus Christ. The embodiment of the divine in human form is the most striking articulation of the New Testament concept of a God of love. It is also the mirror image and anticipation of another key doctrine, Christ's (and man's) resurrection. The celebration of divine love permeates Browning's work, and this is most clear in his references to the Incarnation. Thus the poet Aprile in *Paracelsus*, for instance, exhorts the hero, who strives for knowledge and power, that love is more important than these two qualities, and divine love is manifest in the Incarnation:

■ Man's weakness is his glory – for the strength
Which raises him to heaven and near God's self,
Came spite of it: God's strength his glory is,
For thence came with our weakness sympathy
Which brought God down to earth, a man like us. [II, 613–17, 1849 edition] □

In the most extended study on the subject, *The Central Truth: The Incarnation in Robert Browning's Poetry* (1963), William Whitla posits that the Incarnation informs not only Browning's poetry on religion but also the poems on love and art: 'In dealing with any of these subjects in a poem, Browning's characteristic method is to solve the "problem" of the poem by some kind of incarnational experience.'[53] Whitla traces Browning's interest in the Incarnation back to his early exposure to various forms of Protestantism, such as his mother's Congregationalism and his contact with Unitarian and sceptical thinkers during his twenties, but he also states that the poet's emphasis on divine love is a consequence of his own experience of human love. He quotes Beryl Stone's summary of how the Incarnation impacts both Browning's thought and poetry:

■ The symbolic act of the Incarnation of Christ offered Browning an analogy of his own experience as a creative artist. The artist enjoys a vision of the truth which must be shared with humanity. As God clothed himself in human flesh, so the poet speaks in words the vision that he has seen. If the artist manages to convey in language the truth of his vision, he will have unfolded something of the Divine Word in his human words. He will share in the redeeming work of Christ as he liberates men from the tyranny of error and the bondage of self.[54] □

Writing poetry is a human analogy for the divine Incarnation. Similarly, Whitla posits that the lovers' ideal combination of physical and spiritual unity is a reflection of divine love and of the union of human body and divine spirit in Christ's Incarnation:

■ The love of man and woman is the finite manifesting itself as the shadow of the infinite. The images of human love are the only means which man can validly use in discourse about divine love. Browning has passed from the single vision of the literal text to the deeper inquiry of metaphysical thought.[55] □

When it comes to Browning's religious poems about the Incarnation, a more penetrating analysis than Whitla's is offered by Jochen Haug (born 1972). He considers these texts in his study *Passions Without a Tongue: Dramatisations of the Body in Robert Browning's Poetry* (2004), which argues for the centrality of the body in the constitution of the characters' identity. For Haug, Browning's poems about the Incarnation reveal an unconventionally close association of body and soul which goes against their distancing by philosophical authorities such as Plato and René Descartes. Haug comments on the paradox of 'A Death in the Desert' (1864), the framed dramatic monologue by the dying apostle and evangelist St John:

■ The fleshliness of Christ is crucial for Christian belief, as was the bodily presence of John as an eye-witness [at the crucifixion]; yet for John himself, the flesh represents an impediment against gaining spiritual fulfilment. The dissolution of his body paves the way for the exaltation of the soul, but it also obliterates the last corporeal proof of God's existence and love.[56] □

The authority of St John's gospel – disputed by the Higher Critics to whom Browning responds in this poem (see Chapter 7) – relies on John's personal experience of the embodied God. Yet Browning's St John also argues in his monologue that divine miracles like the Incarnation are no longer necessary for believers who have intuitive faith in God's existence, and he also sees his decaying body as hindering his spirituality.

Haug detects a similar paradox in 'An Epistle Containing the Strange Medical Experience of Karshish, the Arab Physician' (1855), in which the speaker reports his encounter with Lazarus after his resurrection. The poem adopts the perspective of somebody who does not believe in the divinity of Christ and approaches what Christians consider a miracle from a purely rational point of view. But Karshish's intuitive attraction to Christianity eventually shines through his letter.

■ Karshish gains the insight that mere materialism and a wholly rationalistic approach to knowledge will not yield any spiritual truths. It is intuition that can guide him towards truth and provide his soul with an emotional and spiritual basis. What the Arab physician must do is abandon his fixation on the body as the prime source of knowledge and belief. But since he is a man of the body, trapped within it, and reduced in his attention to understand bodily processes, he can only comprehend spirituality and divine love when given a bodily analogue to spiritual essence.[57] □

Karshish thus acts as an alter ego for any Christian who overcomes the limits of the body and attains spirituality because his encounter with Lazarus allows him to connect the unfamiliar concept of divine love with the much more familiar entity of the body. And Lazarus' case is a human analogy for Christ's divine Incarnation.[58]

A foreshadowing of the Incarnation also forms the climax of the complete version of 'Saul' (1855, first published as a fragment in 1845). Here the Old Testament poet and later Israelite king David rescues his predecessor, King Saul, from a state of depression through his song which articulates his love for Saul. David's homo-erotic admiration for Saul's body has been commented on by a number of critics. But Haug insists that the love David expresses needs to be seen as religious, since Saul's pose in his catatonic state, 'both arms stretched out wide / On the great cross-support in the centre' (ll. 28–9) of his tent, clearly anticipates the crucified Christ. David's discovery of his intense love for Saul is crucial to the poem. He

■ concludes that it is inconceivable that he, as God's creation, should possess the capacity of love unless God himself were able to love, too: 'Would I fain in my impotent yearning do all for this man, / And dare doubt he alone shall not help him, who yet alone can?' (269–270). Consequently, David knows, God will come to the world in physical shape and love mankind in the same way as he himself loves Saul [...]

The intensity of his bodily experience has convinced David that it must necessarily be repeated by the Godhead. Since his love for Saul is rooted in physicality, God's love for man must manifest itself, physically, too; otherwise, the 'creature [would] surpass the Creator' (268) – a concept that David can in no way accept. In 'Saul,' the body is dramatised as a crucial agent for the comprehension of God as a God of love. But unlike Lazarus, Saul is restored to life by the human analogue of God's love, namely the bodily love of David. Of course, David, as a symbolic representative of an intuitive approach to love and knowledge, is more complete in his envisioning of the coming of Christ than a rationalist like Karshish. [...] In 'Saul,' body and soul are unified: none of the two is privileged over the other. The Incarnation finally becomes a bodily as well as an emotional and spiritual act.[59] □

Like Karshish, David seems to model for the reader an experience of divine love made comprehensible through an appreciation of the more accessible physical world.

Finally, Haug contrasts these celebrations of the Incarnation with 'Caliban upon Setebos' (1864). Caliban

■ uses the same positivist approach as Karshish in his attempt at fathoming God. However, since Caliban is an unpleasant, inhuman figure, the result is an Incarnation *ex negativo*. Whereas in 'An Epistle of Karshish' and 'Saul,' Browning dramatises bodies as the manifestations of God's love, Caliban, vice versa, uses his own bodily experience to develop a theology whose god, Setebos, is preoccupied by the same petty spite, envy and malevolence as Caliban himself.[60] □

Caliban's invention of his god is an Incarnation gone wrong because he lacks any feeling of love.

The contrast between this final section of the chapter and its opening section shows the wide divergence in explanations for Browning's intense interest in the theme of love. The suggestion that his preoccupation with love and female identity was fostered by his relationship with Barrett Browning, to whose poetry the position of women is so crucial, is certainly a very plausible one. But the importance of religion for the aesthetics of nineteenth-century authors is also a feature that modern readers in their more secular context need to bear in mind. Both the substitution of conventional ideas of masculinity with a Christian ideal which Sifaki identifies and Brady's reading of Pompilia as embodying true Christian love argue how pivotal faith is to Browning's world view. Such readings raise the question whether human love really is Browning's main interest or whether it is rather an accessible vehicle to convey other, more abstract ideas and values. As the section on his unhappy lovers and his recurrent use of the female artist's model have suggested, he may in part be using these poems, which are ostensibly about gender, as a means of discussing aesthetics, whether it be the illusions of Romantic ideals, the difficulty of communication, or the power of the artist or owner of an artwork over the work.

Yet Browning is also quite clearly seen as a poet who scrutinises gender relations. While there are a few critics who accuse him of misogyny, the majority view him as an opponent of patriarchy who either exposes the oppression of women or who even presents female characters resisting male dominance. A similarly modern interpretation of Browning as a critic of masculine ideals emerges from the chapter's penultimate section. Divergent assessments of his views on gender are possible due to the absence of an authorial voice in the dramatic monologue. Browning's distance from or proximity to his speakers can in some cases be argued either way. The same applies to the presence or absence of the author's irony towards his speakers, and, as seen in the readings of Pompilia, whether speakers are passive victims of gender stereotypes or cunningly exploit those stereotypes is also open to interpretation.

The extent to which poems are meant as comments on Victorian society has also emerged as a main critical focus. The poems on gender are far from being the only ones in Browning's work in which contemporary references may be disguised by a historical setting. His preference for this device will be considered more closely in the next chapter. It will explore the purpose of his use of historical and geographical distancing and show how his work is embedded in the cultural context of Victorian discourses about history, national identity and, once again, religion.

# CHAPTER SEVEN

# Historical and Geographical Distancing

Although Browning is considered a quintessentially Victorian author, many of his poems are set in earlier historical periods or foreign locations, especially Italy, where he spent most of the fifteen years of his marriage. This chapter presents criticism that assesses the implications of Browning's choices to use historical and geographical distancing.

The first section considers historical poems of a particular type: those about biblical characters which engage with a new school of biblical criticism, the so-called Higher Criticism. William O. Raymond's assertion that Browning completely rejected the methods and findings of Higher Criticism is contrasted with Elinor Shaffer's demonstration of how Browning accepted the Higher Critics' contentions but still managed to maintain his belief.

The second section focuses on discussions of Browning's concept of historical poetry. Mary Ellis Gibson defines him as a contextual historian, whereas Morse Peckham and Hilary Fraser consider him as responding to developments in nineteenth-century historiography, relating his historical poetry to different theoretical schools. Like Fraser, Stefan Hawlin discusses the political and religious motives for Browning's celebration of the Italian Renaissance. Hawlin's essay links up with the chapter's other section about Browning's Italian poems, which give an insight not only into his view of the Italians but also into his conceptualisation of English national identity. Robert Viscusi explains Browning's portrayal of Italy in terms of a sensory commodity as a logical consequence of his political liberalism; Alison Chapman discusses the cosmopolitan Browning's critical exposure of English patriotism; and Britta Martens argues that Browning draws on established national stereotypes to parody the Italian national character.

## Higher Criticism

Browning's work contains a number of important poems about theological issues which bear witness to the centrality of his faith to his poetry and his interest in contemporary religious debates. Although Browning's beliefs did not match fully with the dogma of any established Christian sect, his values and ideas were strongly influenced by his nonconformist Protestantism. Indeed, a significant number of critics consider his religious convictions to be the main key to his aesthetics. Chapter 4 has already presented J. Hillis Miller's reading of Browning's poetry as representative of the Victorian Crisis of Faith, and Chapter 6 has examined his interest in the Incarnation. This section presents criticism on an intersection of religion and history, Browning's engagement with an interpretation of the Bible from a historical perspective.

Several of Browning's poems on religious subjects – most obviously 'Christmas-Eve' (1850), the 'Epilogue' to *Dramatis Personae* (1864), and the poems about biblical characters, 'Saul' (1845/55), 'An Epistle of Karshish' (1855) and 'A Death in the Desert' (1864) – respond to Higher Criticism, a method of biblical scholarship pioneered by German scholars in the early nineteenth century which made its full impact felt in Britain around the middle of the century. In their attempt to ascertain the historical veracity of the Bible, Higher Critics like Friedrich Schleiermacher (1768–1834), David Friedrich Strauß (1808–74), Ludwig Feuerbach (1804–72) and the Frenchman Ernest Renan (1823–92) subjected biblical scriptures to the same close textual scrutiny as literary and historical scholars, treating these texts not as divinely inspired truth but as historical sources produced by human authors with specific agendas in particular historical circumstances. Their conclusions that biblical texts contradicted each other and were historically inaccurate, and their doubts over the divinity of Christ, shook the belief of those embracing the traditional faith in the literal truth of the Bible.

Most critics on the subject position themselves in opposition to William O. Raymond's 1929 essay 'Browning and the Higher Criticism', which argues that the poet's attitude towards Higher Criticism was 'one of clearly marked antagonism'.[1] Raymond asserts that this attitude was

> ■ very much that of the average English layman in the eighteen-sixties, distrustful of [Higher Criticism] as a product 'made in Germany,' fearful of its iconoclastic tendencies, and with little sympathy for its sifting of documentary evidence and patient work of scientific investigation.[2] □

According to Raymond, Browning subscribed to the classic binary oppositions of love versus reason and feeling versus intellect, rejecting the rational, scientific methods of the Higher Critics in favour of an intuitive faith of the heart:

> Untechnical as Browning's approach to the critical problems of the New Testament, in such a work as *A Death in the Desert*, undeniably is, the depth and discernment of his religious intuition give it genuine significance. The purport of the argument of the poem as put into the mouth of St. John, the beloved disciple, is to represent Christianity as a religion of the spirit, with love as its inspiring motive. While the authority of the New Testament sources is not questioned, the poet tends to minimize the importance of the appeal to history, and refuses to base the truth of Christianity on an intellectual proof of the factual character of a series of past events. It is the realization and appropriation of the divine love of God in the lives of men and women, the abiding presence of the ever living Christ in the hearts of his disciples, that he regards as an irrefutable proof of the validity of the Christian faith.[3]

While later critics do not dispute the emphasis on divine love in Browning's creed, they do take issue with Raymond's assumptions that Browning failed to engage with the methodology of Higher Criticism and its arguments about the historical inaccuracies of the New Testament.

By contrast, in the most important treatment of the subject, 'Browning's St. John: The Casuistry of the Higher Criticism' (1972), Elinor Shaffer argues that Browning's theology as well as his general philosophy and poetics show a clear engagement with the Higher Critics' mode of argument.[4] In Shaffer's view, Browning's awareness of the unreliability of human accounts of any event is most evident in his 'casuistic' poems with their deployment of elaborate reasoning, as well as in the multiperspectivism of *The Ring and the Book*, which undermines the authority of witnesses and judgments. These texts arguably show that he had absorbed the Higher Critics' dismissal of the Bible's claim to historical accuracy and that he transferred their methodology to more recent historical events:

> Browning's notorious 'difficulty' as a poet reflects his full grasp of the significance of the higher critical analysis of the untrustworthiness of historical evidence – of all human testimony. He did not oppose the higher criticism – he could not – but he feared the diminution in the quality of belief that it might entail in its practitioners, friends, and enemies alike.[5]

Shaffer focuses on 'A Death in the Desert' as primarily a response to Renan's *Life of Jesus* (1863), especially Renan's conclusion that, contrary to the claims of the Gospel of St John, John was not present at the crucifixion. Like Renan, who ridicules John as a vulgar liar, eager to promote his importance in the story of Christ, Browning is primarily interested in John's psychology and exposes his lies, but he does so without undermining his dignity. And in a way typical of his casuistic monologues, he does not give the reader a clear indication of how the speaker is to be judged.[6]

As the poem's elaborate explanation of its own transmission demonstrates, Browning fully subscribes to the Higher Critics' view of the Bible as a mosaic of texts written after the death of the apostles and after the original stories had passed through several levels of transmission:

■ Browning's account of the provenance of his poem, the purported deathbed words of St. John, follows faithfully the higher critical analysis of the complex transmission of the Christian story. The 'deathbed words' have four purported auditors, Valens, Xanthus, the Boy, and 'I' (supposed to be Pamphylax the Antiochene); and keeping watch, out of earshot, was a Bactrian convert. Names and vivid description are used to give verisimilitude in the manner ascribed to the author of the Gospel by Renan.[7] ☐

Even though Browning shares the Higher Critics' distrust of the Gospels' claims to historical accuracy, he defends their authenticity on the basis of their long-standing acceptance by the Christian community, replacing the authority of an eye-witness account with that of the community's tradition:

■ 'A Death in the Desert' shows the process by which the claim to ocular witness was transformed into the claim to valid Christian spiritual experience. It is Browning's peculiar merit to have exhibited this change, which took place over centuries, which indeed was complete only in his day, as the experience of 'John.' This 'John,' then, is neither the aged apostle nor his gnostic disciples and interpolators, but 'John' as inherited and interpreted by Christians. That he can be taken thus is shown by Browning as the triumph of Christianity over historical fact.

This is not to say that 'history' is abandoned; rather the narrower conception of ocular witness, of historical reportage, is replaced by the interpretation of history. Rationalist scrutiny of isolated events in the Gospels had given way to [Johann Gottfried] Herder's imaginative grasp of the character and tone of the entire milieu from which they sprang and in which they could be validated, itself a historical undertaking. This imaginative effort to return to another time and to grasp from within the principles of its experience (for another community or a later generation, simply false) was one of the major apologetic methods of the higher criticism, as it was one of the major preoccupations of Browning's poetry. In 'A Death' he adopts a central apologetic device of the higher criticism: the notion of the 'community' in which an idea has its root. Whether or not these are the deathbed words of John, whether or not the apostle John literally wrote the Fourth Gospel or any of the works ascribed to him, these confessions represent the experience of the Christian community [...][8] ☐

Browning, like the Higher Critics, is less interested in the factual, historical events that cannot be recovered than in the way they are transmitted and interpreted. The next section about history will show that critics who examine his concept of history come to the same conclusion.

## Browning's Concept of History

The nineteenth century saw important developments in the ways history was being researched and analysed. Browning undoubtedly followed these developments. He was a friend of the historian Thomas Carlyle (1795–1881) and, in 1836, he helped his friend John Forster (1812–76) write a biography of Thomas Wentworth, first Earl of Strafford (1672–1739) – the hero of his play *Strafford* (1837). Critics have tried to situate the concept of history that is implicit in Browning's many poems with historical subjects both in relation to competing approaches to historiography during the period and in more general terms.

A starting point has been the famous praise of Browning's 'The Bishop Orders His Tomb' by the influential art critic John Ruskin, as already cited in Chapter 5. Ruskin, we recall, lauded the poem as a better representation of Renaissance culture than his own treatise on Venetian art and architecture, *The Stones of Venice*. Mary Ellis Gibson (born 1952), in *History and the Prism of Art: Browning's Poetic Experiments* (1987), labels Ruskin's approach to history here as contextualist, that is as an 'attempt to get at habits of mind and to describe the moral, spiritual, intellectual, or aesthetic preoccupations of an age'.[10] She contends that this is also the position of other contemporary historiographers, cultural critics and writers, including Browning. She compares Browning's interest in heroism in his stage plays of the 1830s and 1840s – an interest typical of Romantic historiography – with his mature poetry, where the emphasis shifts to capturing the cultural climate of an epoch, what Victorians called the 'spirit of the age':

■ Browning's scrutiny of heroism and aristocratic and republican values, and of the possible failures of revolt in the plays presages the shift in his later writing toward an examination of the social and political fabric. Rather than emphasizing sudden political change in the major historical monologues and *The Ring and the Book* Browning examines broader shifts and changes in cultural and historical climate. Individuals may still have their moment of spiritual crisis and of sudden inspiration, but their personal resolves and actions do not in themselves make for revolutionary social and political change. Rather, like Fra Lippo Lippi [1855], they participate in or, like Andrea del Sarto, they attempt to hold themselves aloof from the great cultural or social changes of their times. In this shift from examining revolt to examining broad patterns of cultural change, Browning deemphasizes one aspect of romantic historiography – the centrality of the hero – in favor of another – the spirit of the age. This emphasis underlies the poet-personae, the narrative structures, the historical ironies, and the language of Browning's historical poems, and it makes possible what I call Browning's contextualist understanding of history.[11] ☐

The scrutiny of an individual psyche which characterises the dramatic monologue is thus, in Gibson's view, complemented by an exploration of social and political conditions in both the monologues and the long poems.

Approaching the subject from a different angle, J. Hillis Miller, in *The Disappearance of God* (1963), likewise argues that the dramatic monologue is acutely conscious of the problems of historical analysis. Miller states that the 'dramatic monologue is par excellence the literary genre of historicism' because '[i]t presupposes a double awareness on the part of the author, an awareness which is the very essence of historicism. The dramatic monologuist is aware of the relativity, the arbitrariness of any single life or way of looking at the world.'[12]

Morse Peckham, too, engages with this question of how the relativism of individual perspectives in the dramatic monologue can be related to nineteenth-century historiography. In 'Historiography and *The Ring and the Book*' (1968), he proposes that in the dramatic monologue, and especially in *The Ring and the Book*, Browning models his poetic technique on the methods of the new historiographical school led by the German Leopold von Ranke (1795–1886). Ranke's method is characterised not only by a more rigorous analysis of all available sources than that practised by his predecessors, but also by a critical consideration of the personality and interests of the authors of historical sources – factors which obviously play an important role in the divergent versions of the Roman murder story as they are presented by the various speakers of *The Ring and the Book*. Moreover, although their professional method was simplistically described as 'objective' historiography, Rankean scholars themselves were conscious of the historiographer's own biases in their interpretation of sources and historical processes.

Peckham suggests that, despite *The Ring and the Book*'s repeated claims to convey the objective truth of the story, Browning here transfers the historiographer's critical awareness of his own bias to his position as a poet. He does so through the medium of the speaker of the poem's framing Books I and XII, whose references to his wife and his life in Florence clearly identify him as the poet himself. As a result,

> ■ the carefully identified historical Robert Browning of Book I is fatally compromised by the very plan of the poem, for that plan puts that Robert Browning in the same category as each of the other monologuists [...] if the cognitive act of a monologuist is compromised by his interests, then Browning's cognition of that cognitive act is compromised by *his own* interests.[13] □

Therefore, like the other speakers of *The Ring and the Book*,

> ■ the Robert Browning of Book I is to be conceived as interpreting the documents [of the Old Yellow Book] according to his own interests – necessarily and ineluctably. And further, his self-conception is the primary source of that interpretation, as the careful self-portrait at the very beginning makes sufficiently clear.[14] □

Peckham concedes that this awareness of the poet's subjectivity is a logical consequence of Browning's use of the dramatic monologue, but he suggests that Browning, with his strong interest in historical subjects, reached this conclusion through his reading of the self-conscious reflections on the historiographer's bias by members of Ranke's school. Focusing on the 'structural similarity between Ranke's conception of the historical document',[15] as determined by the biases and personality of the source's author, and the dramatic monologue which exposes the biases and personality of the speaker, Peckham nevertheless points out an essential opposition between the historian who strives for objectivity, even if he knows it cannot be realised, and the poet whose purpose is the exploration of human subjectivity:

> ■ Ranke endeavored to cancel, or at least reduce to a minimum, the distorting interest, or surd, of the authors of historical documents in order to get at historical truth, *wie es eigentlich gewesen* [as it actually happened]. Browning aimed at creating historical situations so that the irreducible surd of the interest of the speaker might be located. This is why it is so difficult to decide if the monologuist speaks for Browning: in one, Browning might be seeking to identify his own interests; in another, to identify interests not his; in yet another the monologuist might share some of Browning's interests and not share others. But the monologuist and Browning always had one interest in common, to manifest their uniqueness, or irrational surd, in the cognitive apprehension and interpretation of a situation.[16] □

Returning to Browning's self-portrayal in the framing books of the *Ring and the Book*, Peckham maintains that his deviations from the facts in his source and his projection of the personally relevant St George myth onto the story (see Chapter 6), for which he has been reproached by some critics, are the poet's way of indicating to himself and those readers who knew of his elopement with Elizabeth that even the poem's author cannot be trusted to give access to historical truth.[17]

The poet's critical self-consciousness that Peckham detects in *The Ring and the Book* is disputed by other critics, but many agree on his closeness to Ranke's ideas. However, the influence of other historiographers has also been argued. Hilary Fraser, in 'Browning and Nineteenth-Century Historiography' (1989), proposes the French Romantic and republican historian Jules Michelet (1798–1874) as an alternative model, both in his concept of the Renaissance, which features so prominently in Browning's monologues, and in his metaphors for the historian's method:

■ Michelet's principal claim was that the historian's role was to 'resurrect' the deceased inhabitants of the past, and to enable these historical 'actors' to speak for themselves. The metaphors of resurrection and theatre which pervade Browning's explanations of his historical method strengthen the argument for finding a historiographical affinity between the poet's mode of historical realism and what Hayden White has identified as the Romantic and Metaphorical historical consciousness of Michelet.[18] □

Fraser refers here to Browning's use, in the framing books of *The Ring and the Book*, of the metaphor of resurrection (I, 707–72) and his reference to his dramatic speakers as 'actors' (I, 948). His literary method in the dramatic monologue, like Michelet's historical narrative and the contemporary realist novel, creates what Roland Barthes calls an *'effet de réel'* [realistic effect], in that the authorial voice seems absent while the story seems to tell itself objectively through the voices and acts of the characters.[19]

Expanding on Browning's use of the resurrection metaphor, not only in *The Ring and the Book* but also in the resurrection of Lazarus in 'An Epistle of Karshish' and in 'Easter-Day' (1850, ll. 1029–40), Fraser explains in what sense Browning's and Michelet's concept of the historian-narrator is influenced by Romance as defined by Hayden White (born 1928) in his analysis of nineteenth-century historiographical discourse through literary categories:

■ Hayden White suggests that the story of the Resurrection of Christ in Christian mythology corresponds to the archetype of Romance, in that it is 'a drama of self-identification symbolized by the hero's transcendence of the world of experience, his victory over it, and his final liberation from it... a drama of the triumph of good over evil [...] (pp. 8–9).

White argues that [...] Michelet cast all of his histories in the Romantic mode (pp. 149–63), an argument strengthened by Michelet's self-definition as a resurrectionist historian. [...]

> Michelet's Romantic, resurrectionist mode of emplotment clearly cannot be separated from his republican ideology, and there is similarly a political dimension to Browning's commitment to resuscitating the past. [...] Browning's political sympathies were, like Michelet's, republican, but in his case it was Italy rather than France which captured his imagination and engaged his commitment. Like many other English liberals of his time, Browning was a strong supporter of Italy's Risorgimento, the movement for national liberation and unification. His efforts to resurrect through his art the spirit of the Renaissance, the era of Italy's greatness, were arguably directed towards recalling, in the midst of its contemporary oppression and degradation, a sense of national pride and dignity.[20]

Following White's analysis, Fraser suggests here that there is a strong moral and political agenda underlying Browning's concept of historical poetry. In particular, his favourable representations of the Italian Renaissance are a way of championing the cause of nineteenth-century Italy, which suffered from a fragmentation into small principalities, foreign occupation, poverty and cultural decline.[21]

Another reading of Browning's concept of the Renaissance as driven by political and religious motives is offered by Stefan Hawlin in 'Love Among the Political Ruins: 1848 and the Political Unconscious of *Men and Women*' (2012). Hawlin reads this 1855 collection in the context of the 1848 European revolutions, disclosing how the poet's politically liberal views and his Protestant ideology are encoded even in apparently apolitical poems. He argues that Browning's celebrations of the Renaissance present it as a period of Protestant enlightenment and liberty in resistance to political and religious (i.e. Catholic) authoritarianism. He links poems like 'Fra Lippo Lippi', 'A Grammarian's Funeral' and 'Old Pictures in Florence' (all 1855) to the late poem 'Fust and His Friends' (1887), which presents Johann Fust (ca. 1400–66) rather than Johannes Gutenberg (1395–1468) as the inventor of the printing press and proposes a connection between printing, the spread of Protestantism and civil liberty:

> ■ What 'Fust and His Friends' makes clear, ultimately, is the Liberal and Protestant myth of the Renaissance with which Browning was working, stripped as it is in this late poem of most subtlety and nuance. [...] the binary in 'Fust' is between, on the one side, bigotry/superstition/ignorance/social control/Catholicism/and the medieval, and on the other side, enlightenment/reason/education/liberty/Protestantism/and modernity [...] Lippi is the modern artist breaking with what is 'medieval' and 'monkish,' distancing (unconsciously perhaps) what is superstitious and ignorant in his cultural milieu, at odds with the social and religious control of the Catholic Church, and beginning to forge his version of modernity: an art that is more realistic, that responds to the visible world, that is not hamstrung by dogma.[22]

While Lippo illustrates the resistance of Italian Renaissance art to Catholic authoritarianism by a member of the Catholic Church, 'A Grammarian's Funeral' makes a more explicit point about the benefits of Protestantism, despite the readings of the eponymous scholar as an anti-hero who is too absorbed in his narrow subject. Insisting on the importance of the poem's subtitle, which situates the text 'Shortly after the revival of learning in Europe', Hawlin argues that the grammarian is one of the scholars who prepared

> ■ the Reformation, the freeing of The Word from the fetters of Catholic philosophical obscurantism and social control. In short, we should associate together 'the day again / Rimming the rock-row' (ll. 7–8) in 'A Grammarian's Funeral' (his body is carried to its rest in the dawn light), with the physical spring-time setting of 'Old Pictures in Florence' and its idea of the Renaissance as 'the season / Of Art's spring-birth' (ll. 177–78), with the literal and symbolic dawn at the end of 'Fra Lippo Lippi.'
>
> Through *Men and Women*, then, Browning's insistent celebration of the rebirth or revival of the Renaissance/Reformation contains elements of displaced political feeling. What he had hoped for in 1848, from his ideological perspective, was the meaningful overthrow of some of the backward regimes of Europe, a dawn of modernity, the breaking of the nexus between social and religious authoritarianism and control. That achievement was thwarted, but the hopes, for example, of Italian nationalism lived on, so that *Men and Women*'s focus on the Renaissance as rebirth and 'dawn' and 'spring-time' is an implicit focus on the hope for such a 'spring-time' in other spheres.[23] □

In Hawlin's reading, Browning's representations of the Renaissance – reinforced by associated metaphors of revival and dawn which allude to the etymological root of 'Renaissance' ('Rebirth') – become a way of projecting onto this distant historical period his disappointed hopes for political progress throughout Europe and especially in Italy. The next section will cover criticism which examines the political and cultural implications of Browning's poetry about contemporary Italian subjects. Here we will see a more critical view both of the Italians and of British perceptions of Italy.

## Englishmen and Italy

Browning's attitude towards Italy is complex and contradictory. While his poetry shows genuine admiration for the culture of Renaissance Italy and support for the political independence and freedom of Italy, remarks such as the following extract from a letter to his friend Isabella Blagden (1816/17-73) show marked contempt for Italian people:

> ■ I agree with you, & always did, as to the uninterestingness of the Italians individually, as thinking, originating souls: I never read a line of a modern Italian book that was of use to me,– never saw a flash of poetry come out of an Italian *word*: in art, in action, *yes*,– not in the region of ideas: I always said, they *are* poetry, don't and can't *make* poetry,– & you know what I mean by *that*,– nothing relating to rhymes and melody and *lo stile* [the style]: but as a nation, politically, they are most interesting to me,– I think they have more than justified every expectation their best friends formed of them,– and their rights are indubitable: my liking for Italy was always a selfish one,– I felt alone with my own soul there [...]$^{24}$ □

A number of critics have set themselves the task of solving the paradox of Browning's political support of the Risorgimento and his apparently racist stereotyping of the Italians as a primitive, passive and superstitious people governed by animal appetites. In '"The Englishman in Italy": Free Trade as a Principle of Aesthetics' (1984), Robert Viscusi acknowledges that Browning is influenced by various English literary traditions depicting Italians as inferior and backward. However, he suggests that a key source of this contradiction is the notion of free trade as championed by Victorian political liberals, the belief that the best price and quality of goods is guaranteed if buyers and producers are not limited by restrictions of any kind. Viscusi denounces this doctrine as morally wrong since it disregards the needs of consumers and the wider society and makes money all powerful. Having quoted John Stuart Mill's defence of free trade in the core text of Victorian liberalism, *On Liberty* (1859), Viscusi criticises that same liberalism's separation of trade from society:

> ■ It leaves money free to circulate eternally separated from all it may contain of human labor, pain, division, loyalty, conception, thought, or love. It is the invention, nothing less, of a sacrament. And, on a slightly less ethereal plane, it is the ideological prophylaxis which enables so committed an antislaver, so great an apostle of human emancipation, as Robert Browning to live as he lived, live on what he lived on, and, most to our purpose, write as he wrote, the herald of liberty sustained throughout his long existence on someone else's labor, someone else's unearned income, fed by servants ('Italians'), dressed by tailors ('I always said, they *are* poetry, don't and can't *make* poetry'), paid and paid for in the name of freedom.$^{25}$ □

Viscusi here alludes to the fact that Browning never worked and lived for much of his life on the income of his wife, whose family owned sugar plantations in the Caribbean. As a self-proclaimed liberal (see his 1885 poem 'Why I am a Liberal'), he would not have seen a contradiction between his humanitarian commitment and his support of free trade. To illustrate his point, Viscusi quotes the apparently incongruous concluding lines of 'The Englishman in Italy' (1845) with their reference to the parliamentary debates leading up to the 1846 repeal of the British Corn Laws, which put an end to high import duties on grain from abroad (ll. 286–92). Contrasting this passage with the sensuous descriptions of Italian food and scantily clad bodies in lines 52–68 and 95–109, Viscusi argues:

> ■ The messages are exceedingly direct: Italy is the land of appetite. All that is missing in England, all that exquisite food and sunshine and random ancient religion, is there. All that is missing in Browning, likewise: the naked, the brown, 'Himself [the fisherman] too as bare to the middle.' [l. 65] [...] all of this is there to be bought, and cheaply. "Tis a sensual and timorous beauty,' he writes. 'How fair! but a slave' (ll. 195–96). It is not insignificant, for every detail is here meant to *tell*, that the fisherman's talisman is but a 'string and its brass coin.' [l. 67] These are delectable places, delectable persons, to be had almost for the asking [...]. In this light, the ending of the poem indeed makes more sense than one can readily gaze upon. Abolishing the Corn Laws, those final bastions between the great landlords and the flood of inexpensive European produce and grain, would make this vast catalogue of the delicious, as indeed it did do, part of the everyday English bill of fare. These were the days, recall, of the potato famine. People starved in the British Isles. Browning's political motive cannot have been more unexceptionable.[26] □

Viscusi here sees Browning not only promoting the belief that free trade (made possible by the abolition of the Corn Laws) will actually improve the food supply in Britain, but also giving in to the lure of money and the sensuality of Italian life and food which clashed with his self-image as a rational, sober, north European with a strong dislike for nudity. What Viscusi does not consider is that the poem is a dramatic monologue and that therefore the speaker's views do not need to coincide with the poet's own. Indeed, most analyses of the poem suggest that Browning distances himself from the speaker, so that the poem's emphasis shifts to a critical exposure of the Englishman's prejudices regarding Italy rather than being a giveaway of Browning's own prejudices.

This focus on Browning's critical analysis of his countrymen's nationalist myopia is exemplified by Alison Chapman's 'Robert Browning's Homesickness' (2012) about the popular anthology piece 'Home-Thoughts, from Abroad' (1845). This poem is usually read as 'a quintessential expression of English patriotism',[27] which clashes with Browning's otherwise cosmopolitan outlook. By contrast, Chapman argues that the poem – which she insists must be read as a dramatic utterance – is actually satirising the speaker's nostalgic patriotism which can idealise the home country because it is out of reach:

■ The speaker longs so intensely for his English home that he creates in his imagination a detailed and idealized pastoral scene ironically grounded on his frustrated (and rather irritable) desire for his homeland. The poem suggests that home can only be appreciated when abroad, and that what is directly in front of him – the exotic – can only be depreciated: 'The buttercups, the little children's dower' are ironically 'Far brighter than this gaudy melon-flower!' (ll. 19–20).[28] ☐

As Chapman points out, the speaker's idyllic pastoral completely ignores the unpleasant reality of the heavily industrial England of the 1840s with its social unrest:

■ Such insistence on England as a perfect pastoral sits uneasily with the poem's context in the hungry forties: with, for example, the People's Charter of May 1838, the Chartist riots of 1839 and 1842, the debate leading up to the Factory Act of 1844 (reducing the hours children aged 8–13 worked from 9 hours to 6.5 hours per day), and the Irish Famine of 1845–1849 [...][29] ☐

Chapman compares the poem's hidden references to social conditions at home to the more obvious critique of English politics in 'The Englishman in Italy'. The latter poem

■ implies a kind of tourist irony, for the speaker's sudden, throwaway, even casual opposition to the Corn Laws (which raised the price of corn and caused famine in Britain) to an Italian peasant girl, while he enjoys the sensual pleasures of Italy, could also be seen as a grandiose ineffectual gesture, never mind tactless.[...] The vision of England in Browning's poem can only exist *from* abroad, at one remove from the poem's political and social contexts. The poem's patriotic confidence falters for good reason.[30] ☐

Like 'The Englishman in Italy', 'Home-Thoughts, from Abroad' portrays a speaker whose detachment from the social problems of his home country should invite the reader to judge him critically. Chapman suggests that in presenting such a blinkered speaker, the poem makes an implicit argument for an engagement with the foreign. She relates the poem to the work of Christopher Keirstead on Browning's *Red Cotton Night-Cap Country* (1873), which 'investigates the uneasy ethics of cosmopolitanism, the sense that crossing into another culture depends on the luxury of mobility [...] and thus elitism and privilege'.[31] The later poem explores the tension between identification with and distance from the foreign culture – a tension Keirstead relates to that between sympathy and judgment which defines the dramatic monologue according to Robert Langbaum (see Chapter 3). Yet, ultimately, the poem praises Browning's French friend Joseph Milsand (1817–86) as an ideal of Anglo-French cosmopolitanism, occupying the liminal space between the two cultures. By contrast, Chapman concludes that 'Home-Thoughts, from Abroad' 'voices a catastrophic failure of the cosmopolitan identity with another culture, but this failure [...] is eminently productive' as a critical examination of the construction of nationhood.[32]

Browning's view of Italian national identity is the focus of Britta Martens' '"Oh, a day in the city-square, There is no such Pleasure in Life!": Robert Browning's Portrayal of Contemporary Italians' (2007). Like Viscusi's article, it grapples with the poet's paradoxical sympathy for the Risorgimento and appreciation of Renaissance art that clash with his denigration of Italian people. Martens suggests that Browning may have used the Italians as a convenient foil to confirm his ideal self-definition as a liberal, rational, Protestant Englishman. She argues that for his conceptualisation of the Italian national character, he drew on two conflicting theories.

The first, historical-political theory explains the Italians' perceived cultural degradation and submissiveness as temporary and a result of political oppression by foreign occupying powers. By contrast, the cultural flowering of Italy during the Renaissance is ascribed to the period's city republics with their emphasis on personal and civic liberty. This reading of Italian history influenced the Romantics and tallies with Fraser's and Hawlin's argument about Browning's recourse to Renaissance settings to encode his support for the movement for liberty in contemporary Italy.

The other, ahistorical and physiological theory about the Italian national temperament contrasts North and South European cultures. It had significant currency in eighteenth-century France and informs the ideas of other Victorian writers such as Ruskin. It 'argues for the influence of climate on the human organism, which in turn determines national temperament and thus the way a society is organised'.[33] According to Montesquieu's *De l'Esprit des lois* (1748),

> ■ the effect of the cold English climate on the blood and the body's humours leads to a concentration of bodily energy which breeds in Englishmen virtues like courage and honesty, while a hot climate makes the nervous system more sensitive and therefore more susceptible to pain and pleasure.[34] As a result, southern people are governed by their passions; they are immoral and inconstant. [...] A hot climate leads to physical and mental passivity, which makes southerners easy prey for 'tyranny', i.e. absolutist government. By contrast, the cold climate makes Englishmen courageous and impatient; therefore 'democracy' (i.e. government by the many where power can change hands easily) is the appropriate form of government for them.[35] □

This view of the Italians as sensuous, mentally lazy and submissive to authoritarian powers, both political and religious, is illustrated by 'Up at a Villa – Down in the City' (1855). In his praise of city life over the boredom of the countryside, the poem's Italian speaker takes a childish pleasure in sensory stimuli, be these the onomatopoeic 'spout and splash' and 'paddle and pash' of the fountain (ll. 26, 28), the sounds of church bells or the crude *'Bang-whang whang* goes the drum, *tootle-te-tootle* the fife' (ll. 53, 63) of a band. The speaker's characterisation thus agrees with Montesquieu's theory that 'the Italian is governed by his sense impressions, and as a result his outlook on life is a hedonistic desire for pleasures of the senses'.[36]

The poem also suggests Montesquieu's causal link between mental passivity and the uncritical acceptance of autocratic authorities. The speaker's insensitivity to the power wielded by the religious and secular authorities appears in his inability to appreciate the signifiers of power, such as the symbolic value of a religious procession, which is protected by the Duke's guard and which he only values as spectacle (ll. 59–62). He is even less critical of the political violence perpetrated by the secular government, which is again only seen as entertainment:

> ■ The speaker's inability to think critically is further illustrated by his acceptance of the description by the authorities of three men who have been executed as 'liberal thieves' (45). He reiterates the conjunction of crime with political orientation that has been made by the authorities, and instead of showing sympathy with the men, cares only for their entertainment value which is the same as that of 'the new play' (44). A brief mention of 'some little new law of the Duke's' (46) and the absence of any indication as to what this law is about conveys the speaker's utter indifference to political decisions and the Duke's legislative power.[37] □

The ridiculous speaker of this poem is quite clearly meant to be read as a parody of a stereotype but he displays an important component of Browning's analysis of the problems faced by contemporary Italy.

Browning's historical poems and his poems about Italy show him responding to contemporary discourses about these subjects. Paradoxically, these texts about distant times and cultures prove him to be a man of his time and his British society, keen to make his poetry relevant to a wider public. The critics covered in this chapter explore how he deals with communicating his political views during a period when their direct expression was not always appreciated by the readership. Historical and / or geographical distancing become oblique ways of recommending his liberal and democratic values to a British audience that would on the whole have been more conservative than he was.

All three sections of this chapter have shown central disagreements among critics. The analyses of the Italian poems with their negative portrayal of the Italians evoke a perennial problem of Browning scholarship, i.e. the question to what extent statements made by the speakers of dramatic poems can be attributed to the poet himself. And in the historical poems, the arguments that Browning should be aligned with Michelet's Romantic historiography or alternatively with the more scientific and self-conscious school of Ranke are equally convincing, but they seem mutually exclusive. Yet the student of Browning's work should not be too surprised to find that the poet oscillates between opposing positions or is content to uphold contradictory views. A key feature of his dramatic monologue and of the multiperspectivism and relativism of *The Ring and the Book* is Browning's ability to explore various perspectives on the same subject without having to commit to a single one. This refusal to be pinned down to fixed ideas makes for a less neat classification of his aesthetics but it also makes his poetry more complex and intriguing for the reader, especially nowadays when readers are more suspicious than Browning's contemporaries of theories and ideas that lay claim to absolute validity.

CONCLUSION

# Browning at 200 and Beyond

This Reader's Guide has provided an overview of the main critical preoccupations in Browning studies up to and beyond his Bicentenary in 2012. Browning's crucial historical position as an innovator responding to the overpowering Romantic tradition, his dominance in the genre of the dramatic monologue, his discussion of aesthetics, and his engagement with contemporary Victorian debates about issues such as gender, politics and national identity or developments in historiography and biblical scholarship have been highlighted as major areas of critical analysis.

Browning's work has proven to lend itself to a wide variety of theoretical perspectives and he will undoubtedly continue to attract new critical approaches. A recent striking example is Suzanne Bailey's 2010 monograph which draws on cognitive research into Attention Deficit / Hyperactivity Disorder.[1] She interprets Browning's stylistic peculiarities as symptoms of a neurological condition rather than deliberate authorial choices, thus positing a wholly new, biographically based explanation for the poet's obscurity.

It is likely, however, that most criticism in years to come will continue to relate Browning's poetry to its cultural and historical contexts, given the power of the poet's realism and the unusually wide range of characters and situations he portrays. Despite Victorian poetry's neglected existence in the shadow of the more accessible and popular novel, this augurs well for the future of Browning studies, with the trend in Victorian studies over recent years moving away from traditional literary analysis towards a consideration of broader media and cultural phenomena.

This was certainly a view put forward by some of the leading names in Browning criticism – Isobel Armstrong, Sandra Donaldson, Warwick Slinn, Herbert Tucker and John Woolford – in a roundtable discussion about the future of Browning studies for the Browning Bicentenary special issue of the journal *Victorian Poetry* (Winter 2012). Their consensus was that Browning's work, with its rich blend of the historical and the topical, offers plenty to sustain new analyses as 'Victorian literature' finds itself increasingly superseded by multi-media 'Victorian studies'. In her contribution to this discussion, Armstrong very pertinently stressed Browning's own interest in various aspects of material culture that have a high visibility in his realism:

> ■ Behind the monologue he explored his interest in a many-times mediated world, from the virtual image to the celebrity, which was emerging in the nineteenth century. This interest was not simply a matter of superficial 'topical' references to newspapers, the photograph, and spectacle: he saw that new forms of mediation shape the language and the form of culture in a dynamic way and his poems exemplify this new mediation in their structure and poetic speech acts.[2] □

The section on realism in this Guide (see Chapter 5), with its references to material culture, suggests where such readings might take us. There have already been a few analyses of Browning poems which relate them to developments in material culture, such as an article by Ivan Kreilkamp and a book section by Isobel Armstrong on photography and optics, and two contributions to an essay collection about literary bric-à-brac by Bernard Beatty and Jennifer McDonnell suggesting analogies between Browning's interest in collectible curiosities and the oddity of his style.[3] The poet's interest in other media, above all sculpture, which he at one time pursued quite earnestly, offers another potential field of exploration.

Part of the burgeoning interest in Victorian culture is reflected by a growth in publications about the period's religious poetry. Recent books about Victorian religious writing and articles about specific Browning poems have added to our understanding of the poet's work in relation to contemporary religious debates and more conventional devotional verse.[4] In particular, research into his engagement with Higher Criticism, represented notably in this Guide by Shaffer's article (see Chapter 7), has been flourishing of late.[5] Building on these contributions, more research might fruitfully be developed on Browning's position at the intersection of religion and poetry.

Yet another growth area in Browning criticism promises to be the literary afterlife of his works, both with regard to their reception in various cultures and their adaptations by later authors and other media.[6] Although the new field of Neo-Victorian research concentrates primarily on modern novels and films which represent or engage with Victorian literature and culture, John Morton's recent work on the Scottish poet Mick Imlah (1956–2009) shows the potential for analysing twentieth- and twenty-first-century poetry that responds to Browning's work and adapts the dramatic monologue.[7]

One potential problem for the reader aspiring to a comprehensive appreciation of Browning's oeuvre and aesthetics is that almost all recent scholarship focuses of necessity on a restricted corpus of texts. This is a further feature of Browning criticism in the changing world of literary scholarship: as it becomes harder for researchers to find publishers for single-author monographs – especially if the subject is a dead, white, male, heterosexual and middle-class poet – studies of Browning's work are most likely to be limited to a small selection of texts analysed in articles and book chapters or, if they feature in book-length studies, juxtaposed with the work of other authors.[8] Recent publications that might illustrate this trend are Richard Cronin's close-reading study *Reading Victorian Poetry* (2012) or the over 900-page *Oxford Handbook of Victorian Poetry* (2013).[9] Browning occupies a central position in both Cronin's book and many of the essays in the *Oxford Handbook* – confirmation that he is maintaining his status as a major Victorian poet despite the difficult critical climate for canonical authors in recent years.

The one safe preserve of exclusive and close attention to Browning will be the ongoing editions of *The Brownings' Correspondence* and the Oxford and Longman critical editions of Browning's work. The editors' extensive contextual research for these projects will surely shed further light on the poet's participation in contemporary debates about current events, media, politics and aesthetics. Critics can also look forward to an enriched sense of Browning's eclectic reading and of his social interaction with contemporary figures, especially in his later years as a London socialite when he rubbed shoulders with many famous Victorians.

In the final analysis, Browning's rootedness in the writings of both predecessors and contemporaries, the idiosyncrasies of his poetic language and his perennial preoccupation with the medium of language more widely convinced the above roundtable of eminent Browning specialists that the poet will continue to be studied as a poet of textuality despite the shift in critical fashion from the printed medium to aural and visual media. As Warwick Slinn puts it, Browning is a 'supremely verbal person (living at the vortex of a semiotic world, perceiving and arranging his life through reading, by means of letters, dictionaries, books, newspapers, poems)'.[10] A poet whose main work culminates in the exclamation 'For how else know we save by worth of word?' (*The Ring and the Book*, I, 837), whose poetry discusses and demonstrates above all else how the self makes sense of the world through language, cannot but continue to fascinate readers and critics, no matter how our understanding of the self, the mind and language evolves.

# Notes

## INTRODUCTION

1. See William S. Peterson, *Interrogating the Oracle: A History of the London Browning Society* (Athens, OH: Ohio University Press, 1969); Louise Greer, *Browning and America* (Chapel Hill: University of North Carolina Press, 1952). For an extended survey of Browning's critical reception until 1995, see Patricia O'Neill, *Robert Browning and Twentieth-Century Criticism* (Columbia Camden House, 1995).
2. O'Neill (1995), pp. 5–7.
3. Peterson (1969), p. 5.
4. Henry Jones, *Browning as a Philosophical and Religious Thinker* (Glasgow: James MacLehose & Son, 1891); George Santayana, 'The Poetry of Barbarism', *Interpretations of Poetry and Religion* (New York: Scribner, 1900).
5. See George Bornstein, 'Pound's Parleyings with Robert Browning', *Ezra Pound Among the Poets*, ed. George Bornstein (Chicago and London: University of Chicago Press, 1985), pp. 106–27; Mary Ellis Gibson, *Epic Reinvented: Ezra Pound and the Victorians* (Ithaca: Cornell University Press, 1995), pp. 39–78.
6. T.S. Eliot, *Selected Essays* (London: Faber and Faber, 1951), p. 288.
7. Eliot (1951), p. 287.
8. Eliot (1951), p. 17.
9. F.R. Leavis, *New Bearings in English Poetry* (London: Chatto and Windus, 1932).
10. Robert Langbaum, *The Poetry of Experience: The Dramatic Monologue in Modern Literary Tradition* [1957] (Chicago: University of Chicago Press, 2nd edn 1985).
11. Harold Bloom, *The Ringers in the Tower: Studies in Romantic Tradition* (Chicago: University of Chicago Press, 1971); *The Anxiety of Influence: A Theory of Poetry* (New York: Oxford University Press, 1973); *A Map of Misreading* (New York: Oxford University Press, 1975); *Poetry and Repression: Revisionism from Blake to Stevens* (New Haven: Yale University Press, 1976).
12. Herbert F. Tucker, *Browning's Beginnings: The Art of Disclosure* (Minneapolis: Minnesota University Press, 1980); E. Warwick Slinn, *Browning and the Fictions of Identity* (Basingstoke: Palgrave Macmillan, 1982).
13. Clyde de L. Ryals, *Browning's Later Poetry 1871–1889* (Ithaca: Cornell University Press, 1975); *Becoming Browning: The Poems and Plays of Robert Browning, 1833–1846* (Columbus: Ohio State University Press, 1983).
14. Dorothy Mermin, *The Audience in the Poem: Five Victorian Poets* (New Brunswick: Rutgers University Press, 1983); Lee Erickson, *Robert Browning: His Poetry and His Audiences* (Ithaca: Cornell University Press, 1984).
15. John Woolford, *Browning the Revisionary* (London: Palgrave Macmillan, 1988); David E. Latané, 'Browning's *Sordello* and the Aesthetics of Difficulty', *English Literary Studies* 40 (1987).
16. Mary Ellis Gibson, *History and the Prism of Art: Browning's Poetic Experiments* (Columbus: Ohio State University Press, 1987); Loy D. Martin, *Browning's Dramatic Monologues and the Post-Romantic Subject* (Baltimore: Johns Hopkins University Press, 1985).
17. Roma A. King *et al.* (general eds), *The Complete Works of Robert Browning*, 17 vols (Athens, OH, and Waco, TX: Ohio University Press and Baylor University, 1969–2012);

John Woolford, Daniel Karlin and Joseph Phelan (eds), *The Poems of Browning* (4 vols to date) (London: Longman, 1991–); Ian Jack and Michael Meredith (general eds), *The Poetical Works of Robert Browning*, 15 vols (9 vols to date) (Oxford: Clarendon Press, 1983–); Philip Kelley, *et al.* (eds), *The Brownings' Correspondence*, 40 vols (21 vols to date) (Winfield: Wedgestone Press, 1984–).

## 1 ROMANTICISM: BROWNING AND SHELLEY

1 *Letters of Percy Bysshe Shelley. With an introductory essay*, by Robert Browning (London: Moxon, 1852).
2 See Samuel Taylor Coleridge, *Biographia Literaria or Biographical Sketches of My Literary Life and Opinions* (London: Everyman, 1965), p. 92.
3 'Introductory Essay [Essay on Shelley]', in Adam Roberts (ed.), *Robert Browning: The Major Works* (Oxford: Oxford University Press, 1997), pp. 574–90, at p. 574–5.
4 Roberts (1997), p. 576.
5 Roberts (1997), p. 577.
6 Roberts (1997), p. 574.
7 Roberts (1997), pp. 576–7.
8 'Advertisement' to *Dramatic Lyrics*, in John Pettigrew and Thomas J. Collins (eds), *Robert Browning: The Poems*, vol. 1 (New Haven and Harmondsworth: Yale University Press and Penguin, 1981), p. 347.
9 Philip Drew, 'Browning's *Essay on Shelley*', *Victorian Poetry* 1 (1963), pp. 1–6, at p. 5.
10 Drew (1963), p. 4.
11 Drew (1963), p. 4.
12 Thomas J. Collins, 'Browning's *Essay on Shelley*: In Context', *Victorian Poetry* 2 (1964), pp. 119–24, at p. 121.
13 Roberts (1997), pp. 577–8.
14 Roberts (1997), p. 578.
15 Drew (1963), p. 5.
16 'Essay on Chatterton', in John Woolford, Daniel Karlin and Joseph Phelan, (eds), *The Poems of Browning* (4 vols to date) (London: Longman, 1991–), 2: 475–503, at p. 484.
17 Mrs Sutherland Orr, *Life and Letters of Robert Browning* (London: Smith, Elder, 1891), p. 42.
18 Frederick A. Pottle, *Shelley and Browning: A Myth and Some Facts* (Chicago: Pembroke, 1923); John Maynard, *Browning's Youth* (Cambridge, MA: Harvard University Press, 1977).
19 Maynard (1977), p. 204.
20 Woolford, Karlin and Phelan (1991–), 1: 17–18.
21 William Clyde DeVane, *A Browning Handbook*, 2nd edn (New York: Appleton-Century-Crofts, 1955), p. 11.
22 DeVane (1955), p. 11.
23 Herbert F. Tucker, 'Browning as Escape Artist: Avoidance and Intimacy', *Robert Browning in Contexts*, ed. John Woolford (Winfield: Wedgestone Press, 1998), pp. 1–25, at p. 5.
24 Woolford, Karlin and Phelan (1991–), 1: 20.
25 Tucker (1998), pp. 5–6.
26 Tucker (1998), p. 9.
27 Michael G. Yetman, 'Exorcising Shelley Out of Browning: *Sordello* and the Problem of Poetic Identity', *Victorian Poetry* 13 (1975), pp. 79–98, at pp. 81–5.
28 Yetman (1975), pp. 86–7.
29 Yetman (1975), pp. 94–8.
30 Betty Miller, *Robert Browning: A Portrait* (London: Murray, 1952), p. 11.
31 Harold Bloom, *The Anxiety of Influence: A Theory of Poetry* [1973] (Oxford: Oxford University Press, 2nd edn 1997), p. 30.

32 See the table on p. 84 of Harold Bloom, *A Map of Misreading* (New York: Oxford University Press, 1975).
33 Bloom (1975), p. 106.
34 Bloom (1975), pp. 117–18.
35 Bloom (1975), p. 106.
36 Bloom (1975), p. 108.
37 Bloom (1975), p. 109.
38 Bloom (1975), p. 110.
39 Bloom (1975), pp. 111–12.
40 Bloom (1975), p. 112.
41 Bloom (1975), p. 113.
42 Bloom (1975), pp. 119–22.
43 Bloom (1975), pp. 175–6. See also Harold Bloom, 'Browning's *Childe Roland*: All Things Deformed and Broken', *The Ringers in the Tower: Studies in Romantic Tradition* (Chicago: University of Chicago Press, 1971), pp. 157–67.
44 Harold Bloom, *Poetry and Repression: Revisionism from Blake to Stevens* (New Haven: Yale University Press, 1976), p. 175.
45 Bloom (1976), pp. 177–8.
46 Bloom (1976), pp. 201–4.

## 2 ROMANTICISM: DEBT AND DEFIANCE

1 John Haydn Baker, *Browning and Wordsworth* (Madison: Fairleigh Dickinson University Press, 2004), p. 20.
2 Baker (2004), pp. 20–1.
3 Baker (2004), p. 21.
4 Baker (2004), p. 59.
5 Harold Bloom, *Poetry and Repression: Revisionism from Blake to Stevens* (New Haven: Yale University Press, 1976), p. 17.
6 Lawrence Kramer, 'The "Intimations" Ode and Victorian Romanticism', *Victorian Poetry* 18 (1980), pp. 315–35, at pp. 316–17.
7 Kramer (1980), pp. 332–3.
8 Kramer (1980), p. 333.
9 Kramer (1980), p. 333.
10 Kramer (1980), pp. 334–5.
11 Clyde de L. Ryals, *Becoming Browning: The Poems and Plays of Robert Browning, 1833–1846* (Columbus: Ohio State University Press, 1983); *Browning's Later Poetry, 1871–1889* (Ithaca: Cornell University Press, 1975); *A World of Possibilities: Romantic Irony in Victorian Literature* (Columbus: Ohio State University Press, 1990).
12 Ryals (1983), pp. 3–4.
13 [Kathleen] Wheeler, Preface to *German Aesthetic and Literary Criticism* [(London: Cambridge University Press, 1984)], p. viii. [Rigg's note].
14 Patricia Diane Rigg, *Robert Browning's Romantic Irony in 'The Ring and the Book'* (London: Associated University Press, 1999), p. 21. Rigg here cites Novalis, *Miscellaneous Writings* in Wheeler (1984), p. 12.
15 Ryals (1983), pp. 4–6.
16 Rigg (1999), p. 24.
17 Ryals (1983), p. 255.
18 Ryals (1983), p. 255.
19 'Introductory Essay [Essay on Shelley]', in Adam Roberts (ed.), *Robert Browning: The Major Works*, (Oxford: Oxford University Press, 1997), pp. 574–90, at p. 576.
20 Catherine Maxwell, *The Female Sublime from Milton to Swinburne: Bearing Blindness* (Manchester: Manchester University Press, 2001), p. 149. Maxwell is citing Edmund

Burke, *A Philosophical Enquiry into the Origin of Our Ideas of the Sublime and Beautiful*, ed. James T. Boulton (Oxford: Basil Blackwell, 1987), p. 62.
21 Maxwell (2001), p. 150.
22 Maxwell (2001), pp. 150–1.
23 Maxwell (2001), p. 151.
24 Herbert F. Tucker, *Browning's Beginnings: The Art of Disclosure* (Minneapolis: University of Minnesota Press, 1980), p. 5.
25 Barbara Herrnstein Smith, *Poetic Closure: A Study of How Poems End* (Chicago and London: University of Chicago Press, 1968).
26 Tucker (1980), p. 6.
27 Tucker (1980), p. 6.
28 Tucker (1980), pp. 8–9.
29 Tucker (1980), p. 9.
30 Tucker (1980), p. 10.
31 David E. Latané, 'Browning's *Sordello* and the Aesthetics of Difficulty', *English Literary Studies* 40 (1987), p. 11.
32 See Wolfgang Iser, *The Act of Reading: A Theory of Aesthetic Response* (Baltimore: Johns Hopkins University Press, 1978).
33 Latané (1987), p. 35.
34 'Preface' to *Paracelsus*, in John Pettigrew and Thomas J. Collins (eds), *Robert Browning: The Poems*, vol. 1 (New Haven and Harmondsworth: Yale University Press and Penguin, 1981), p. 1030.
35 For the text of the 1840 version of *Sordello* and all other first editions of Browning's work, see John Woolford, Daniel Karlin and Joseph Phelan (eds), *The Poems of Browning* (4 vols to date) (London: Longman, 1991–).
36 Ian Jack, 'Browning on *Sordello* and *Men and Women*: Unpublished Letters to James T. Fields', *Huntington Library Quarterly* 45 (1982), pp. 185–99, at p. 196.
37 Latané (1987), pp. 38–9.
38 Britta Martens, *Browning, Victorian Poetics and the Romantic Legacy: Challenging the Personal Voice* (Farnham: Ashgate, 2011), pp. 12–13.
39 Martens (2011), pp. 15–16.
40 Martens (2011), p. 20.
41 Martens (2011), p. 20.

## 3 THE DRAMATIC MONOLOGUE: FORM AND THE READER

1 For the influence of Browning on later dramatic monologues, see Ekbert Faas, *Retreat into the Mind: Victorian Poetry and the Rise of Psychiatry* (Princeton: Princeton University Press, 1988), pp. 145–215.
2 'Advertisement' to *Dramatic Lyrics*, in John Pettigrew and Thomas J. Collins (eds), *Robert Browning: The Poems*, vol. 1 (New Haven and Harmondsworth: Yale University Press and Penguin, 1981), p. 347.
3 A. Dwight Culler, 'Monodrama and the Dramatic Monologue', *PMLA* 90.3 (1975), pp. 366–85, at p. 366.
4 Isobel Armstrong, *Victorian Poetry: Poetry, Poetics and Politics* (London: Routledge, 1993), p. 294.
5 Armstrong (1993), 318–32; Cynthia Scheinberg, 'Recasting "sympathy and judgment": Amy Levy, Women Poets, and the Victorian Dramatic Monologue', *Victorian Poetry* 35 (1997), pp. 173–91; Glennis Byron, 'Rethinking the Dramatic Monologue: Victorian Women Poets and Social Critique', *Victorian Women Poets*, ed. Alison Chapman, *Essays and Studies* 56 (2003), pp. 79–98.
6 Ina Beth Sessions, 'The Dramatic Monologue', *PMLA* 62.2 (1947), pp. 503–16, at p. 508.

7. Michael Mason, 'Browning and the Dramatic Monologue', *Writers and Their Background: Robert Browning*, ed. Isobel Armstrong (London: Bell, 1974), pp. 231–66, at p. 232.
8. Mason (1974), p. 234.
9. Mason (1974), p. 235.
10. Mason (1974), pp. 235–6.
11. Alan Sinfield, *Dramatic Monologue* (London: Methuen, 1977), p. 24.
12. Sinfield (1977), p. 25. Sinfield borrows the term 'feint' from Käte Hamburger, *The Logic of Literature*, 2nd edn, trans. Marilyn J. Rose (Bloomington: Indiana University Press, 1973).
13. Sinfield (1977), p. 25.
14. Philip Drew, *The Poetry of Browning: A Critical Introduction* (London: Methuen, 1970), p. 15.
15. Drew (1970), p. 16.
16. Robert Langbaum, *The Poetry of Experience: The Dramatic Monologue in Modern Literary Tradition* [1957] (Chicago and London: University of Chicago Press, 2nd edn 1985), at pp. 28–37.
17. Langbaum (1985), p. 11.
18. Langbaum (1985), pp. 21–2.
19. Langbaum (1985), pp. 51–2.
20. Langbaum (1985), p. 105.
21. Langbaum (1985), p. 105.
22. Langbaum (1985), p. 79.
23. Langbaum (1985), p. 77.
24. Langbaum (1985), pp. 3–4.
25. Langbaum (1985), p. 82.
26. Langbaum (1985), p. 83.
27. Langbaum (1985), p. 86.
28. Langbaum (1985), p. 106.
29. Langbaum (1985), pp. 107–8.
30. E. Warwick Slinn, *Browning and the Fictions of Identity* (London and Basingstoke: Palgrave Macmillan, 1982), p. 7.
31. Slinn (1982), p. 7.
32. Slinn (1982), p. 8. Slinn's bracketed page references are to Langbaum (1957).
33. Slinn (1982), p. 9.
34. Slinn (1982), pp. 9–10.
35. Slinn (1982), p. 13.
36. Slinn (1982), p. 76.
37. Slinn (1982), pp. 156–7.
38. See E. Warwick Slinn, *The Discourse of Self in Victorian Poetry* (London: Palgrave Macmillan, 1991).
39. Herbert Tucker, 'From Monomania to Monologue: "St. Simeon Stylites" and the Rise of the Victorian Dramatic Monologue', *Victorian Poetry* 22.2 (1984), pp. 121–37, at p. 134fn.
40. Tucker (1984), p. 134fn.
41. Ralph Rader, 'The Dramatic Monologue and Related Lyric Forms', *Critical Inquiry* 3.1 (1976), pp. 131–51, at p. 132.
42. Rader (1976), p. 133.
43. Rader (1976), pp. 138–9.
44. Scheinberg (1997), pp. 176–7.
45. Scheinberg (1997), p. 178.
46. Scheinberg (1997), p. 178.

47 John Maynard, 'Reading the Reader in Robert Browning's Dramatic Monologues', in *Browning e Venezia*, ed. Sergio Perosa (Firenze: Olschki, 1991), pp. 165–77, at p. 172. Reprinted in Mary Ellis Gibson (ed.), *Critical Essays on Robert Browning* (New York: G. K. Hall, 1992), pp. 69–78.
48 Maynard (1991), p. 177.
49 Jennifer Wagner-Lawlor, 'The Pragmatics of Silence, and the Figuration of the Reader in Browning's Dramatic Monologues', *Victorian Poetry* 35 (1997), pp. 287–302, at p. 288.
50 Paolo Scarpi, 'The Eloquence of Silence: Aspects of Power Without Words', in [Maria Grazia] Ciani, [(ed.), *The Regions of Silence: Studies of the Difficulty of Communicating* (Amsterdam: J. C. Gieben, 1987),] p. 23. [Wagner-Lawlor's note].
51 Wagner-Lawlor (1997), pp. 289–90.
52 Wagner-Lawlor (1997), pp. 290–1.
53 Wagner-Lawlor (1997), p. 293.
54 Wagner-Lawlor (1997), p. 297.
55 Dorothy Mermin, *The Audience in the Poem: Five Victorian Poets* (New Brunswick: Rutgers University Press, 1983), p. 13.
56 Mermin (1983), p. 2.
57 Mermin (1983), p. 4.
58 Mermin (1983), p. 11.
59 Mermin (1983), pp. 48–9.
60 Mermin (1983), p. 53.
61 Mermin (1983), p. 55.
62 Mermin (1983), pp. 58, 63.
63 Lee Erickson, *Robert Browning: His Poetry and His Audiences* (Ithaca and London: Cornell University Press, 1984), p. 156.
64 Erickson (1984), p. 20.
65 Erickson (1984), pp. 17–18.
66 Erickson (1984), p. 84.
67 G. W. F. Hegel, *The Phenomenology of Mind*, trans J. Baille, 2nd edn (New York: Macmillan, 1931), p. 229. […] [Erickson's note].
68 Erickson (1984), pp. 155–6.
69 See the discussion of the master/slave relationship in *Phenomenology of Mind*, pp. 234–40. [Erickson's note].
70 Langbaum (1985), pp. 75–159, 182–209. [Erickson's note].
71 Erickson (1984), pp. 157–8.
72 J. L. Austin, *How to Do Things with Words*, ed. J. O. Urmson and Marina Sbisà, 2nd edn (Cambridge, MA: Harvard University Press, 1975), p. 6. […] [Pearsall's note]. Cornelia Pearsall, *Tennyson's Rapture: Transformation in the Victorian Dramatic Monologue* (Oxford: Oxford University Press, 2008), p. 20.
73 Pearsall (2008), p. 20.
74 Langbaum (1985), p. 183.
75 Cornelia D. J. Pearsall, 'The Dramatic Monologue', *The Cambridge Companion to Victorian Poetry*, ed. Joseph Bristow (Cambridge: Cambridge University Press, 2000), pp. 67–88, at p. 68.
76 Pearsall (2000), p. 71.
77 Pearsall (2000), p. 72.
78 Pearsall (2000), p. 72.
79 E. Warwick Slinn, *Victorian Poetry as Cultural Critique: The Politics of Performative Language* (Charlottesville: University of Virginia Press, 2003), p. 1.
80 Slinn (2003), p. 37.
81 Slinn (2003), p. 37.
82 Slinn (2003), p. 44.

83  Slinn (2003), p. 46.
84  Slinn (2003), pp. 51–2.
85  Slinn (2003), p. 54.

## 4  THE DRAMATIC MONOLOGUE: CAUSES AND CONTEXT

1  Benjamin Willis Fuson, *Browning and His English Predecessors in the Dramatic Monolog* (Iowa City: State University of Iowa Humanistic Studies 8 (1948)), p. 23.
2  Alan Sinfield, *Dramatic Monologue* (London: Methuen, 1977), p. 42.
3  A. Dwight Culler, 'Monodrama and the Dramatic Monologue', *PMLA* 90.3 (1975), pp. 366–85, at p. 368.
4  Culler (1975), pp. 369–84.
5  Robert Langbaum, *The Poetry of Experience: The Dramatic Monologue in Modern Literary Tradition* [1957] (Chicago: University of Chicago Press, 2nd edn 1985), at pp. 57–74.
6  W. David Shaw, *Origins of the Monologue: The Hidden God* (Toronto: University of Toronto Press, 1999), p. 65. See also pp. 62–85.
7  Shaw (1999), pp. 86–126. See John Keats, Letter to George and Tom Keats, 21–27 December 1817, in *The Complete Poetical Works and Letters of John Keats*, ed. Horace Elisha Scudder (Cambridge, MA: Houghton, Mifflin, 1899), p. 277.
8  Shaw (1999), pp. 42–61.
9  Isobel Armstrong, *Victorian Poetry: Poetry, Poetics and Politics* (London: Routledge, 1993), pp. 112–61.
10  Armstrong (1993), p. 12.
11  J. Hillis Miller, *The Disappearance of God: Five Nineteenth-Century Writers* [1963] (Cambridge, MA, and London: Harvard University Press, 1975), p. 4.
12  Miller (1975), pp. 5–6.
13  Miller (1975), p. 9.
14  Miller (1975), p. 98.
15  Miller (1975), pp. 100–1.
16  Miller (1975), pp. 104–5.
17  Loy D. Martin, *Browning's Dramatic Monologues and the Post-Romantic Subject* (Baltimore and London: Johns Hopkins University Press, 1985), pp. 25–6.
18  Martin (1985), p. 28.
19  Britta Martens, 'Dramatic Monologue, Detective Fiction and the Search for Meaning', *Nineteenth-Century Literature* 66.2 (2011), pp. 195–218, at p. 200.
20  Martens (2011), p. 202.
21  Martens (2011), pp. 202–3.
22  Martens (2011), p. 218.
23  Martens (2011), p. 211.
24  Martens (2011), p. 216.
25  Michael Mason, 'Browning and the Dramatic Monologue', *Robert Browning*, ed. Isobel Armstrong (London: Bell, 1974), pp. 231–66, at pp. 255–66.
26  Mason (1974), p. 260.
27  Ekbert Faas, *Retreat into the Mind: Victorian Poetry and the Rise of Psychiatry* (Princeton: Princeton University Press, 1988).
28  Barry L. Popowich, 'Porphyria is Madness', *Studies in Browning and his Circle* 22 (1999), pp. 59–66.
29  Ellen L. O'Brien, *Crime in Verse: The Poetics of Murder in the Victorian Era* (Columbus: Ohio State University Press, 2008).
30  O'Brien (2008), p. 25.
31  O'Brien (2008), p. 118.
32  O'Brien (2008), p. 131.
33  O'Brien (2008), p. 137.

34 O'Brien (2008), p. 133.
35 O'Brien (2008), p. 142.
36 O'Brien (2008), p. 25.
37 Gregory Tate, *The Poet's Mind: The Psychology of Victorian Poetry 1830–1870* (Oxford: Oxford University Press, 2012), p. 3.
38 Tate (2012), p. 6.
39 Tate (2012), p. 32.
40 Tate (2012), p. 51.
41 Tate (2012), pp. 56–7.
42 Tate (2012), p. 154.
43 George Henry Lewes, 'The Heart and the Brain', *Fortnightly Review* 1 (1865), pp. 66–74.
44 Tate (2012), pp. 169–70.
45 Tate (2012), p. 173.
46 Tate (2012), p. 175.
47 Oscar Wilde, 'The True Function and Value of Criticism', *Nineteenth Century* 28 (1890): 123–47, reprinted in *Robert Browning's Poetry: Authoritative Texts, Criticism*, ed. James F. Loucks and Andrew M. Stauffer (New York: Norton, 2007), pp. 517–19, at p. 518.

## 5 AESTHETICS: REALISM AND THE GROTESQUE

1 Oscar Wilde, 'The True Function and Value of Criticism', *Nineteenth Century* 28 (1890), pp. 123–47, reprinted in *Robert Browning's Poetry: Authoritative Texts, Criticism*, ed. James F. Loucks and Andrew M. Stauffer (New York: Norton, 2007), pp. 517–19, at pp. 518–19.
2 Walter Bagehot, 'Wordsworth, Tennyson, and Browning; or, Pure, Ornate, and Grotesque Art in English Poetry', *The National Review* 19 (1864), pp. 27–67, reprinted in Loucks and Stauffer (2007), pp. 504–9, at pp. 504–5.
3 Letter of 19 November 1868 in Richard Curle (ed.), *Robert Browning and Julia Wedgwood: A Broken Friendship as Revealed in their Letters* (London: John Murray & Cape, 1937), p. 158.
4 John Woolford, *Robert Browning* (Tavistock: Northcote House, 2007), p. 47.
5 Woolford (2007), pp. 47–8.
6 Woolford (2007), p. 50.
7 Woolford (2007), pp. 52–3.
8 E. Warwick Slinn, *Browning and the Fictions of Identity* (Basingstoke: Palgrave Macmillan, 1982), pp. 3–4.
9 J. Hillis Miller, *The Disappearance of God: Five Nineteenth-Century Writers* [1963] (Cambridge, MA, and London: Harvard University Press, 1975), pp. 119–20.
10 Bagehot in Loucks and Stauffer (2007), p. 504.
11 Bagehot in Loucks and Stauffer (2007), p. 505.
12 Bagehot in Loucks and Stauffer (2007), p. 507.
13 George Santayana, 'The Poetry of Barbarism', *Interpretations of Poetry and Religion* (London: Adam and Charles Black, 1900), p. 189.
14 Santayana (1900), p. 211.
15 Bagehot in Loucks and Stauffer (2007), p. 507.
16 See John Ruskin, 'Grotesque Renaissance', *The Stones of Venice*, Vol. III, chapter 3, and 'On the Nature of the Gothic', *The Stones of Venice*, Vol. II, chapter 6, *The Works of John Ruskin*, ed. E. T. Cook and Alexander Wedderburn (London: Allen, 1903–12), vol. 11.
17 Woolford (2007), p. 15.
18 Woolford (2007), p. 16.
19 Woolford (2007), p. 57.
20 Woolford (2007), p. 56.
21 Woolford (2007), p. 56.
22 Woolford (2007), p. 60.

23 Isobel Armstrong, 'Browning and the "Grotesque Style"', in *The Major Victorian Poets: Reconsiderations*, ed. Isobel Armstrong (London: Routledge, 1969), pp. 93–123; Armstrong, *Victorian Poetry: Poetry, Poetics and Politics* (London: Routledge, 1993), pp. 284–317.
24 *Modern Painters*, Vol. IV [1856], *The Works of John Ruskin*, ed. E. T. Cook and Alexander Wedderburn (London: Allen, 1903–12), 6: 446–9, reprinted in Loucks and Stauffer (2007), pp. 502–4, at p. 503.
25 Armstrong (1993), p. 286.
26 Armstrong (1993), pp. 287–8.
27 David L. DeLaura, 'The Context of Browning's Painter Poems: Aesthetics, Polemics, Historics', PMLA 95 (1980), pp. 367–88, at p. 367.
28 Alexis François Rio, *The Poetry of Christian Art* (London: Bosworth, 1854), p. 91.
29 DeLaura (1980), p. 371.
30 DeLaura (1980), p. 377.
31 DeLaura's page reference is to Rio (1854).
32 DeLaura (1980), pp. 378–9.
33 DeLaura (1980), p. 379. The page reference to *Locke* is to Charles Kingsley, *Alton Locke* (London: Macmillan, 1873).
34 DeLaura (1980), p. 380.
35 DeLaura (1980), p. 380.
36 Laurence Lerner, 'Browning's Painters', *Yearbook of English Studies* 36.2 (2006), pp. 96–108, at p. 99.
37 Lerner (2006), pp. 99–100.
38 Harold Bloom, *Poetry and Repression: Revisionism from Blake to Stevens* (New Haven: Yale University Press, 1976), pp. 192–3.
39 Lerner (2006), pp. 103–4.
40 Lerner (2006), pp. 105–6.
41 Loy D. Martin, *Browning's Dramatic Monologues and the Post-Romantic Subject* (Baltimore and London: Johns Hopkins University Press, 1985), p. 38.
42 Martin (1985), pp. 41–2.
43 Martin (1985), p. 43.
44 Martin (1985), pp. 43–4.
45 Martin (1985), p. 44.
46 Martin (1985), p. 46.
47 Martin (1985), pp. 46–7.

## 6 LOVE AND GENDER RELATIONS

1 Betty Miller, *Robert Browning: A Portrait* (London: Murray, 1952), p. 11.
2 See e.g. J. E. Shaw, 'The "Donna Angelicata" in *The Ring and the Book*', PMLA 41 (March 1926), pp. 55–81.
3 William Clyde DeVane, 'The Virgin and the Dragon', *Yale Review* n.s. 37 (1947), pp. 33–46.
4 Daniel Karlin, *The Courtship of Robert Browning and Elizabeth Barrett* (Oxford: Oxford University Press, 1985).
5 Corinne Davies and Marjorie Stone, '"Singing Song for Song": The Brownings "in the Poetic Relation"', *Literary Couplings: Writing Couples, Collaborators, and the Construction of Authorship*, ed. Marjorie Stone and Judith Thompson (Madison: University of Wisconsin Press, 2006), pp. 151–74, at pp. 161–2.
6 Davies and Stone (2006), p. 162.
7 Nina Auerbach, 'Robert Browning's Last Word', *Victorian Poetry* 22.2 (1984), pp. 161–73, at p. 168.
8 Auerbach (1984), p. 168.

9  Auerbach (1984), p. 171.
10 Auerbach (1984), pp. 172–3.
11 John Woolford and Daniel Karlin, *Robert Browning* (London: Longman, 1995), pp. 130–1.
12 Karlin (1985), pp. 49–50.
13 Isobel Armstrong, 'Browning and the Victorian Poetry of Sexual Love', in *Writers and Their Background: Robert Browning*, ed. Armstrong (London: Bell, 1974), pp. 267–98, at pp. 283–4.
14 Armstrong (1974), p. 284.
15 Daniel Karlin, *Browning's Hatreds* (Oxford: Clarendon Press, 1993), p. 179.
16 Karlin (1993), p. 180.
17 Karlin (1993), p. 180.
18 Joseph Bristow, *Robert Browning* (New York: Harvester Wheatsheaf, 1991), pp. 128–9.
19 U. C. Knoeplfmacher, 'Projection and the Female Other: Romanticism, Browning, and the Victorian Dramatic Monologue', *Victorian Poetry* 22.2 (1984), pp. 139–59, at 142.
20 Knoeplfmacher (1984), pp. 142–3.
21 Knoepflmacher (1984), pp. 155–6.
22 Ann Brady, *Pompilia: A Feminist Reading of Robert Browning's The Ring and the Book* (Athens, OH: Ohio University Press, 1988), pp. 125–6, 131.
23 Brady (1988), p. 133.
24 Susan Brown, '"Pompilia": The Woman (in) Question', *Victorian Poetry* 34 (1996), pp. 15–37, at pp. 22–3.
25 Brown (1996), pp. 29–30.
26 Penelope Gay, 'Desire and the Female Voice in Browning's *Men and Women* and *Dramatis Personae*', *AUMLA* 71 (1989), pp. 47–63, at p. 55.
27 Gay (1989), p. 51.
28 Mary Rose Sullivan, 'Irony in "A Woman's Last Word"', *Browning Society Notes* 5.2 (1975), pp. 14–17. […] [Gay's note].
29 Gay (1989), pp. 51–2.
30 Gay (1989), p. 54.
31 Shifra Hochberg, 'Male Authority and Female Subversion in Browning's "My Last Duchess"', *LIT* 3 (1991), pp. 77–84, at p. 77.
32 Hochberg (1991), p. 78.
33 Sandra Gilbert, 'Introduction' to Hélène Cixous and Catherine Clément, *The Newly Born Woman*, trans. Betsy Wing (Manchester: Manchester University Press, 1986). As Hochberg points out in a longer note at this point, the French term *jouissance* can have several meanings, including orgasm.
34 Hochberg (1991), pp. 78–9.
35 Hochberg (1991), pp. 79–80.
36 Catherine Maxwell, *The Female Sublime from Milton to Swinburne: Bearing Blindness* (Manchester: Manchester University Press, 2001), p. 153.
37 Ernest Fontana, '"Beatrice Signorini" as Portrait Poem', *Victorian Newsletter* 95 (Spring 1999), pp. 33–5.
38 Fontana (1999), p. 35.
39 Fontana (1999), p. 35.
40 Michael Ackerman, 'Monstrous Men: Violence and Masculinity in Robert Browning's *The Ring and the Book*', in *Horrifying Sex: Essays on Sexual Difference in Gothic Literature*, ed. Ruth Bienstock Anolik (Jefferson: McFarland, 2007), pp. 122–34, at pp. 122–3.
41 Ackerman (2007), p. 128.
42 Herbert Sussman, *Victorian Masculinities: Manhood and Masculine Poetics in Early Victorian Literature and Art* (Cambridge: Cambridge University Press, 1995), p. 81.
43 Sussman (1995), p. 82.

44 Sussman (1995), pp. 73–4.
45 Sussman (1995), p. 74.
46 Sussman (1995), p. 77.
47 Sussman (1995), p. 74.
48 Sussman (1995), p. 83.
49 Sussman (1995), pp. 86–7.
50 Sussman (1995), pp. 90–1.
51 Evgenia Sifaki, 'Masculinity, Heroism, and the Empire: Robert Browning's "Clive" and Other Victorian Re-Constructions of the Story of Robert Clive', *Victorian Literature and Culture* 37.1 (2009), pp. 141–56, at pp. 149, 152.
52 Sifaki (2009), p. 153.
53 William Whitla, *The Central Truth: The Incarnation in Robert Browning's Poetry* (Toronto: University of Toronto Press, 1963), p. v.
54 Whitla (1963), pp. 4–5, quoting Beryl Stone, 'Browning and Incarnation', unpublished M.A. thesis, University of Toronto (1957), p. iii.
55 Whitla (1963), p. 149.
56 Jochen Haug, *Passions Without a Tongue: Dramatisations of the Body in Robert Browning's Poetry* (Frankfurt: Peter Lang, 2004), p. 177.
57 Haug (2004), p. 182.
58 Haug (2004), p. 182.
59 Haug (2004), pp. 186–7.
60 Haug (2004), p. 187.

## 7 HISTORICAL AND GEOGRAPHICAL DISTANCING

1 William O. Raymond, 'Browning and Higher Criticism' [1929], reprinted in Raymond, *The Infinite Moment and Other Essays in Robert Browning* [1950] (Toronto: University of Toronto Press, 2nd edn 1965), pp. 19–51, at p. 19.
2 Raymond (1965), p. 36.
3 Raymond (1965), p. 37.
4 Elinor Shaffer, 'Browning's St. John: The Casuistry of the Higher Criticism', *Victorian Studies* 16 (1972), pp. 205–21, at p. 205.
5 Shaffer (1972), p. 206.
6 Shaffer (1972), p. 213.
7 Shaffer (1972), p. 215.
8 Shaffer (1972), pp. 216–17.
9 *Modern Painters*, Vol. IV [1856], *The Works of John Ruskin*, ed. E. T. Cook and Alexander Wedderburn (London: Allen, 1903–12), 6: 446–9, reprinted in *Robert Browning's Poetry: Authoritative Texts, Criticism*, ed. James F. Loucks and Andrew M. Stauffer (New York: Norton, 2007), pp. 463–4.
10 Mary Ellis Gibson, *History and the Prism of Art: Browning's Poetic Experiments* (Columbus: Ohio State University Press, 1987), pp. 28–9.
11 Gibson (1987), p. 22.
12 J. Hillis Miller, *The Disappearance of God: Five Nineteenth-Century Writers* [1963] (Cambridge, MA, and London: Harvard University Press, 1975), p. 108.
13 Morse Peckham, 'Historiography and *The Ring and the Book*', *Victorian Poetry* 6 (1968), pp. 242–57, at p. 246.
14 Peckham (1968), p. 246.
15 Peckham (1968), p. 253.
16 Peckham (1968), p. 253.
17 Peckham (1968), pp. 255–6.
18 Hilary Fraser, 'Browning and Nineteenth-Century Historiography', *AUMLA* 71 (1989), pp. 13–29, at p. 14.

19 Fraser (1989), pp. 16–17.
20 Fraser (1989), pp. 25–7. Fraser is citing Hayden White, *Metahistory: The Historical Imagination in Nineteenth-Century Europe* (Baltimore: Johns Hopkins University Press, 1973).
21 The main step towards Italian unification – albeit not as a republic – was only taken in 1861 with the foundation of the kingdom of Italy. Unification was completed with the annexation of the Papal state of Rome in 1870.
22 Stefan Hawlin, 'Love Among the Political Ruins: 1848 and the Political Unconscious of *Men and Women*', *Victorian Poetry* 50 (2012), pp. 503–20, at pp. 511–12.
23 Hawlin (2012), pp. 512–13.
24 Letter of 19 May 1866 in Edward C. McAleer (ed.), *Dearest Isa: Robert Browning's Letters to Isabella Blagden* (Austin: Texas University Press, 1951), pp. 238–9.
25 Robert Viscusi, '"The Englishman in Italy": Free Trade as a Principle of Aesthetics', *Browning Institute Studies* 12 (1984), pp. 1–28, at p. 19.
26 Viscusi (1984), pp. 24–5.
27 Alison Chapman, 'Robert Browning's Homesickness', *Victorian Poetry* 50 (2012), pp. 469–84, at p. 470.
28 Chapman (2012), p. 471.
29 Chapman (2012), p. 475.
30 Chapman (2012), pp. 475–6.
31 Chapman (2012), p. 471. See Christopher Keirstead, 'Stranded at the Border: Browning, France, and the Challenge of Cosmopolitanism in *Red Cotton Night-Cap Country*', *Victorian Poetry* 43 (2005), pp. 411–34.
32 Chapman (2012), p. 472. A related argument about the creative potential of Browning's status as an expatriate in Italy is made in Jane Stabler's *The Artistry of Exile: Romantic and Victorian Writers in Italy* (Oxford: Oxford University Press, 2013). Stabler considers 'doubled vision as a key element in the artistry of exile. [...] Exile has always been a dialogical condition, fostering reflection on the difference between here and there, then and now, presence and absence' (ix). References to Browning occur throughout the study, including his response to the visual and aural aspects of Italian Catholicism and his self-portrayal as a character in-between two cultures in *The Ring and the Book*.
33 Britta Martens, '"Oh, a day in the city-square, there is no such pleasure in life!": Robert Browning's Portrayal of Contemporary Italians', *Browning Society Notes* 32 (2007), pp. 4–16, at p. 7.
34 Charles-Louis de Secondat, Baron de La Brède et de Montesquieu, *De l'Esprit des lois*, XIV, 2; *Œuvres complètes*, ed. Roger Caillois, vol. 2 (Paris: Gallimard, 1951), pp. 474–7.
35 Martens (2007), p. 8.
36 Martens (2007), p. 11.
37 Martens (2007), p. 12.

## CONCLUSION

1 Suzanne Bailey, *Cognitive Style and Perceptual Difference in Browning's Poetry* (New York: Routledge, 2010).
2 Mary Ellis Gibson and Britta Martens (eds), 'Future Directions for Robert Browning Studies: A Virtual Roundtable', *Victorian Poetry* 50 (2012), pp. 431–49, at p. 435.
3 Ivan Kreilkamp, '"One More Picture": Robert Browning's Optical Unconscious', *ELH* 73.2 (2006), pp. 409–35; Isobel Armstrong, *Victorian Glassworlds: Glass Culture and the Imagination 1830–1880* (Oxford: Oxford University Press, 2008); Bernard Beatty, 'The Bric-à-Brac Wars: Robert Browning and Blessed John Henry Newman', *Literary Bric-à-Brac and the Victorians: From Commodities to Oddities*, ed. Jonathon Shears and Jen Harrison (Farnham: Ashgate, 2013), pp. 83–98; Jennifer McDonnell 'Browning's Curiosities: *The Ring and the Book* and the "Democracy of Things"' in Shears and Harrison (2013), 67–81.

4  Charles LaPorte, *Victorian Poets and the Changing Bible* (Charlottesville: University of Virginia Press, 2011); Kirstie Blair, *Form and Faith in Victorian Poetry and Religion* (Oxford: Oxford University Press, 2012); Michael Wheeler, *St. John and the Victorians* (Cambridge: Cambridge University Press, 2012); Adrienne Munich and Nicole Garret, 'Apocalyptic "Christmas-Eve" / Extravagant Criticism', *Victorian Poetry* 50 (2012), pp. 485–501; Robin Colby, 'Browning's *Christmas-Eve and Easter-Day* as Meditational Verse', *Christianity and Literature* 61 (2012), pp. 625–39.
5  Michael Meredith and Seamus Perry, *Browning at Balliol* (Oxford: Balliol College, 2012); Erin Nerstad, 'Decomposing but to Recompose: Browning, Biblical Hermeneutics, and the Dramatic Monologue', *Victorian Poetry* 50 (2012), pp. 543–61; Philip Jenkins, 'A Critic in the Desert: Robert Browning and the Limits of Plain Historic Fact', *Fides et Historia* 45 (2013), pp. 14–29.
6  See Suzanne Bailey's observations on this area in her 'Guide to the Year's Work: Robert Browning', *Victorian Poetry* 52 (2014), pp. 535–51, at pp. 536–7, 544, 548.
7  John Morton, 'Robert Browning and Mick Imlah: Forming and Collecting the Dramatic Monologue', *Australasian Journal of Victorian Studies* 18.3 (2013), pp. 84–98.
8  For Mary Ellis Gibson's discussion of the decreasing number of doctoral dissertations on Browning, see Gibson and Britta Martens, 'Browning's Bodies and the Body of Criticism', *Victorian Poetry* 50 (2012), pp. 415–29, at pp. 420–2.
9  Richard Cronin, *Reading Victorian Poetry* (Oxford: Blackwell, 2012), *The Oxford Handbook of Victorian Poetry*, ed. Matthew Bevis (Oxford: Oxford University Press, 2013).
10 Gibson and Martens, 'Future Directions' (2012), p. 444.

# Bibliography

A key resource for Browning studies is 'The Brownings: A Research Guide', hosted by the Armstrong Browning Library at Baylor University in Waco, Texas. http://www.browningguide.org/. It includes:

- **The Browning Collections**—a catalogue of both Brownings' library, presentation volumes, manuscripts, likenesses, works of art, personal effects and other associated items.
- **The Brownings' Correspondence**—a register of the poets' correspondence, with text of those letters which have already been published in the ongoing print edition of *The Brownings' Correspondence*, ed. Philip Kelley *et al.*, 40 vols (22 vols to date). Winfield: Wedgestone Press, 1984–.
- **Supporting Documents**—a register of secondary material relating to the Brownings, with text of those documents published in *The Brownings' Correspondence*.
- **Contemporary Reviews**—a register of the reviews of the Brownings' works, with text of those reviews reprinted in *The Brownings' Correspondence*.
- **Printed Works**—a bibliography of works by and about the Brownings.

## CRITICAL EDITIONS OF BROWNING'S WORK
### COMPLETE EDITIONS
Jack, Ian, and Michael Meredith, general eds. *The Poetical Works of Robert Browning*. 15 vols (9 vols to date). Oxford: Clarendon Press, 1983–.

King, Roma A. *et al.*, general eds. *The Complete Works of Robert Browning*. 17 vols. Athens, OH, and Waco, TX: Ohio University Press and Baylor University, 1969–2012.

Woolford, John, Daniel Karlin and Joseph Phelan, eds. *The Poems of Browning*. 4 vols to date. London: Longman, 1991–.

### SELECTED EDITIONS
Loucks, James F., and Andrew Stauffer, eds. *Robert Browning's Poetry: Authoritative Texts, Criticism*. New York: Norton, 2007.

Pettigrew, John, and Thomas J. Collins, eds. *Robert Browning: The Poems*. 2 vols. New Haven and Harmondsworth: Yale University Press and Penguin, 1981.

Roberts, Adam. Ed. *Robert Browning: The Major Works*. Oxford: Oxford University Press, 1997.

Woolford, John, Daniel Karlin and Joseph Phelan, eds. *Robert Browning: Selected Poems*. London: Longman, 1991–.

### BIOGRAPHIES
Finlayson, Iain. *Browning: A Private Life*. London: Harper Collins, 2004.

Griffin, W. Hall, and Harry Christopher Minchin. *The Life of Robert Browning With Notices of His Writings, His Family, & His Friends*. London: Methuen, 1910.

Irvine, William, and Park Honan. *The Book, the Ring, and the Poet: A Biography of Robert Browning*. London: Bodley Head, 1975.
Kennedy, Richard S., and Donald S. Hair. *The Dramatic Imagination of Robert Browning: A Literary Life*. Columbia, MO: University of Missouri Press, 2007.
Miller, Betty. *Robert Browning: A Portrait*. London: Murray, 1952.
Neville-Sington, Pamela. *Robert Browning: A Life After Death*. London: Weidenfeld & Nicolson, 2004.
Orr, Mrs [Alexandra] Sutherland. *Life and Letters of Robert Browning*. London: Smith, Elder, 1891.
Ryals, Clyde de L. *The Life of Robert Browning: A Critical Biography*. Oxford: Blackwell, 1993.
Ward, Masie. *Robert Browning and His World*. 2 vols. London: Cassell, 1968–69.

### CRITICAL BIBLIOGRAPHIES
O'Neill, Patricia. *Robert Browning and Twentieth-Century Criticism*. Columbia, SC: Camden House, 1995.
'Guide to the Year's Work: Robert Browning'. Published annually in issue 3 of *Victorian Poetry* (1974–).

### CRITICISM ON SPECIFIC ASPECTS OF BROWNING'S WORK
### ROMANTICISM
Baker, John Haydn. *Browning and Wordsworth*. Madison: Fairleigh Dickinson University Press, 2004.
Bloom, Harold. *A Map of Misreading*. New York: Oxford University Press, 1975.
Bloom, Harold. *Poetry and Repression: Revisionism from Blake to Stevens*. New Haven: Yale University Press, 1976.
Bloom, Harold. *The Anxiety of Influence: A Theory of Poetry*. 1973. Oxford: Oxford University Press, 2nd edn 1997.
Bloom, Harold. *The Ringers in the Tower: Studies in Romantic Tradition*. Chicago: University of Chicago Press, 1971.
Collins, Thomas J. 'Browning's *Essay on Shelley*: In Context'. *Victorian Poetry* 2 (1964): 119–24.
Collins, Thomas J. *Browning's Moral-Aesthetic Theory 1833–1855*. Lincoln: Nebraska University Press, 1967.
Drew, Philip. 'Browning's *Essay on Shelley*'. *Victorian Poetry* 1 (1963): 1–6.
Kramer, Lawrence. 'The "Intimations" Ode and Victorian Romanticism'. *Victorian Poetry* 18 (1980): 315–35.
Latané, David E. 'Browning's *Sordello* and the Aesthetics of Difficulty'. *English Literary Studies* 40 (1987).
Martens, Britta. *Browning, Victorian Poetics and the Romantic Legacy: Challenging the Personal Voice*. Farnham: Ashgate, 2011.
Maxwell, Catherine. *The Female Sublime from Milton to Swinburne: Bearing Blindness*. Manchester: Manchester University Press, 2001.
Pottle, Frederick A. *Shelley and Browning: A Myth and Some Facts*. Chicago: Pembroke, 1923.
Rigg, Patricia Diane. *Robert Browning's Romantic Irony in 'The Ring and the Book'*. London: Associated University Press, 1999.
Ryals, Clyde de L. *Becoming Browning: The Poems and Plays of Robert Browning, 1833–1846*. Columbus: Ohio State University Press, 1983.

Ryals, Clyde de L. *Browning's Later Poetry 1871–1889*. Ithaca: Cornell University Press, 1975.
Ryals, Clyde de L. *A World of Possibilities: Romantic Irony in Victorian Literature*. Columbus: Ohio State University Press, 1990.
Smalley, Donald. *Browning's Essay on Chatterton*. Cambridge, MA: Harvard University Press, 1948.
Tucker, Herbert F. 'Browning as Escape Artist: Avoidance and Intimacy'. *Robert Browning in Contexts*. Ed. John Woolford. Winfield: Wedgestone Press, 1998. 1–25.
Yetman, Michael G. 'Exorcising Shelley Out of Browning: *Sordello* and the Problem of Poetic Identity'. *Victorian Poetry* 13 (1975): 79–98.

## THE DRAMATIC MONOLOGUE

Culler, A. Dwight. 'Monodrama and the Dramatic Monologue'. *PMLA* 90.3 (1975): 366–85.
Faas, Ekbert. *Retreat into the Mind: Victorian Poetry and the Rise of Psychiatry*. Princeton: Princeton University Press, 1988.
Fuson, Benjamin Willis. *Browning and His English Predecessors in the Dramatic Monolog*. State University of Iowa Humanistic Studies 8. Iowa City: State University of Iowa, 1948.
Langbaum, Robert. *The Poetry of Experience: The Dramatic Monologue in Modern Literary Tradition*. 1957. Chicago: University of Chicago Press, 2nd edn 1985.
Martens, Britta. 'Dramatic Monologue, Detective Fiction and the Search for Meaning'. *Nineteenth-Century Literature* 66.2 (2011): 195–218.
Martin, Loy D. *Browning's Dramatic Monologues and the Post-Romantic Subject*. Baltimore: Johns Hopkins University Press, 1985.
Mason, Michael. 'Browning and the Dramatic Monologue'. *Writers and Their Background: Robert Browning*. Ed. Isobel Armstrong. London: Bell, 1974. 231–66.
Maynard, John. 'Reading the Reader in Robert Browning's Dramatic Monologues'. *Browning e Venezia*. Ed. Sergio Perosa. Firenze: Olschki, 1991. 165–77. Reprinted in *Critical Essays on Robert Browning*. Ed. Mary Ellis Gibson. New York: G. K. Hall, 1992. 69–78.
Mermin, Dorothy. *The Audience in the Poem: Five Victorian Poets*. New Brunswick: Rutgers University Press, 1983.
Miller, J. Hillis. *The Disappearance of God: Five Nineteenth-Century Writers*. 1963. Cambridge, MA and London: Harvard University Press, 1975.
Morton, John. 'Robert Browning and Mick Imlah: Forming and Collecting the Dramatic Monologue'. *Australasian Journal of Victorian Studies* 18.3 (2013): 84–98.
O'Brien, Ellen L. *Crime in Verse: The Poetics of Murder in the Victorian Era*. Columbus: Ohio State University Press, 2008.
Pearsall, Cornelia D. J. 'The Dramatic Monologue'. *The Cambridge Companion to Victorian Poetry*. Ed. Joseph Bristow. Cambridge: Cambridge University Press, 2000. 67–88.
Pearsall, Cornelia D. J. *Tennyson's Rapture: Transformation in the Victorian Dramatic Monologue*. Oxford: Oxford University Press, 2007.
Popowich, Barry L. 'Porphyria is Madness'. *Studies in Browning and his Circle* 22 (1999): 59–66.
Rader, Ralph. 'The Dramatic Monologue and Related Lyric Forms'. *Critical Inquiry* 3.1 (1976): 131–51.
Scheinberg, Cynthia. 'Recasting "sympathy and judgment": Amy Levy, Women Poets, and the Victorian Dramatic Monologue'. *Victorian Poetry* 35 (1997): 173–91.
Sessions, Ina Beth. 'The Dramatic Monologue'. *PMLA* 62.2 (1947): 503–16.

Shaw, W. David. *Origins of the Monologue: The Hidden God*. Toronto: University of Toronto Press, 1999.
Sinfield, Alan. *Dramatic Monologue*. London: Methuen, 1977.
Tate, Gregory. *The Poet's Mind: The Psychology of Victorian Poetry 1830–1870*. Oxford: Oxford University Press, 2012.
Tucker, Herbert F. 'From Monomania to Monologue: "St. Simeon Stylites" and the Rise of the Victorian Dramatic Monologue'. *Victorian Poetry* 22 (1984): 121–37.
Wagner-Lawlor, Jennifer. 'The Pragmatics of Silence, and the Figuration of the Reader in Browning's Dramatic Monologues'. *Victorian Poetry* 35 (1997): 287–302.

## AESTHETICS

Armstrong, Isobel. 'Browning and the "Grotesque Style"'. *The Major Victorian Poets: Reconsiderations*. Ed. Isobel Armstrong. London: Routledge, 1969. 93–123.
Bagehot, Walter. 'Wordsworth, Tennyson, and Browning; or, Pure, Ornate, and Grotesque Art in English Poetry'. *The National Review* 19 (1864): 27–67. Reprinted in *Robert Browning's Poetry: Authoritative Texts, Criticism*. Ed. James F. Loucks and Andrew M. Stauffer. New York: Norton, 2007. 504–9.
DeLaura, David J. 'The Context of Browning's Painter Poems: Aesthetics, Polemics, Historics'. *PMLA* 95 (1980): 367–88.
Lerner, Laurence. 'Browning's Painters'. *Yearbook of English Studies* 36.2 (2006): 96–108.
Ruskin, John. *The Works of John Ruskin*. 39 vols. Ed. E. T. Cook and Alexander Wedderburn. London: Allen, 1903–12.
Santayana, George. 'The Poetry of Barbarism'. *Interpretations of Poetry and Religion*. New York: Scribner, 1900. http://www.gutenberg.org/files/48563/48563-h/48563-h.htm#VII [accessed 21 August 2015].
Whitla, William. *The Central Truth: The Incarnation in Robert Browning's Poetry*. Toronto: University of Toronto Press, 1963.

## LOVE AND GENDER

Ackerman, Michael. 'Monstrous Men: Violence and Masculinity in Robert Browning's *The Ring and the Book*'. *Horrifying Sex: Essays on Sexual Difference in Gothic Literature*. Ed. Ruth Bienstock Anolik. Jefferson: McFarland, 2007. 122–34.
Armstrong, Isobel. 'Browning and the Victorian Poetry of Sexual Love'. *Writers and Their Background: Robert Browning*. Ed. Isobel Armstrong. London: Bell, 1974. 267–98.
Auerbach, Nina. 'Robert Browning's Last Word'. *Victorian Poetry* 22 (1984): 161–73.
Brady, Ann. *Pompilia: A Feminist Reading of Robert Browning's The Ring and the Book*. Athens, OH: Ohio University Press, 1988.
Brown, Susan. '"Pompilia": The Woman (in) Question'. *Victorian Poetry* 34 (1996): 15–37.
Byron, Glennis. 'Rethinking the Dramatic Monologue: Victorian Women Poets and Social Critique'. *Victorian Women Poets*. Ed. Alison Chapman. *Essays and Studies* 56 (2003): 79–98.
Davies, Corinne, and Marjorie Stone. '"Singing Song for Song": The Brownings "in the Poetic Relation"'. *Literary Couplings: Writing Couples, Collaborators, and the Construction of Authorship*. Ed. Marjorie Stone and Judith Thompson. Madison: University of Wisconsin Press, 2006. 151–74.
DeVane, William Clyde. 'The Virgin and the Dragon'. *Yale Review* n.s. 37 (1947): 33–46.

Fontana, Ernest. '"Beatrice Signorini" as Portrait Poem'. *Victorian Newsletter* 95 (Spring 1999): 33–5.
Gay, Penelope. 'Desire and the Female Voice in Browning's *Men and Women* and *Dramatis Personae*'. *AUMLA* 71 (1989): 47–63.
Haug, Jochen. *Passions Without a Tongue: Dramatisations of the Body in Robert Browning's Poetry*. Frankfurt: Peter Lang, 2004.
Hochberg, Shifra. 'Male Authority and Female Subversion in Browning's "My Last Duchess"'. *LIT* 3 (1991): 77–84.
Karlin, Daniel. *Browning's Hatreds*. Oxford: Clarendon Press, 1993.
Karlin, Daniel. *The Courtship of Robert Browning and Elizabeth Barrett*. Oxford: Oxford University Press, 1985.
Knoepflmacher, U. C. 'Projection and the Female Other: Romanticism, Browning, and the Victorian Dramatic Monologue'. *Victorian Poetry* 22 (1984): 139–59.
Pollock, Mary Sanders. *Elizabeth Barrett and Robert Browning: A Creative Partnership*. Aldershot: Ashgate, 2003.
Scheinberg, Cynthia. 'Recasting "sympathy and judgment": Amy Levy, Women Poets, and the Victorian Dramatic Monologue'. *Victorian Poetry* 35 (1997): 173–91.
Shaw, J. E. 'The "Donna Angelicata" in *The Ring and the Book*'. *PMLA* 41 (March 1926): 55–81.

## HISTORICAL AND GEOGRAPHICAL DISTANCING
Chapman, Alison. 'Robert Browning's Homesickness'. *Victorian Poetry* 50 (2012): 469–84.
Fraser, Hilary. 'Browning and Nineteenth-Century Historiography'. *AUMLA* 71 (1989): 13–29.
Gibson, Mary Ellis. *History and the Prism of Art: Browning's Poetic Experiments*. Columbus: Ohio State University Press, 1987.
Gridley, Roy E. *The Brownings and France: A Chronicle with a Commentary*. London: Athlone Press, 1982.
Hawlin, Stefan. 'Love Among the Political Ruins: 1848 and the Political Unconscious of *Men and Women*'. *Victorian Poetry* 50 (2012): 503–20.
Jenkins, Philip. 'A Critic in the Desert: Robert Browning and the Limits of Plain Historic Fact'. *Fides et Historia* 45 (2013): 14–29.
Keirstead, Christopher. 'Stranded at the Border: Browning, France, and the Challenge of Cosmopolitanism in *Red Cotton Night-Cap Country*'. *Victorian Poetry* 43 (2005): 411–34.
Korg, Jacob. *Browning and Italy*. Athens, OH: Ohio University Press, 1983.
Martens, Britta. '"Oh, a day in the city-square, there is no such pleasure in life!": Robert Browning's Portrayal of Contemporary Italians'. *Browning Society Notes* 32 (2007): 4–16.
Peckham, Morse. 'Historiography and *The Ring and the Book*'. *Victorian Poetry* 6 (1968): 242–57.
Shaffer, Elinor. 'Browning's St. John: The Casuistry of the Higher Criticism'. *Victorian Studies* 16 (1972): 205–21.
Sifaki, Evgenia. 'Masculinity, Heroism, and the Empire: Robert Browning's "Clive" and Other Victorian Re-Constructions of the Story of Robert Clive'. *Victorian Literature and Culture* 37.1 (2009): 141–56.
Stabler, Jane. *The Artistry of Exile: Romantic and Victorian Writers in Italy*. Oxford: Oxford University Press, 2013.
Sussman, Herbert. *Victorian Masculinities: Manhood and Masculine Poetics in Early Victorian Literature and Art*. Cambridge: Cambridge University Press, 1995.

Viscusi, Robert. '"The Englishman in Italy": Free Trade as a Principle of Aesthetics'. *Browning Institute Studies* 12 (1984): 1–28.

## GENERAL CRITICAL WORKS ON BROWNING

Armstrong, Isobel. *Victorian Poetry: Poetry, Poetics and Politics*. London: Routledge, 1993.
Armstrong, Isobel. Ed. *Writers and Their Background: Robert Browning*. London: Bell, 1974.
Bailey, Suzanne. *Cognitive Style and Perceptual Difference in Browning's Poetry*. London: Routledge, 2010.
Berdoe, Edward. *The Browning Cyclopædia: A Guide to the Study of the Works of Robert Browning*. London: Swan Sonnenschein, 2nd edn 1902.
Bristow, Joseph. *Robert Browning*. Brighton: Harvester Press, 1991.
Cook, A. K. *A Commentary upon Browning's 'The Ring and the Book'*. Oxford: Oxford University Press, 1920.
Cook, Eleanor. *Browning's Lyrics: An Exploration*. Toronto: University of Toronto Press, 1974.
Crowell, Norton B. *The Convex Glass: The Mind of Robert Browning*. Albuquerque: New Mexico University Press, 1968.
DeVane, William Clyde. *A Browning Handbook*. New York: Appleton-Century-Crofts, 2nd edn 1955.
DeVane, William Clyde. *Browning's Parleyings: The Autobiography of a Mind*. New York: Russell & Russell, 1964.
Drew, Philip. *The Poetry of Robert Browning: A Critical Introduction*. London: Methuen, 1970.
Erickson, Lee. *Robert Browning: His Poetry and His Audiences*. Ithaca: Cornell University Press, 1984.
Gibson, Mary Ellis. Ed. *Critical Essays on Robert Browning*. New York: G. K. Hall, 1992.
Gibson, Mary Ellis, and Britta Martens. 'Browning's Bodies and the Body of Criticism'. *Victorian Poetry* 50 (2012): 415–29.
Gibson, Mary Ellis, and Britta Martens, eds. 'Future Directions for Robert Browning Studies: A Virtual Roundtable'. *Victorian Poetry* 50 (2012): 431–49.
Greer, Louise. *Browning and America*. Chapel Hill: University of North Carolina Press, 1952.
Hair, Donald S. *Browning's Experiments with Genre*. Toronto: University of Toronto Press, 1972.
Hair, Donald S. *Robert Browning's Language*. Toronto: University of Toronto Press, 1999.
Hassett, Constance W. *The Elusive Self in the Poetry of Robert Browning*. Athens, OH: Ohio University Press, 1982.
Hawlin, Stefan. *The Complete Critical Guide to Robert Browning*. London: Routledge, 2002.
Jack, Ian. *Browning's Major Poetry*. Oxford: Clarendon Press, 1973.
Jones, Henry. *Browning as a Philosophical and Religious Thinker*. Glasgow: James MacLehose & Son, 1891.
King, Roma A. *The Focusing Artifice: The Poetry of Robert Browning*. Athens, OH: Ohio University Press, 1968.
Litzinger, Boyd, and Donald Smalley, eds. *Robert Browning: The Critical Heritage*. London: Routledge, 1970.
Maynard, John. *Browning's Youth*. Cambridge, MA: Harvard University Press, 1977.
Orr, Mrs [Alexandra] Sutherland. *A Handbook to the Works of Robert Browning*. London: Bell and Sons, 1902.

Peterson, William S. Ed. *Interrogating the Oracle: A History of the London Browning Society*. Athens, OH: Ohio University Press, 1969.

Raymond, William O. *The Infinite Moment and Other Essays in Robert Browning*. 1950. Toronto: University of Toronto Press, 2nd edn 1965.

Shaw, W. David. *The Dialectical Temper: The Rhetorical Art of Robert Browning*. Ithaca: Cornell University Press, 1968.

Slinn, E. Warwick. *Browning and the Fictions of Identity*. Basingstoke: Palgrave Macmillan, 1982.

Sullivan, Mary Rose. *Browning's Voices in 'The Ring and the Book': A Study of Method and Meaning*. Toronto: University of Toronto Press, 1969.

Tucker, Herbert F. *Browning's Beginnings: The Art of Disclosure*. Minneapolis: Minnesota University Press, 1980.

Wood, Sarah. *Robert Browning: A Literary Life*. Basingstoke: Palgrave Macmillan, 2001.

Woolford, John. *Browning the Revisionary*. London: Palgrave Macmillan, 1988.

Woolford, John. *Robert Browning*. Tavistock: Northcote House, 2007.

Woolford, John, and Daniel Karlin. *Robert Browning*. London: Longman, 1996.

# Index

Ackerman, Michael, 104, 122–3
Armstrong, Isobel, 42, 67–9, 76, 82, 89, 92–4, 104, 111, 147–8
Arnold, Matthew, 27
Arnold of Brescia, 91
Auerbach, Nina, 104, 107–9, 113, 114
Austin, J.L., 61–2

Bagehot, Walter, 82, 83, 86–9, 91
Bailey, Suzanne, 147, 162
Baker, John Haydn, 25–7, 29
Bakhtin, Mikhail, 72
Barrett Browning, Elizabeth, 2, 59–60, 104, 105–11, 114, 129, 138
Barthes, Roland, 38, 138
Beatty, Bernard, 148
Blagden, Isabella, 140
Bloom, Harold, 5, 8, 18–24, 25–8, 34, 82, 98–100
Bonaparte, Napoleon, 92
Brady, Ann, 104, 115–16, 129
Bristow, Joseph, 104, 113
Brown, Susan, 104, 115–17
Browning, Robert, works by
  'Andrea del Sarto', 32, 57–8, 94, 98–100, 110, 113–14, 120, 124, 136
  'Any Wife to Any Husband', 111, 118
  Aristophanes' Apology, 23
  Asolando, 27–9
  'Beatrice Signorini', 120–1
  'Bishop Blougram's Apology', 48, 59, 74, 95
  'Bishop Orders His Tomb at Saint Praxed's Church, The', 44, 48, 62–5, 74, 92–3, 95, 113–14, 124, 135
  'By the Fire-Side', 109, 112, 117–18
  'Caliban Upon Setebos', 46, 88, 90, 129
  '"Childe Roland to the Dark Tower Came"', 20–3, 62, 99

  'Christmas Eve', 132
  'Clive', 124–5
  'Confessional, The', 74
  'Death in the Desert, A', 127, 132–4
  Dramatic Lyrics, 10, 15, 41
  Dramatis Personae, 2, 109, 117, 132
  Dramatic Romances and Lyrics, 10
  'Easter-Day', 138
  'Englishman in Italy, An', 141–3
  'Epilogue' Dramatis Personae, 132
  'Epistle Containing the Strange Medical Experience of Karshish, the Arab Physician, An', 45, 128–9, 132, 138
  Essay on Chatterton, 9, 12–13
  Essay on Shelley, 9–12, 32, 69, 98
  'Evelyn Hope', 109, 111
  'Flight of the Duchess, The', 106–7
  'Forgiveness, A', 74, 112
  'Fra Lippo Lippi', 45, 58, 69, 74, 83–5, 94–7, 113, 124, 136, 139–40
  'Fust and His Friends', 139
  'Grammarian's Funeral, A', 139–40
  'Home-Thoughts, from Abroad', 142–4
  'In a Year', 118
  'Johannes Agricola in Meditation', 55, 74
  'Laboratory, The', 74, 75, 76–8
  'Love Among the Ruins', 109–11
  'Love in a Life', 118
  'Lovers' Quarrel, A', 111
  Men and Women, 2, 58, 60, 97, 104, 109, 117, 139–40
  'Mesmerism', 111, 118
  'Mr Sludge, "The Medium"', 48, 59, 85–6
  'My Last Duchess', 44, 48, 52–5, 56–7, 58, 74–5, 76–8, 113–14, 118–20, 120–21, 124

170

# INDEX 171

'Old Pictures in Florence', 32, 94, 97–8, 139–40
'One Word More', 39, 60, 111–12
*Paracelsus*, 2, 26, 37–8, 110, 126
*Parleying With Certain People of Importance in Their Day*, 75
'Patriot, The', 90–2
*Pauline*, 2, 8, 13–16, 76, 78, 120
'Pictor Ignotus', 73, 94, 100–2
*Pippa Passes*, 2, 120
*Poetical Works*, 15–16
'Porphyria's Lover', 45, 55, 58–61, 74–5, 76–7, 113–14, 120
*Prince Hohenstiel-Schwangau*, 91
'Prologue' to *Asolando*, 27–9
*Red Cotton Night-Cap Country*, 75, 143
*Return of the Druses, The*, 91
*Ring and the Book, The*, 2, 4, 30–31, 39, 74, 79, 83, 105, 107–8, 114–17, 122–3, 133, 135, 136–8, 146, 149
'Saul', 128–9, 132
'Soliloquy of the Spanish Cloister', 58, 62, 124
*Sordello*, 2, 3, 5, 8, 16–18, 26–7, 31
*Soul's Tragedy, A*, 91
*Strafford*, 135
'Thamuris marching', 23
'"Transcendentalism": A Poem in Twelve Books', 33
'Two in the Campagna', 110–11, 118
'Up at a Villa – Down in the City', 144–5
'Why I am a Liberal', 141
'Woman's Last Word, A', 118
Browning Society, 2–3
Burke, Edmund, 32
Byron, Glennis, 42

Carlyle, Thomas, 135
Catholicism, 63, 74, 94–7, 139–40, 161
Chapman, Alison, 131, 142–4
Chatterton, Thomas, 12–13
Clive, Robert, 124
Coleridge, Samuel Taylor, 10, 12, 47, 68
Collins, Thomas J., 8, 11
cosmopolitanism, 131, 142–4
crime, 73–4, 76–8, 85, 145
Cronin, Richard, 149
Culler, A. Dwight, 41, 68

Dante Alighieri, 111
Darwin, Charles, 88
Davies, Corinne, 104, 106–7
deconstruction, 5, 25, 31, 34–6, 51–2
DeLaura, David J., 82, 94–7
Derrida, Jacques, 34–5, 52
Descartes, René, 72, 127
DeVane, William Clyde, 8, 14–15, 104, 105
Donaldson, Sandra, 147
Donne, John, 3
dramatic monologue, 2, 4–6, 10, 12, 31, 38–40, 41–81, 86–7, 94, 98, 100, 102, 104, 108, 113–14, 116, 127, 130, 133, 136–8, 142, 143, 146, 147–8
Drew, Philip, 8, 10–12, 41, 45–6, 49

Eliot, T. S., 3–4
Erickson, Lee, 5, 41, 59–61

Faas, Ekbert, 67, 75–6
feminism, 5, 7, 41, 52, 53–5, 104, 107–9, 112–21, 122, 126
Feuerbach, Ludwig, 132
Fontana, Ernest, 104, 120–21
Forster, John, 135
Fraser, Hilary, 131, 138–9, 144
Freud, Anna, 19
Freud, Sigmund, 5,18–19, 98, 105
Fuson, Benjamin Willis, 67–8
Fust, Johann, 139

Gay, Penelope, 104, 117–18
Gender (see also *women*), 5, 7, 53–4, 78, 104–26, 129–30, 147
George III, King, 76
Gibson, Mary Ellis, 5, 131, 135–6, 162
Gilbert, Sandra, 119
Gothic, 74, 89, 93, 121–3
grotesque, 6, 20–21, 82–3, 86–94, 102
Gutenberg, Johannes, 139

Haug, Jochen, 105, 127–9
Hawlin, Stefan, 74, 131, 139–40, 144
Hegel, Georg Wilhelm Friedrich, 60–1
heroism, 90, 124–5, 135–6
Herder, Johann Gottfried, 134
Herrnstein Smith, Barbara, 34
Higher Criticism, 127, 131–5, 148

historiography, 7, 131–9, 146, 147
history, 5, 7, 8, 23, 131–40, 144, 145–6
Hochberg, Shifra, 104, 118–20
humanitarianism, 26–7, 141

idealism, 13, 26, 88, 91, 96–7, 99
Imlah, Mick, 148
imperfect, 25, 32–6, 88, 100
imperialism, 124–5
Incarnation, 105, 126–9, 132
Iser, Wolfgang, 36–8
Italy, 2, 7, 115, 131, 139–45, 161

Jones, Henry, 3

Karlin, Daniel, 104, 106, 109–12
Keats, John, 68
Keirstead, Christopher, 143–4
Kingsley, Charles, 95–6
Knoepflmacher, U. C., 104, 113–14
Kramer, Lawrence, 25, 27–9
Kreilkamp, Ivan, 148
Kristeva, Julia, 72

Lacan, Jacques, 72
Langbaum, Robert, 4, 41, 46–9, 49–55, 61, 62, 67, 68, 73, 143
Latané, David E., 5, 25, 36–8, 40
Leavis, F. R., 4
Leonardo da Vinci, 99, 114
Lerner, Laurence, 82, 97–100
Lewes, George Henry, 79
liberalism, 90–2, 96, 113, 131, 139, 141, 144, 145
Lippi, Filippo, 83, 95
love, 7, 30–1, 59–61, 104–30, 132–3,

Martens, Britta, 25, 38–40, 67, 73–4, 131, 144–5
Martin, Loy D., 5, 67, 71–4, 82, 100–2
Marx, Karl, 72
Marxism, 5, 67, 72, 82, 100–1
masculinity, 7, 96, 105, 106, 113, 121–6, 129–30
Mason, Michael, 41, 43–4, 46, 67, 75–6
Maxwell, Catherine, 25, 32–3, 104, 120
Maynard, John, 8, 13–14, 41, 54–5
McDonnell, Jennifer, 148
McGann, Jerome, 63
Medici, Cosimo de, 95

Mermin, Dorothy, 5, 41, 57–9
Michelangelo, 9, 114
Michelet, Jules, 138–9, 146
Mill, John Stuart, 14–15, 141
Miller, Betty, 18–19, 23, 104, 105
Miller, J. Hillis, 67, 69–72, 74, 87, 132, 136
Milsand, Joseph, 143
Milton, John, 20, 36
modernism, 3–5, 46–7
Montesquieu, Charles-Louis de Secondat Baron de La Brède et de, 144–5
Morton, John, 148

national identity, 7, 124–6, 130, 131, 139–45, 147
New Historicism, 5, 63

objective poetry, 8, 9–12, 14, 16–17, 47, 50, 69, 76, 98, 138
O'Brien, Ellen L., 67, 76–8
obscurity, 2, 32, 35–6, 79, 89, 106, 147
Ovid, 68, 120

painting, 6, 32, 58, 82, 83, 85, 94–102, 110, 119, 120–21, 124
patriarchy, 7, 65, 104, 106, 108, 112–26, 130
Patmore, Coventry, 117
Pearsall, Cornelia D. J., 41, 61–5
Peckham, Morse, 131, 136–8
Plato, 68, 88, 127
politics, 6, 13–14, 16–17, 26, 36, 53, 59, 63–5, 68, 74, 76, 78, 82, 89–95, 103, 106–7, 110, 113, 117, 121, 125, 131, 135–6, 139–45, 147, 149
Popowich, Barry L., 67, 76
postcolonialism, 5, 125
Pottle, Frederick A., 13
Pound, Ezra, 3
Procter, Bryan, 75
Protestantism, 63, 70, 74, 94–7, 126, 132, 139–40, 144
psychology, 1, 6, 10, 14, 19, 21, 30, 35, 44, 49, 51, 53, 60, 64, 67, 73, 74–80, 83, 133

Rader, Ralph, 41, 49, 52–3
Ranke, Leopold von, 136–8, 146

Raphael, 99–101, 114
Raymond, William O., 131, 132–3
reader-response theory, 5, 25, 36–9, 55
realism, 4, 6, 10, 26, 28, 43, 44–5, 46, 50–1, 53, 82–7, 88,91, 95–7, 101–3, 119, 124, 138–9, 147–8
relativism, 4, 49, 54, 70, 73, 136, 146
religion, 1, 3, 6–7, 19, 28–9, 32, 34, 46, 54, 55, 59, 61, 63–5, 69–71, 73, 78, 82, 84–6, 88–90, 93, 94–8, 100, 101, 103, 105, 110–11, 115, 118, 124, 125, 126–30, 131–6, 138, 139–40, 142, 144–5, 148
Renaissance, 19, 65, 74, 77, 92–9, 111, 131, 135, 138–40, 144
Renan, Ernest, 132–4
Rigg, Patricia Diane, 25, 30–1
Rio, Alexis François, 94–6
Robespierre, Maximilien de, 92
Romantic irony, 5, 6, 24, 25, 29–31
Romanticism, 2, 3, 4, 6, 8–40, 42, 46–7, 49–50, 55, 58, 60, 68–9, 71–2, 73, 76, 78–9, 85, 90–91, 111, 113, 123, 129, 135–6, 138–9, 144–6, 147
Rossetti, Dante Gabriel, 75–6
Rousseau, Jean-Jacques, 68
Rowley, Thomas, 13
Ruskin, John, 89, 92–5, 135, 144
Ryals, Clyde de L., 5, 25, 29–31, 36, 40

Santayana, George, 3, 82, 86, 88–9, 91
Sarto, Andrea del, 98
Scarpi, Paolo, 56
Scheinberg, Cynthia, 41, 42, 52, 53–5
Schlegel, Friedrich, 30–1
Schleiermacher, Friedrich, 132
Schopenhauer, Arthur, 69
self-expression, 2, 3, 8, 9, 10, 13, 14, 16, 25, 38–40, 68, 119
Sessions, Ina Beth, 41, 42–3, 47
sexuality, 64, 83, 93, 95–7, 99, 106, 111–26, 149
Shaffer, Elinor, 131, 133–5, 148
Shakespeare, William, 10, 76, 86
Shaw, W. David, 68

Shelley, Mary, 74
Shelley, Percy Bysshe, 2, 5, 6, 8–24, 30, 99
Sifaki, Evgenia, 105, 124–6, 129
Sinfield, Alan, 41, 44–5
Slinn, E. Warwick, 5, 41, 49–52, 61–5, 76, 82, 86, 147, 149
speech act theory, 41, 52, 61–5, 148
Stabler, Jane, 161
Stone, Beryl, 126–7
Stone, Marjorie, 106
Strauβ, David Friedrich, 132
sublime, 20–21, 25, 31, 32–3, 90–91
subjective poetry, 9–12, 16–17, 30, 32, 47, 50, 69, 98, 106

Tasso, Torquato, 12
Tate, Gregory, 67, 78–80
Tennyson, Alfred, 1, 2, 3, 27, 41–2, 47, 62, 69, 75, 78, 87
Theocritus, 68
Thornbury, George W., 42
Sussman, Herbert, 105, 123–5
Tucker, Herbert F., 5, 8, 15–16, 25, 33–6, 38, 51–2, 147

Vasari, Giorgio, 94
Viscusi, Robert, 131, 141–2, 144

Wagner-Lawlor, Jennifer, 41, 56–7
Wentworth, Thomas, Earl of Strafford, 135
Wheeler, Kathleen, 30
White, Hayden, 138–9
Whitla, William, 105, 126–7
Wilde, Oscar, 80, 82–3
women (see also *gender*), 53–5, 65, 74, 104, 23, 127, 129–30
Woolf, Virginia, 4
Woolford, John, 5, 82, 83–6, 89–94, 109, 147
Wordsworth, William, 12, 24, 25–9, 47, 84–5, 87

Yetman, Michael G., 8, 16–18, 36

www.ingramcontent.com/pod-product-compliance
Lightning Source LLC
Chambersburg PA
CBHW051812230426
43672CB00012B/2702